SOCIOCYBERNETICS

**Recent Titles in
Contributions in Sociology**

Cultural Practices and Socioeconomic Attainment: The Australian Experience
Christopher J. Crook

The Civic and the Tribal State: The State, Ethnicity, and the Multiethnic State
Feliks Gross

The American Ritual Tapestry: Social Rules and Cultural Meanings
Mary Jo Deegan, editor

Birth Alternatives: How Women Select Childbirth Care
Sandra Howell-White

Crossing the Line: Interracial Couples in the South
Robert McNamara, Maria Tempenis, and Beth Walton

Authentic Ethnicities: The Interaction of Ideology, Gender Power, and Class in the Italian-American Experience
Patricia Boscia-Mulé

Stalking the Sociological Imagination: J. Edgar Hoover's FBI Surveillance of American Sociology
Mike Forrest Keen

Korean Immigrants and the Challenge of Adjustment
Moon H. Jo

Citizenship and Ethnicity: The Growth and Development of a Democratic Multiethnic Institution
Feliks Gross

Making a Life in Yorkville: Experience and Meaning in the Life-Course Narrative of an Urban Working-Class Man
Gerald Handel

Movies, Masculinity, and Modernity: An Ethnography of Men's Filmgoing in India
Steve Derné

Ideology and the Social Sciences
Graham C. Kinloch and Raj P. Mohan, editors

SOCIOCYBERNETICS:

Complexity, Autopoiesis, and Observation of Social Systems

Edited by
Felix Geyer and Johannes van der Zouwen

Contributions in Sociology, Number 132

GREENWOOD PRESS
Westport, Connecticut • London

Library of Congress Cataloging-in-Publication Data

Sociocybernetics : complexity, autopoiesis, and observation of social systems / edited by Felix Geyer and Johannes van der Zouwen.
    p. cm — (Contributions in sociology, ISSN 0084–9278 ; no. 132)
    Includes bibliographical references and index.
    ISBN 0–313–31418–7 (alk. paper)
    1. Social systems. 2. Autopoiesis. 3. Cybernetics—Social aspects. I. Geyer, R. Felix. II. Zouwen, J. van der. III. Series.
HM701.S66 2000
301—dc21   00–058713

British Library Cataloging in Publication Data is available.

Copyright © 2001 by Felix Geyer and Johannes van der Zouwen

All rights reserved. No portion of this book may be reproduced, by any process or technique, without the express written consent of the publisher.

Library of Congress Catalog Card Number: 00–058713
ISBN: 0–313–31418–7
ISSN: 0084–9278

First published in 2001

Greenwood Press, 88 Post Road West, Westport, CT 06881
An imprint of Greenwood Publishing Group, Inc.
www.greenwood.com

Printed in the United States of America

The paper used in this book complies with the Permanent Paper Standard issued by the National Information Standards Organization (Z39.48–1984).

10 9 8 7 6 5 4 3 2 1

CONTENTS

Preface   vii

Introduction to the Main Themes in Sociocybernetics   1
Felix Geyer & Johannes van der Zouwen

PART I: GROWING SOCIETAL COMPLEXITY

1. Sociophysics and Sociocybernetics: An Essay on the Natural Roots and Limits of Political Control   17
   Paris Arnopoulos

2. Mind and Brain: A Dynamic System Model   41
   Walter Buckley

3. Management by Complexity: Redundancy and Variety in Organizations   59
   Heinrich W. Ahlemeyer

4. The Emergence of Societal Information   73
   Robert Artigiani

5. On the Interpenetration of Social Subsystems: A Contemporary Reconstruction of Parsons and Luhmann   89
   Michael Rempel

PART II: AUTOPOIESIS

6. Information, Meaning, and Communication: An Autopoietic Approach 109
   John Mingers

7. Are Firms Autopoietic Systems? 125
   Lucio Biggiero

8. The Autopoiesis of Social Systems: An Aristotelian Interpretation 141
   Colin Dougall

9. Autopoiesis and Governance: Societal Steering and Control in Democratic Societies 159
   John H. Little

PART III: OBSERVATION OF SOCIAL SYSTEMS

10. Implications of Autopoiesis and Cognitive Mapping for a Methodology of Comparative Cross-Cultural Research 173
    Bernd R. Hornung & Charo Hornung

11. Social Differentiation as the Unfolding of Dimensions of Social Systems 191
    Jürgen Klüver & Jörn Schmidt

12. The Dynamics of Educational Expansion: A Simulation Model 205
    Cor van Dijkum, Niek Lam & Harry B.G. Ganzeboom

13. Towards a Methodology for the Empirical Testing of Complex Social Cybernetic Models 223
    Johannes van der Zouwen & Cor van Dijkum

Index 241

About the Contributors 249

PREFACE

First of all, the editors wish to thank the authors of the thirteen chapters in this volume for the thorough and often time-consuming rewriting they were prepared to engage in as a result of our editorial comments. They want to pay tribute especially to one of the authors, Walter Buckley, who can be considered the "father of sociocybernetics," as a result of his groundbreaking publications in the late 1960s. While other social scientists like Talcott Parsons, David Easton, and Karl Deutsch admittedly did try to apply cybernetics and General Systems Theory (GST) to the social sciences at an earlier stage, Buckley was the first to systematically connect cybernetics and GST with the social sciences.

The editors took up Buckley's challenge almost a decade later, and were invited by professor John Rose, the director of the World Organization of General Systems and Cybernetics (WOGSC), to organize the first of a series of sessions on "social systems" at the 1978 congress, which resulted in a two-part volume, entitled *Sociocybernetics*. This was to their knowledge the first time the term was coined for this newly developing field. Subsequently, they organized sessions again at WOGSC congresses in Mexico City (1981), Paris (1884), London (1987), and New York (1990), each resulting in a volume with a selection of papers. See Geyer's website at <http://www.unizar.es/sociocybernetics/chen/felix.html> for details of these publications.

Thus, the present volume can be viewed as the most recent in a series that spans nearly a quarter century. A problem during these early days, however, was that most sociocybernetic research was published in cybernetics and systems journals, rather than in social science ones. This was perhaps caused by the fact that the social science community still entertained rather negative stereotypes about cybernetics and GST as being too engineering-oriented and mechanistic to be useful for the more subtle problems of the social sciences. Moreover the

"Woodstock generation" saw the use of cybernetics for apparently repressive purposes by institutions like the U.S. Central Intelligence Agency (CIA) and the Rand Corporation as proof of their inherently conservative character.

Some of this criticism may have been warranted at the time. Since the early 1970s, however, with the rise of second-order cybernetics, the emphasis has shifted from the maintenance of equilibrium and its associated emphasis on "steering from above" to the explanation of morphogenesis, or problems of change, which has given cybernetics and GST a more "progressive" image, while on the social science side new and related fields of research study emerged, like complexity studies.

This led in the 1990s to the revitalization of a so-called Thematic Group on Sociocybernetics within the International Sociological Association (ISA), which organized a successful conference in Bucharest in 1996, with a large participation from the social sciences. As stated above, it is from this group, recognized as the ISA Research Committee on Sociocybernetics at the 1998 World Congress of Sociology in Montreal, that the papers derive on which the present volume is based.

The editors feel that with this belated recognition from the international social science community, Walter Buckley's original goal has been accomplished: the recognition of sociocybernetics as a valuable and fertile paradigm for the social sciences by the international social science community. The Research Committee itself expressed its gratitude to Buckley by making him its honorary president.

It certainly was a time-consuming task to put this volume together. But is would have been a nearly impossible task without the excellent help of Ms. Brigitte van den Akker-Schouten, the departmental secretary of one of the editors, who prepared the final manuscript from the original text of the different chapters, inevitably delivered in somewhat different style, with slightly different referencing systems, and so on. The editors want to thank her here for an excellent job well done.

The editors also want to thank Ms. Katie Chase for the meticulous editorial services she provided during the later stages of this project.

In this volume, thirteen authors describe recent advances in the rapidly developing new field of sociocybernetics. The first part deals with increasing societal complexity, and contains chapters on its overall development, the complexity of brain-environment interaction loops, complexity in organizational change, complexity and human values, and increasing interpenetration of social systems.

The second part concentrates on a hot issue in sociocybernetics: "autopoiesis" or self-production—a concept derived from biology, indicating the relative independence and self-organization of societal subunits, which resist efforts at steering "from above," and thus contribute to overall societal complexity. It contains chapters on "embodied cognition," on the applicability of autopoiesis to business firms, on its roots in Aristotelian philosophy, and on the possibility of societal control and steering in democratic societies.

The third, more methodological, part discusses the difficulties inherent in observing complex social systems. The chapters deal with the problems of cross-cultural comparative research, simulation of the evolution of social systems from primitive to present-day forms, longitudinal simulation of education systems, and finally the methodological difficulties inherent in analyzing the unexpected complexities of mutually interacting nonlinear systems. This last chapter argues that much of social science methodology has misunderstood Karl Popper and still assumes linear cause-effect relations without reckoning with feedbacks.

The editors hope this volume will finds its way in the academic community, even in nonsocial science departments. After all, this is what cybernetics and GST are about: a truly interdisciplinary and novel approach to the vexing problems of an increasingly interdependent and complex world.

INTRODUCTION TO THE MAIN THEMES IN SOCIOCYBERNETICS

Felix Geyer & Johannes van der Zouwen

THE ORIGINS OF THIS VOLUME

This volume contains a selection out of more than 100 papers presented in the sessions organized by the Research Committee on Sociocybernetics of the International Sociological Association (ISA), at the 1998 World Congress of Sociology in Montreal.[1]

The term cybernetics derives from the Greek word for steersman. It can roughly be translated as the art of steering, and refers here to a set of related approaches, including especially general systems theory. It can offer some interesting concepts and models to social science, and may also in that sense have a steering function.

Sociocybernetics consists of the applications of first-order and especially second-order cybernetics to the social sciences, and their further development within the social sciences (Buckley, 1998). First-order cybernetics was developed in the 1940s, largely outside of the social sciences, whereas second-order cybernetics was developed to remedy the shortcomings of first-order cybernetics when applied in a biological or social science context. For reasons of space, the essentials of first-order cybernetics—and its main concepts: system boundaries; the distinction between systems, subsystems, and suprasystems; circular causality; positive and negative feedback loops; simulation—cannot be dealt with here (Geyer & van der Zouwen, 1991).[2] Second-order cybernetics originated later, in the early 1970s. The term was coined by Heinz von Foerster (1970; also 1974) in "Cybernetics of Cybernetics." He defined first-order cybernetics as the cybernetics of *observed* systems, and second-order cybernetics as the cybernetics of *observing* systems. Indeed, second-order cybernetics explicitly includes the observer(s) in the systems to be studied. These are generally living systems, ranging from simple cells to human beings, rather than the control systems for inanimate technological devices studied by most first-order cybernetics. It could be said to have a biological approach, or at least a biological basis. Some of its main concepts—self-organization, self-reference, self-steering, and autopoiesis—are referred to frequently in this volume.

The thirteen papers selected as chapters for this volume are divided into three parts, because they deal with three core aspects of sociocybernetics that are recently foremost in the discussions within this field: complexity, autopoiesis, the observation of social systems.

PART I: GROWING SOCIETAL COMPLEXITY

Growing societal complexity is certainly not only one of the core problems for sociocybernetics, but for the social sciences as a whole. In the perspective of the average individual, social systems have not only tremendously *diversified* over the last century—if only because different cultures come within one's horizon to a different degree through exposure to foreign travel, mass media, and the like—but because of their accelerated interaction they have also *become more complex at an accelerating rate*.

The Effects of Growing Societal Complexity on the Individual

If indeed one bothers to compare 1900 with 2000, the differences are enormous: the majority of the population was then still engaged in barely a dozen agriculture-related professions, lived in small villages, found a marriage partner at best in the next village, and perhaps made a trip to the big city once a year. Social control was most probably rather stifling, at least for postmodern standards, but on the other hand alienation was not yet a mass phenomenon, and social isolation was still rare (Geyer, 1992). When Durkheim (1951) concluded at the end of the last century that it caused suicide statistics to peak in summer rather than in winter as one would expect, he implicitly pointed to the social cohesion in winter when people lived together in small family units.

Both these processes, societal differentiation and increasingly rapid complexification, have not made life any easier for Luhmann's (1986) "psychic systems," or individuals defined as unique perception systems.[3] Viewed from the abovementioned constructivist perspective, chances for a really thorough mutual understanding between any two individuals—especially if not socialized within the same (sub)culture—were already low during the premodernity of the early 1900s, and are even lower in present postmodern times. Arriving at mutual understanding is hard work, and requires intensive interaction, as well as repetitive iterations to check rationally whether the other's message is more or less understood. As most people neither have the time, nor the patience, nor the desire to engage in such checking, at least in their superficial contacts with relative outsiders, chances for irrational attitudes are greatly enhanced, due to the relative prevalence of non-face-to-face contacts and resulting relative lack of immediate feedback.

As processes of urbanization, industrialization, knowledge accumulation, and technological development continued, not to forget the effects of World War II, mass society theory originated to explain these processes of differentiation and complexification, and the effect they had on the average individual. In the 1950s, Riesman's *The Lonely Crowd* (1973) describes the potential loneliness of the individual in an urban environment—less restrictive social control than in the more agricultural countryside from which most of the city dwellers still originated, but a frightening degree of freedom one cannot deal with. In the meantime, despite the explicit attention focussed by Riesman and the mass society theorists on the problems of the big cities and the loneliness of the big city crowd, an opposite process was at work as well: the chains of interdependence that bound people together, though often not in very personal ways, were silently growing, until John Lachs (1976) drew attention to this process and spoke about the "mediated society." In former days and simpler times: (1) people used to plan their actions, within the limited degrees of freedom provided by their culture, (2) execute them to the extent possible, within the equally limited possibilities, and (3) be confronted with their intended or unintended, positive or negative consequences. This may have been a harsh learning process, but at least it was a learning process, on an individual as well as a group level. When this "holy triangle" is broken, increasing societal complexity often results not only in decreased responsibility and increased alienation, as John Little demonstrates in chapter 9—one needs to think only of industries causing present-day ecological problems—but also in decreased observability of the social systems in the environment. This goes not only for the individual trying to get a firm grasp on the surrounding world, but also for the social scientist whose professional task it is to observe social systems.

The Effects of Growing Societal Complexity on the Governability of Society

Indeed, the effects of growing societal complexity on an individual level also hold for the politicians, managers, and others who try to govern or steer society, and for the social scientists who try to study it. These effects are far-reaching, and interconnect the three parts of this volume: autopoiesis, or "self-production," recognizes that many units in society are self-organizing, self-reproducing, and self-steering, which obviously does not make it any easier to steer society in a top-down way. The observation of social systems is likewise not made any easier under the present-day conditions of an increasingly rapid complexification of society, as these imply the proliferation of a large number of highly differentiated, mutually interacting, and partially autonomous social systems and subsystems, which self-organize in often unforeseen ways.

Growing societal complexity has been driven by the technology-cum-knowledge explosion of the last century, as demonstrated by Paris Arnopoulos, the first author in this volume. Chapter 1 deals with societal complexity, with an intellectually stimulating and even fascinating overview of the development of both hard and soft sciences, by placing them in a systems-theoretical perspective, demonstrating their continuity, and presenting just enough detail to make the essentials of each of these sciences understandable. Arnopoulos progresses from what he calls physiocybernetics through sociophysics to sociocybernetics. The subtitle of his chapter, "An Essay on the Natural Roots and Limits of Political Control," indicates the thrust of his argument. As he concludes at the end: "due to systemic complexity, social control is necessary; due to scientific progress, such control is possible, and due to human imperfection, it is desirable." However, he considers perfect control to be unnecessary, impossible, and undesirable, and thus views it as the task of sociocybernetics to find the point of "cyberoptimality."

As argued above, the effects of growing societal complexity on the individual are certainly not negligible either. They have resulted in a growing amount of self-reference ("why am I acting like this?"), if not on an individual level (as demonstrated by an increase of all sorts of scientific and pseudoscientific therapies), then certainly on a scientific level ("why is the mind acting like this?"). As Niklas Luhmann maintains: the individual tries to master environmental complexity by building up internal complexity, and an increase of self-reference certainly implies a buildup of internal complexity. One of the effects in the social sciences has been an increasing stress on studies of how the mind works to cope with this increase of environmental complexity.

Our second author, Walter Buckley, who can be considered the "father of sociocybernetics," presents an intriguing overview of research in this field, and develops his own systems-oriented model of the human mind. Buckley became well-known as a result of two books published in 1967 and 1969, in which he applied a general systems approach to the social sciences, and he recently published another volume (1998) in which he summarizes and elaborates on his lifelong research in the field. Chapter 2 summarizes the essentials of this last work. It presents a dynamic systems model of the interactive loops between mind, brain, and environment, which states that conscious awareness emerges second by second from the continual organism-environment looping, which includes sensory input, perception and cognition, decision, and motor output back on the environment.

Societal complexity is of course especially evident in the interactions of large business organizations with their environments, certainly when they have to adapt to changing circumstances in order not to lose their market share and to keep ahead of the competition. This often implies a willingness to engage in sometimes risky innovation, which may run counter to stabilizing mechanisms of the corporate culture. This is the area covered by systems-oriented management studies, exemplified here by our third author, Heinrich Ahlemeyer. Chapter 3 analyzes the notion of complexity and its applicability to management studies, and addresses the problems of redundancy and variety in organizations. Complexity itself is not a simple, but a complex notion, with four central features: (1) a system is complex when it is not in a state of either complete order or complete disorder, that is, when it presents a mixture of redundancy and variety; (2) complexity enforces a selective and contingent connection between the system's elements, which always could have been different; (3) complexity is a notion without a difference, without counternotions like transparency or simplicity, and it is always bound to an observer; (4) a distinction can be made between "simple complexity" and "complex complexity" (with even the former too complex to explain simply in a few words here!). The author subsequently distinguishes five reasons why change and innovation are considered improbable in organizations. He nevertheless concludes that many organizations show a marked trend toward an increase of variety, and thus also of complexity: smaller and more independent structures, with more autonomy and complexity, less communication-restraining hierarchical structures, and an increasing importance of project teams and networks.

To many outsiders the cybernetic approach, including the sociocybernetic one, often makes a highly technical impression, speaking in terms of feedbacks, feedforwards, and the like. This may be due in part to the fact that first-order cybernetics as well as much of the general systems approach were originally developed with an engineering perspective. It all started during World War II with Norbert Wiener trying to program the activities of antiaircraft batteries, and it culminated in the development of artifical intelligence and robotics. One may wonder to what extent norms and values enter in this approach, as indeed the founding fathers of second-order cybernetics did when trying to apply cybernetics to the social sciences.

Our fourth author, Robert Artigiani, deals with this issue in a wide-ranging historical perspective, and concludes that norms and values inevitably emerged in an early stage of the process towards increasing societal complexity, as the byproduct of a historical development towards larger units where norms and values had an important survival value. Chapter 4 utilizes the new science of organizing systems to trace the origin of Values, Ethics and Morals (VEMs), and argues that linguistically linked humans could have been unintentionally caught up in the process of organizing agricultural systems. These emerged as wholes greater than the sum of their parts, and formed the basis for the emergence of more complex social systems. Two equally simplistic explanations have been presented to explain the origins of culture, including VEMs: the biological determinist one, which ultimately reduces culture to genes, and the conspiracy theory, which reduces culture to exploitation of the exploited by the privileged. Human behavioral choices depend on rules appropriate to their emergent level of reality, and such rules are moral rather than biological. Such rules are stored in the systems themselves, not in the individuals, but in the relations between them. Operating in the social world, on whose maintenance survival depended, it is argued, in line with Buckley's explanation, that humans acquired new attributes, like mind and consciousness.

The social sciences have for a long time been thinking in terms of a rather monolithic conception of culture (Schacht, 1989). This was indeed possible before the advent of multigroup society, when "integration"—whatever this vague term was supposed to mean—was one of the ideals. Of course, there were the deviants, in one form or another, but they were the exceptions that confirmed the rule. It was Merton, for example, who demonstrated that criminals certainly do have norms and values, though different from those of mainstream society. In the meantime, the monolithic conception of culture has been left behind, and has largely been replaced by postmodern conceptions of fragmentation. For example, it has become abundantly clear that the differentiation of modern society has resulted in a large set of relatively independent ethnic, organizational, institutional, and corporate subcultures.

Our fifth author, Michael Rempel, feels these images of fragmentation are highly exaggerated and—while not returning to the idea of an integrated, monolithic culture—wants to stress the opposite trend of an increasing interpenetration. Chapter 5 compares the social action system of Talcott Parsons with the social communication system of Niklas Luhmann with regard to social differentiation, and cogently argues for a synthesis of the two approaches. Both Parsons and Luhmann assume a radical segmentation of society's major institutions in economic, legal, political, scientific, and religious spheres. In the legal sphere, for example, Parsons' action-based component assumes purely legal organizations, while Luhmann's communication-based component rests on the assumption of a separate technical language and logic for the legal system. Rempel, however, argues for the existence of a recently accelerating interpenetration between the different action and communication subsystems. He points to increasing interdisciplinarity, interlocking organizational structures, multifunctional workers, global interpenetration of money and markets. He analyzes the implications for the study of institutions—including "extrainstitutional" communication subsystems like gender—and for social stability.

PART II: AUTOPOIESIS

Next to complexity, autopoiesis is another important concept in sociocybernetics which occupies a central place in recent discussions. This is logical, since—as stated above—autopoiesis stresses the self-organizing, self-reproducing, and self-steering qualities of individuals and groups, and thus tends to thwart efforts to steer society from above. In the first postwar decades, especially governmental agencies felt attracted to cybernetics, since they felt it could be useful for steering societal development in a desired direction. Understandably, this drew protests from the Woodstock generation, which objected against the use of cybernetics by institutions like the CIA and the Rand Corporation. The development of the autopoiesis concept provided a theoretical underpinning for the conviction that societies cannot be steered in a kataskopic way, "from above," but that the emergence of complexity is a bottom-up process

Autopoiesis stands for "self-production," and is a concept introduced in the 1970s by the biologists Maturana and Varela (1974) to differentiate the living from the nonliving.[4] An autopoietic system was defined as a network of interrelated component-producing processes such that the components in

INTRODUCTION TO THE MAIN THEMES

interaction generate the same network that produced them. Although they considered the concept applicable only in biology, and not in the social sciences, an interesting "theory transfer" was made by Luhmann (1986). He defended the quite novel thesis that, while social systems are self-organizing and self-reproducing systems, they do not consist of individuals—or roles or even acts, as commonly conceptualized—but exclusively of communications. When generalizing the usages of autopoiesis, developed while studying biological systems, to make it also applicable to social systems, the biology-based theory of autopoiesis should therefore be expanded into a more general theory of self-referential autopoietic systems. Social and psychic systems are based upon another type of autopoietic organization than living systems: namely on communication and consciousness, respectively, as modes of meaning-based reproduction.

While Luhmann thus views communications instead of actions as the elementary units of social systems, the concept of action admittedly remains necessary to ascribe certain communications to certain actors. Thus, the chain of communications can be viewed as a chain of actions. This enables social systems to communicate about their own communications and to choose their new communications (i.e., to be active in an autopoietic way). Such a general theory of autopoiesis has important consequences for the epistemology of the social sciences: it draws a clear distinction between autopoiesis and observation, but also acknowledges that observing systems are themselves autopoietic systems, subject to the same conditions of autopoietic self-reproduction as the systems they are studying.

The theory of autopoiesis thus belongs to the class of global theories—theories that point to a collection of objects to which they themselves belong. Classical logic cannot really deal with this problem, and it will therefore be the task of a new systems-oriented epistemology to develop and combine two fundamental distinctions: between autopoiesis and observation, and between external and internal (self-)observation. Classical epistemology searches for the conditions under which external observers arrive at the same results, and does not deal with self-observation. Consequently, societies cannot be viewed, in this autopoietic perspective, as either observing or observable. Within a society, all observations are by definition self-observations.

Our sixth author, John Mingers, is nevertheless critical of recent efforts to import this after all biological concept wholesale into the social sciences. Chapter 6 aims to develop the connection between a conceptualization of information and meaning at the level of the interaction between individuals and communication at a societal level. Mingers considers the notion that societies are autopoietic systems as highly controversial, and he prefers to use the less restrictive notion of organizational closure. Societies, and even institutions and organizations, lack two essential components of autopoietic systems: a self-generated and self-maintained boundary, and a process of production of components which themselves participate in further production processes. Mingers then describes in some detail a typology of organizationally closed, self-referential systems, ranging from self-referring to self-conscious systems, and distinguishes four levels of organizational closure: the embodied individual, the social individual, social networks, and society including organizations.

Our seventh author, Lucio Biggiero, looks at autopoiesis from the viewpoint of the management sciences, and is extremely reluctant to apply autopoiesis there. Chapter 7 defends two main theses. The first one states: "Autopoiesis is not applicable to profit organizations, or, in other words, firms are not autopoietic systems." The second one is even more critical: "Autopoiesis does not coincide with second-order cybernetics, whose basic concepts, if not taken as on-off conditions, can be applied to social systems." Biggiero wants to "rescue" cybernetics from autopoiesis in order to renew the application of second-order cybernetics to the social sciences. He deals with a few core concepts of autopoiesis—like invariance and change, closure, boundaries, perturbations, identity, and belonging—and demonstrates that these do not hold for profit organizations. The management sciences differ from the autopoiesis paradigm in that they are less radical and consider operational closure not as a given, but as something to be empirically tested.

Our eighth author, Colin Dougall, looks at autopoiesis from a completely different and unexpected philosophical angle, and "unpacks" some relevant remarks of Aristotle, whom he tends to consider almost as the first author to describe the autopoiesis problematique. Chapter 8 presents an Aristotelian interpretation of the autopoiesis of social systems. Maturana's description of autopoiesis, with reference to the knowing subject that subsequently emerges, has excited great interest and controversy in the social and management sciences, especially as attempts have been made at developing a theory of "social" autopoiesis. What has proved to be elusive, however, is a hook upon which to hang the autopoiesis of social systems. Maturana's celebrated hook is "self-production" with all that entails. Luhmann, in spite of his considerable sophistication, has failed to demonstrate that "communication" is the most appropriate hook for social autopoiesis. Aristotle, in his *Physics,* makes some implicit and at first sight enigmatic allusions to autopoiesis, equally obscure as what is found in Maturana. Dougall's chapter is devoted to unpacking these allusions, which then turn out to be pointers to a reading of autopoiesis that is both internally consistent and coherent, and at the same time has enough generality to encompass both physical and social autopoiesis.

It will be evident that autopoiesis is an especially relevant concept in political science, which is after all concerned with governing, with cybernetic efforts at large-scale societal steering. The autopoiesis of subunits within a society—individuals, groups, or institutions—can after all resist efforts at societal steering by the government or the bureaucracy.

Our ninth author, John Little, inverses this problem, and wonders to what extent the governors in a democracy can be steered themselves, and can be controlled by the public. Chapter 9 discusses the relationship between autopoiesis and governance, and poses the question to what extent societal steering and control are possible in democratic societies. Many citizens have an alienated perception of government, as explained by the macro-level theory of Niklas Luhmann, which helps to delegitimize its actors and actions. A competing micro-level theory, formulated by Peter Hejl, seems potentially useful for understanding what might be done to change that perception. Little compares these theories, and analyzes their possible application to a normative theory of participation in the administration of government. Are governments themselves controllable by the public? Luhmann is pessimistic about this, and views social systems, including the political subsystem, as consisting of self-referential communication systems rather than of people. Self-referential systems inevitably run into paradoxes, which can only be solved by developing greater complexity, thus becoming more unresponsive; every bureaucracy has to codify exceptions to its rules, which in turn generate further exceptions. Hejl's theory of "synreferentiality" views individuals rather than communications as the core of social systems, and speaks of "autonomization" rather than autonomy. One of his rather idealistic notions is to promote one-to-one encounters between individuals in government and citizens.

PART III: OBSERVATION OF SOCIAL SYSTEMS

The third part of this volume deals with the observation of social systems, and is largely methodological in nature—logically so, as the observation of complex social systems, which are moreover autopoietic to a large extent and thus largely tend to defy the predictions of external observers, is a complex affair in itself which requires a sophisticated methodology.

One of the areas where the observation of social systems poses unexpected difficulties is international-comparative research. The constructivist school in social science is convinced that everyone construes his or her own world through a strictly personal and subjective interpretation of the surrounding world. One does not need to be a constructivist to generalize this conviction and to realize that every culture has its own distinct image of the world. In an age of increasingly vast globalization and international contacts, cultural differences often seem to be understandable, if sometimes a little quaint, at first sight. However, apparently similar ideas in different cultures often turn out to be embedded in different emotional and cognitive structures. The emic or insider's view can be significantly different from the etic, or outside observer's view, and both views need to be taken into account to arrive at truly international-comparative research.

It is to this fascinating field of cross-cultural research methodology that our next authors, Bernd and Charo Hornung devote their attention, with specific reference to androgyny in cross-cultural comparisons. Chapter 10 opens Part III of this volume on the observation of social systems and investigates the implications of autopoiesis and cognitive mapping for a methodology of comparative cross-cultural research. Evident key categories of sociocybernetics are social systems, societies, social actors, and their actions. Less evident, but intrinsically linked to these, are culture, personality, and psychology, including cognition. Sociocybernetics and the cognitive mapping approach propose methodological tools to integrate concepts like culture and personality with the notion of social systems. In the age of globalization this revives the danger of ethnocentrism and the urgent need for cross-cultural studies along with an appropriate methodology. Empirical studies, such as in psychology and anthropology, involving aspects of personality and cognitive systems, rapidly encounter very practical methodological problems which lead to questions originally posed by cultural relativists. These problems have seen a certain revival in the methodological controversy on etic and emic approaches in psychology and anthropology. Hornung and Hornung illustrate this with a cross-cultural study on androgyny carried out in Germany and Peru. The implications of autopoietic theory and cognitive mapping are explored with regard to this problem. An evolutionary sociocybernetic view is then proposed as a basis for a methodology for cross-cultural research.

One way to get a firm grip on the issues involved in observing social systems is by computer simulation, a technique now widely employed in the social sciences, but first employed within the systems and cybernetics community. Simulation is often used to study the development of specific social systems, or to simulate policy decisions without actually taking them in order to see how the consequences can vary when introducing different (values for the) parameters involved. However, the authors of our eleventh chapter, Jürgen Klüver and Jörn Schmidt, embarked on an even more ambitious task. They simulated the development of human society, from the original simplicity of hunter-gatherer societies to the present-day complexity of postmodern multigroup societies, and came to remarkable conclusions. Chapter 11 concentrates on the geometry and dimensions of social systems. While geometrical concepts are mainly used metaphorically in the social sciences, the authors demonstrate that it is possible to apply the mathematical concepts of geometrical space and dimensions to social fields. The concept of mathematical dimensions can be introduced into social systems theory: As dimensions of social systems (i.e., societies), the authors define the three main levels of social differentiation, namely the levels of social segments, social strata, and functional social subsystems. Modern societies can be described accordingly as three-dimensional social systems. A computer model was constructed to analyze the consequences of social differentiation in a space of three dimensions. The model is a (stochastic) cellular automaton which is changed by a genetic algorithm. The most important results are: (1) Social evolution of different levels of social structures is very improbable because a lot of different parameter values must be combined at the same time. This explains the well-known fact that the evolution of the different social levels happened only very seldom in human history. (2) The more different levels a system contains, the more sensitive the system is to external perturbations and the more difficult it becomes for the system to reach and maintain simple attractor states, as is evident from modern societies. (3) Social relations on one level are disturbed and partly dissolved when the system evolves to the next level(s) of differentiation. Therefore, there may be mathematical reasons for the fact that in modern societies traditional relations are permanently changed and dissolved.

Simulation was also used by the authors of chapter 12. They made use of detailed data from 1900 onward about population growth and about the level of primary, presecondary, secondary and tertiary education in the Netherlands. Their research provides a typical example of how longitudinal processes can be simulated and theories about these processes can be partially tested, assuming that sufficient and sufficiently detailed data are available over a long period. Cor van Dijkum, Niek Lam, and Harry Ganzeboom developed a simulation model which portrays the dynamics of educational expansion in the Netherlands over the last century. Especially in the more developed industrial societies there is a rising demand for education, while the level of popular education will rise over time, though its causes are less known. Optimists argue that all citizens have good personal reasons to demand education for their children and themselves: education enhances the chances of success on the labor market, and in modern societies the educated have more opportunities for self-development. Thus they consider the demand for more education to be the result of aggregated individual choices. Pessimists point to the system dynamics of the educational system, and view the demand for education as an autonomous phenomenon, relatively unaffected by government measures like high fees or *numerus clausus*. To evaluate both points of view, the educational system dynamics and the impact of choice behavior of several sections of the population were simulated over time. The relatively simple simulation model has only four submodels: (1) a population submodel, (2) an educational submodel, (3) a choice submodel, and (4) a macro submodel (which contains only a set of long-term parameters). However, it also has behavioral feedback loops: the behavior of early generations will affect the behavior of future ones. The output of the educational submodel feeds the population submodel, which in its turn is connected to the educational submodel. The rate of feedback is determined by the choice submodel. In developing this computer simulation, the authors had two objectives. The first one was to reconstruct the consistent rise of the level of education, which led to the conclusion that the pessimists had the best cards; the second was to experiment with the computer simulation to get a better understanding of the dynamics and the limits of their simulation.

As is not uncommon in a relatively new branch of scientific endeavor, sociocybernetic studies are often of a theoretical nature, while empirical validation of sociocybernetic models is still rare. It will have become clear by now that empirical sociocybernetic research poses many methodological problems. If one realizes that the social sciences mainly study complex adaptive systems—self-organizing, self-referential, autopoietic, and thus with their own strategies and expectations, with intertwining processes of emergence and adaptation—then one is confronted with a core problem of the social sciences: how to make a science out of studying a bunch of imperfectly smart agents exploring their way into an essentially infinite space of possibilities which they—let alone the social scientists researching them—are not even fully aware of.

There is indeed quite a methodological problem here. It is already very difficult to apply the principles and methods (e.g., feedbacks and nonlinearities) of first-order cybernetics to empirical social research, much more so than to sociological theory, and nearly impossible to incorporate a second-order cybernetics approach in one's research design. Indeed, as far as empirical research is concerned, second-order cybernetics may be a bridge too far, given the research methodology and the mathematics presently available.

Applying the principles of first-order cybernetics in empirical research already poses heavy demands on the data sets and the methods of analysis: every feedback ($X_t \rightarrow Y \rightarrow X_{t+1}$), every interaction between variables [$Z \rightarrow (X \rightarrow Y)$], and every nonlinear equation ($Y = cX^2 + bX + a$), let alone nonlinear differential equation ($Y' = cY^2 + bY + a$), demands extra parameters to be estimated, and quickly exhausts the information embedded in the data set. Admitting on top of that the second-order notions that the research subjects can change by investigating them, let alone being aware of the fact that these subjects may reorganize themselves on the basis of knowledge acquired by them during the research, exceeds the powers of analysis and imagination of even the most sophisticated methodologists: it equals the effort to solve one equation with at least three unknowns.

In the case of second-order cybernetics, these problems indeed multiply: how does one obtain reliable data within such a framework, where nothing is constant and everything is on the move, let alone base policy-relevant decisions on such data? How can one still forecast developments when at best retrospective analysis of how a new level of complexity has emerged seems possible? Certainly, these are problems that are far from solved, and a lot of work lies ahead before hypotheses derivable from second-order cybernetics will be fully testable. Nevertheless, the opportunities offered by this paradigm to present a truly realistic analysis of the complex adaptive behavior of interacting groups of agents seems too good to pass up.

But the inherent problem remains: the more realistic—and therefore less parsimonious—a theory, the more complex it becomes, and the more difficult to test the hypotheses and subhypotheses derived from it which are used in collecting and interpreting the data. If one accepts that social systems have a high degree of complexity, cybernetic theories become more relevant and fitting, but less testable as they grow more complex themselves, as is the case with second-order cybernetics as compared to first-order cybernetics. There is certainly a challenge here, for theorists and methodologists alike.

The authors of our final chapter take up this challenge, and modestly limit themselves to tackling the methodological problems one already encounters in first-order cybernetic research. In doing so, they criticize the still-prevalent methodological thinking in the social sciences, with its preference for unidirectional causality and simple theories, and argue that Popper's ideas about falsification, simplicity and causality have been misunderstood. Johannes van der Zouwen and Cor van Dijkum end this volume with a chapter entitled "Towards a Methodology for the Empirical Testing of Complex Social Cybernetic Models"—a subject that is highly overdue in sociocybernetics, in view of the relative scarcity of empirical studies. The application of cybernetics for the description of social systems offers a great opportunity to the social sciences to get a firm grip on the complexity of the ever-evolving time-dependent character of social phenomena. Modern cybernetics concepts, like system, feedback, and nonlinear relations between variables, are in principle very helpful to analyze the dynamic character of those systems, and many promising models can be found in the literature. However, the empirical foundation and validation of such models of social systems is still a big problem, one of the reasons being that social science methodology does not yet have a scientifically acceptable solution for the empirical validation of complex models. Moreover, the creators of complex sociocybernetic models prefer breathtaking theories to infer sociocybernetics models over their empirical validation and falsification. With these problems in mind, this chapter explores three questions: (1) How can modern cybernetics concepts and explanations be translated into a sound logic of model building and incorporated in transparent complex models of social phenomena? (2) Which methodological problems and solutions can sociocybernetics and social scientists share when they both try to validate complex models in a scientifically acceptable way? (3) How can such complex models be made plausible, and empirically testable, in a methodologically adequate way?

The editors hope that this volume will prove to be a first step towards answering these questions, and that it will form a stimulus for those working in the field to apply sociocybernetics to theory-driven empirical research in the social sciences.

NOTES

1. The abstracts of these papers are available at the website of the Research Committee, located at <http://www.unizar.es/sociocybernetics/>, and should give a good first impression of what sociocybernetics is all about.

2. The interested reader is also referred to "The Challenge of Sociocybernetics," which elaborates the present chapter (available at <http://www.unizar.es/sociocybernetics/chen/felix.html>) and to the website of the ISA Research Committee on Sociocybernetics, <http://www.unizar.es/sociocybernetics> which includes a 400-item bibliography on sociocybernetics.

3. At <http:/www.webb.net/sites/sociocyberforum/books.html> all Luhmann's publications in English can be found.

4. For an overview of Maturana's and Varela's work, see their extensive bibliographies at the following websites:
<http://www.informatik.umu.se/~rwhit/HMOfficialBib.html> and
<http://www.ccr.jussieu.fr/varela/index.html>, respectively.

REFERENCES

Buckley, W. (1967). *Sociology and Modern Systems Theory*. Englewood Cliffs, NJ: Prentice Hall.

Buckley, W. (Ed.) (1968). *Modern Systems Research for the Behavioral Scientist: A Sourcebook*. Chicago: Aldine.

Buckley, W. (1998). *Society—A Complex Adaptive System*. London: Gordon and Breach. (This is an excellent introduction to the field by the "father of sociocybernetics.")

Durkheim, E. (1951). *Suicide: A Study in Sociology* (Le Suicide, 1896). Trans. J.A. Spaulding and G. Simpson. New York: Free Press.

Foerster, H. von (1970). Cybernetics of Cybernetics. Paper delivered at the annual meeting of the American Society for Cybernetics.

Foerster, H. von (Ed.) (1974). On Constructing a Reality, reprinted In *Observing Systems*, pp. 288-309. Salinas, CA: Intersystems Publications. Also available at <http://platon.ee.duth.gr/~soeist.7t/lessons.lesson2_2.htm>.

Geyer, F. (1992). Alienation in Community And Society: Effects of Increasing Environmental Complexity. *Kybernetes, 21*, No. 2: 33-49.

Geyer, F. & van der Zouwen, J. (1991). Cybernetics and Social Science: Theories and Research in Sociocybernetics. *Kybernetes, 20*, No. 6, 81-92.

Lachs, J. (1976). Mediation and Psychic Distance. In R.F. Geyer and D.R. Schweitzer (eds.), *Theories of Alienation - Critical Perspectives in Philosophy and the Social Sciences*. The Hague: Martinus Nijhoff.

Luhmann, N. (1986). The Autopoiesis of Social Systems. In F. Geyer and J. van der Zouwen (eds.) *Sociocybernetic Paradoxes* (pp. 172-192). London and Beverly Hills, CA: Sage.

Riesman, D. (1973). *The Lonely Crowd*. New Haven, CN: Yale University Press.

Schacht, R. (1989). Social Structure, Social Alienation, and Social Change. In F. Geyer and D. Schweitzer (Eds.), *Alienation Theories and De-alienation Strategies* (pp. 35-56). Northwood, UK: Science Reviews, Ltd.

Varela, F., Maturana, H. & Uribe, R. (1974). Autopoiesis: The Organization of Living Systems, Its Characterization and a Model. *Biosystems, 5*: 187-196.

PART I

GROWING SOCIETAL COMPLEXITY

Chapter 1

SOCIOPHYSICS AND SOCIOCYBERNETICS: AN ESSAY ON THE NATURAL ROOTS AND LIMITS OF POLITICAL CONTROL

Paris Arnopoulos

Natura non nisi parendo vincitur. Francis Bacon

OVERVIEW

One of the critical problems of sociocybernetics is to determine the necessity, possibility, and desirability of social control by political institutions. This conundrum has been tackled repeatedly in history with various responses; some of which have been tried and failed, while others are still going on locally and temporally. Although the problem of social control is pervading and continuing, changing circumstances make all solutions parochial and ephemeral at best.

On this assumption, the question is how much further can this issue be pursued in a more general or theoretical manner. Given the complexity, extensity, and intensity of contemporary social systems, could some general sociocybernetic principles be found to apply here and now, as well as everywhere and always?

It is fortunate that recent scientific discoveries give new insights to old puzzles. The latest advances of General Systems, Complexity, Quantum, and Chaos Theories emphasize the multiplicity of reality and thereby show great promise for various social applications. Combining these theories, this chapter will apply the sociophysics paradigm, which is particularly suitable here because it renders explicit the already implicit metaphors and fundamental isometries between the natural and social sciences, thus contributing to their mutual consolidation and convergence.

The central hypothesis here is that some measure of social control is necessary, possible, and desirable; so the practical question becomes when, where, and how it can be optimized. On the thesis that complex natural and cultural systems are difficult to know and understand, trying to manipulate them is precarious; so any attempt to control them must be thought and carried out in conformity with nature: humbly, carefully, and responsibly.

Under the circumstances, human interference with fragile or chaotic systems found in both nature and culture should be based on the principles of minimizing environmental disturbance and maximizing holistic balance. The best policy would then seem to be choosing a postmodern sociocybernetic strategy which approaches a golden mean between the libertarian and totalitarian extremes.

INTRODUCTION

Sociology is often considered the weakest link of the social sciences, because it lacks an adequate formal theory to serve as a scientific foundation upon which to accumulate knowledge. Since its last heyday thirty years ago, building grand social theories has fallen into lean times, but recently a new generation seems to have rekindled the fires of a general macrosynthetic trend to complement a plethora of microanalytic establishments.

It is in this renewed neopositivist *Zeitgeist* that a recent theory of sociophysics goes beyond sociobiology in contributing its systemic unification model (SUM) to interscientific integration. The socioscientific paradigm rests on the tripod of rationality, sensitivity, and mystery, trying to lessen the discrepancies between our inner (personal) and outer (cultural-natural) realms. It continuously confronts not only actuality but probes possibility, thereby constructing models of the world which approach but never attain an ultimate understanding.

Following a General Systems Theory perspective, our reality may be illustrated as three concentric circles: egosphere, sociosphere, ecosphere. In this scheme, the middle ring representing society becomes our focus, whose elements are human beings and whose environment is nature. Because of the breadth of this viewpoint, we can only touch upon the physics-politics interface, relating the cultural system to its natural environment.

Taking a cue from J.P. Gibbs' thesis that control is sociology's central notion, our point here emphasizes cybernetics as the study of governance or control, focusing on the intermediate regions (meso, present, social) of the above three parameters as they relate to the famous C3 (command-control-communication) triad. Wedging through all three spheres of reality, control may be studied by physiocybernetics, psychocybernetics, and sociocybernetics. As social scientists, we situate the context of this concept in the cultural system and its natural environment, without forgetting its human content.

According to Freud, the human content or condition is controlled by psychology, biology, and ecology. Accordingly, human misery or malaise results from replacing natural instincts by cultural frustrations. We can rearrange these insights by subdividing generic self-governing, regulatory control into the following stages of hierarchical order: primary (objective physiocybernetics of inanimate matter by engineering); secondary (subjective psychocybernetics of human beings by biofeedback); tertiary (interactive sociocybernetics of group conduct by social control).

Primary control is covered in the first section of this chapter as the steady-state tendency of the ecosystem via existential, self-reflexive, adjusting reaction. By discovering the laws of these controls, humans can construct buildings or artifacts and manipulate or engineer their components.

Secondary control involves the innate, yet imperfect, self-control of human beings, as of all living organisms. This autonomic behavior will not be considered here, because natural evolution has deprived humans of much of their instinctive control, leaving it to intelligent, self-steering purposive action and cultural socialization to pick up the slack, as shown in the second section.

Last and most important here, tertiary control is covered in the third section. Given the increased powers of humans over nature but not over themselves, the only significant control remaining to be improved is in collective interpersonal relations by technical, regulative, adaptive behavior.

In correlating physics-politics-cybernetics, we form a triangular locus which runs through our universe of discourse with three interconnected foci forming its integrated system. Since control manifests itself in the interface between sociophysics and sociocybernetics via their common connecting link of physiocybernetics, the three sections of this chapter treat all these trilateral relationships.

This chapter can only present a two-dimensional picture of a complex reality. As the Thematic Matrix (Figure 1.1) indicates, the vertical dimension treats each of the loci between physics, politics, and cybernetics, while the horizontal dimension looks at each of the foci within the infrastructure, structure, and superstructure of our model.

Figure 1.1
The Thematic Matrix

Locus \ Focus	Primary	Secondary	Tertiary
Physiocybernetics	Mechanics	Organics	Semantics
Sociophysics	Statics	Dynamics	Dialectics
Sociocybernetics	Macro	Micro	Meta

These two salient dimensions are based on the causal and conclusive themes, whose intersections produce the nine combined cells. The study is thus organized in three vertical sections, with three horizontal subsections in each, making a total of nine subsections as shown here.

PHYSIOCYBERNETICS

Mechanics

The grand edifice of classical physics rests upon the tripod of Newtonian materialism, Cartesian rationalism, and Laplacian determinism. Mass, space, and time designate its three primordial physical quantities, so that almost everything else can be derived from and expressed in terms or ratios of these measures.

Simple mathematical manipulations of an innate set (space-existence-time) triad puts material content within a spatial field context and temporal concept, combining to produce the notions of density, motion and momentum, as well as their equivalent conservation laws. By combining certain natural constants and variables, physics defines its primal vectors of acceleration, force, impulse, and pressure.

In this scheme, force is a central concept because it serves to produce a change of state by overcoming the natural inertia or material momentum of mass. When force is applied or a mass accelerated through space, work is done, whose rate is measured by power. That is to say, power is fast work or moving force.

These Newtonian forces operating in various Cartesian fields could explain matter in motion in a perfect Laplacian deterministic causality. The realization that all matter has an inherent attribute or charge to influence its environment in some way by certain nuclear, electromagnetic, or gravitational fields is fundamental to scientific relationships of local causality.

This idea stems from the search for an agent to explain change. Classical laws reduce to recursive causality. From that perception arises the desire to affect and effect change by influencing its course of action. So whether we speak of conservation or alteration of any status quo, the constants and variables of a given situation must be considered in their internal and external, structural and functional conditions.

Based on these preliminary definitions, we arrive at our central concept of control. Among others, one given by Gibbs (1989) gives its generic definition as overt human behavior by the commission or omission of an intentional act, towards a desired change in the probability of some condition. From this denotation arises a connotation implying some limitation and direction of action by a conscious agent for a certain purpose: meaning that control is an act performed according to a norm.

Accepting this qualitative definition, we add a quantitative one given by Young (1976), who equates control with the second derivative of velocity. This simplification and formalization means that control is the ability to alter an acceleration or the capacity to change the rate of change.

That formal definition of control implies a conscious activity which requires a legislator, interpretor, and executor—all of which amount to a governor or controller: hence cybernetics. This process operates by certain rules, within set boundaries, beyond which control is lost and chaos results. Consequently, setting standards, keeping limits, and seeking optimals become the hallmark of cybernetics.

Control is very important in the exercise of power, because power becomes the ability to control the behavior of mass in space. This ability accrues to servomechanisms because they process feedbacks which vary the rates of systemic change according to set values. A controller or governor is supposed to determine the state of a system at will, by varying its rate of change from zero to plus or minus, within some given minimax parameters. The range to which one can do that by obtaining and maintaining an optimal performance, indicates the degree of control it has.

Since power is directly proportional to the rate of either material accumulation, energy conversion, or information communication, massive-dynamic systems require and often acquire a great deal of control in order not to self-destruct. It will become evident as we move along, that when systems become more complex, energetic, and informed, they tend to get out of control unless strong cybernetic mechanisms are put in place to regulate their activities. This compulsion to control stems from the determination of systems to increase the likelihood of their survival and propagation. Unfortunately, this tendency often results in the excessive regulation and regimentation of totalitarian tyrannies which carry a good thing too far.

Organics

Deterministic materialism is by no means the whole story in classical physics. Mechanostatics was later supplemented by thermodynamics, when the notions of heat, energy, and entropy were added to those of mass, motion, and force.

In order to apply force, one needs some energy, thus bringing in another great concept of physics. But as energy is related to mass and velocity, it is equivalent to work. As Einstein so succinctly put it in his elegant formulation, $E=mc^2$, kinetic energy is matter in motion, just as potential energy is matter in position.

When we move from the macromechanical to the microchemical level, causality becomes more complicated by the addition of random motion. In this new condition, three statistical-probabilistic indices—heat, temperature, or pressure—are introduced to describe the simple and average macroscopic properties which derive from many, complex microscopic configurations.

Heat and its derivative pressure are created by the chance collisions of a large number of bodies, so disorderly activity is a high temperature or excited state of chaotic motion. Since heat cannot be transformed into energy without some loss, the temporal symmetry of mechanics is destroyed by time's unidirectional orientation. Natural processes thus follow the path of least resistance or effort, so decreasing energy or potential becomes the entropy arrow of time or history.

It seems that force, energy, and power abhor a vacuum which they try to fill wherever it is found and, in doing so, spread out and lose their potency: thus increasing entropy. Moreover, since freedom is any parameter which can vary independently of others, a system with a multitude of independent actors has a large degree of it. This means that in order to apply mechanical laws to large numbers, some constancy is necessary to simplify the enormous degrees of freedom contained in stochastic systems.

Begun as ideal gas thermodynamics, correlating pressure, volume, and temperature, these statistical concepts were extended to describe any action. In that sense, action requires the expenditure of energy or the performance of work, thus making power the dividend of energy and time. Maupertuis' law of least action captures this relationship by saying that in any change of state, the quantity of action tends to be the smallest necessary.

Since every interaction involves an exchange of something, there is a minimal exchange threshold, measured by Planck's quantum of action. In this case, Heisenberg's principle manifests the inevitable limit in measuring any activity. Accordingly, as Bohr put it, we cannot pretend to describe reality directly, but only its momentary phenomena by probabilistic rather than deterministic means.

This probabilism indicates a natural unpredictability in the dynamics of complex nonlinear systems because they are always open to unexpected innovations, as it happened with the infusion of life into matter, as characterized by the emergent functions of metabolic production, genetic reproduction, and cybernetic reduction. As a result, organic systems are syntropic or negentropic in that they counter and lessen entropy by building and maintaining matter, energy, and order. Organisms are spatiotemporal, structural-functional, self-organizing, and self-generating entities.

Although a syntropic process is only local and temporary, for any particular living being, it evolves by alternating between genotypes and phenotypes. Gradual evolution tends towards symmetry-breaking, stability-perturbing and morphogeny-cascading—steps which lead to the progressive complexity-building of higher systems. Like bifurcation, evolution is a transition from a state of high symmetry, strong connectivity, and low complexity to one of low symmetry, weak connectivity, and high complexity. Hence, the emergence of order out of chaos and eventual life out of matter.

All this is to say that contrary to Laplacian determinism, modern physics now recognizes the limitations of stability, rationality and causality. Thus, by extension, due to our shallow logic, hollow knowledge and low energy, we must also exclude the possibility of perfect control; even in mechanical, let alone organic systems. The all too human delusion of omnipotence, like omniscience, inevitably leads to a downfall due to hubris. As two recent popular novels by David Baldacci (1996, 1997) illustrate: "Total Control" is as ephemeral as "Absolute Power" is chimeral!

Semantics

Beyond classical physics, the quantum revolution brought out the importance of information to complete our model of reality. Classical physics of objects have thus given way to quantum mechanics of subjects. Reality is now seen to be ultimately composed of facts or data, rather than objects or things.

The principles of physics must then be applied to symbols as to matter and energy. When this is done to the Law of Conservation, for instance, it means that no system can generate more than the total amount of information it already has. All it can do is manipulate and redistribute it from one level or center to another.

Claude Shannon's formula for information is the negative of Ludwig Boltzmann's formula for entropy, because information decreases entropy and increases order. Entropy then becomes the lack of information or the amount of disorder in a given system. It appears not only as loss of energy, but also of information, because the symbolic content of a message is defined by the probability of its statistical entropy. Consequently, thermodynamic and infostatistic entropy can be made to correspond by using the quantum of information which is associated with the minimal knowable degree of freedom.

Like everything else, information has a cost: every increase in systemic knowledge is paid for by an increase of environmental entropy. The price of information however is minuscule, so the production of knowledge is quite economical. Nevertheless, since the higher the freedom of a system, the higher its form and energy cost, chaotic complexity incurs high costs. This means that the infinite precision necessary for deterministic information is impossible because of its infinite cost; something that limits our knowledge horizon, both in time and place, thus making it impossible to extrapolate from here-now to always-everywhere. Whether we are dealing with James Maxwell's or Pierre Laplace's demon, exact knowledge comes at a prohibitive price.

Classical physics assumes that all natural change is smooth and continuous. Quantum Theory has shattered that assumption by introducing many discontinuities, since there is increasing evidence that we are living in a quantum, as well as a classical, universe. The overall picture emerging from both Quantivity and Relativity is that reality is a network of relations where the traits of each part are determined by their relations to the rest, rather than by a set structure of intrinsic properties.

Moreover, the recent advances of Chaos Theory have given a new meaning to old concepts by recognizing a hidden order behind apparently random phenomena and emphasizing variability as the only constancy of reality. Since Jules-Henri Poincaré's complex equations a hundred years ago, chaotic dynamics have now come of age with the increasing power of computers which enable us to discover an underlying cosmos in a phenomenal chaos. As a result, a lot of supposed randomness stems from simple nonlinear dynamic systems. So instead of trying to simplify reality to fit classic deterministic models, science can now search for the laws of complex probabilistic systems.

Reality allows such systems to be ranged along one of three conditions: a steady state of balanced uniformity, a transitory state of phase change by bifurcation or pulsation, and a random activity of chaos. Complex systems of more than three parameters can fall into any of these patterns. But ordered complexity may emerge in the middle state via a self-stabilizing cascade of symmetry-breaking bifurcations which contain intrinsically hierarchical properties.

Both holistic organicism and dialectic materialism suggest that beyond a certain level of complexity, matter exhibits emergent properties and behaviors which do not exist and cannot be explained in terms of their lower constituents. The human mind and its self-consciousness are the ultimate emergent virtual property of life, whose intelligence is composed of symbolic memorization and computation, carried out by an organic hardware brain and its dedicated software mind. The triune brain represents this evolution from the reptilic (sensual) via the limbic (emotional) to the neocortic (rational) mind. Self-consciousness is thus an emergent property integrating all three.

As a result of this revolutionary development, a third source of causality may be added to determinism and randomism. This final factor—voluntarism—derives from human "free will" and accords some responsibility to decisions taken by people as a result of their self-controlled or intentioned acts which are neither externally determined nor entirely random.

Nevertheless, extraordinary as it is, the human mind and its willpower have severe constraints which limit the ability to understand, let alone control complex systems. According to Kurt Gödel's incompleteness theorem, no system can comprehend anything more complicated than itself. Similarly, Alan Turing's undecidable-incomputable propositions cannot determine their truth or falsity. Thus the limits to knowledge are physical and intellectual, as well as social. Humans can only explain and control relatively simple systems, anything more is beyond our circumscribed capability.

For that reason, Ashby's Law of Requisite Variety requires that effective controls must be at least as many as the disturbances affecting a system. This means that it is possible to control adequately few and simple mechanical or physical systems, as is done successfully by technology or engineering.

So far, humanity, has somehow survived and thrived, without knowing, understanding or controlling much. But as we will see next, because of their increasingly complex degrees of freedom, controlling human or social systems, let alone understanding them, is becoming a much more difficult task; hence a highly risky and uncertain undertaking. Perhaps we have now reached, if not surpassed, the natural threshold of our innate collective competence in dealing with our cultural creations. But in case we have not, we should try to probe the limits of our capability.

SOCIOPHYSICS

Statics

We begin sociophysics by its simplest manifestation in Newtonian mechanics. This basic aspect of system analysis rests on the assumption of three fundamental concepts of our set model.

First, the material aspect of society is composed of human, artificial, and natural stocks: meaning people plus their creations and possessions. Together, these aspects compose sociomass. Accordingly, societies have a certain mass which can be measured by some unit of weight. Like other statistical quantities, sociomass is a useful index because it measures the gross social weight accumulating as sociosystems grow. Agricultural societies, for instance, have much less sociomass than industrial societies. Similarly, other ratios show the capital wealth of society which varies by rates of production and levels of industrialization.

Next, space is reflected in the geography or topology of a country. Social space underlies the fundamental nature of a community which remains rather constant for long periods. Territory and location set the stage upon which human affairs are conducted, so it forms the infrastructural arena of geopolitics and macroeconomics.

When sociomass is distributed over sociospace, it measures sociodensity. This is another useful index because it differentiates between massive or heavy urban societies, spread or sparse rural, and light nomadic hunter-gatherer ones. Obviously, sedentarization and urbanization solidify societies into more dense and rigid states.

Finally, adding time to mass and area introduces history to physiology and geography. Human action is the systemic content which takes place in a space-time continuum and can never be isolated from its environmental context. The flow of time measures the rate of change of vital indices, adding motion to position. Sociomotion is an index measuring the average or aggregate velocity of social components. A mobile society indicates the amount of people's travel and goods' transport in sociospace. This index also measures social mobility by correlating horizontal movement in geospace with vertical movement in sociostrata.

Traditional societies are slow changing, whereas modern societies are fast moving. Social inertia dictates that heavy systems are slower to maneuver than light ones, hence changing the status quo of large establishments is very difficult. In this case, the Conservation of Momentum Law plays a great role in social as in all material systems. Following Newton's First Law, this conservative tendency makes all societies maintain their status quo indefinitely, unless something happens to change it.

That something is of course force. According to Newton's Second Law, some force, proportional to mass and acceleration, is required to change a system's state of inertia. This means that the more massive a society, the greater force must be brought to bear upon it in order to effect any social change. Without some application of force, no alteration of the status quo is possible.

The required force can only be exerted by expending some energy as a result of work. When this happens, energy is expended by bringing force to bear upon mass. So social change requires energy in order to work its way from one condition to another. No change can be made without the use of some energy in doing some work. The heavier the system, the farther and faster it is to be moved; the greater the amount of work to be done and energy to be expended.

When time is added to this equation, we get social power which measures the rate of social change. In this sense, social power is the ability to make people move far and fast. The more people one can move, farther and faster, the more power one has or needs. Leaders have such power because they can get great masses to do in a short time what they would not otherwise have done for long periods.

Unlike physical power which displaces material bodies by contact or transport, social power gets humans to act by information and communication. Doing things by the force of verbal power is the great distinction of human society and the basic difference between brute violence and subtle influence. Power is used in both cases, but in different ways.

Energy and power are not equally spread through society. Social structures and institutions accumulate and agglutinate energy in certain centers of power, while they also produce power vacuums in between. Social strata and classes are systemic hierarchies of potential power differentials which form the classical social pyramid, where power percolates to the top.

Arrow's Paradox points to this tendency of elite control of society. Similarly, Michel's Iron Law of Oligarchy and Pareto's 20/80 Ratio of Inequality describe the general trend of power to concentrate or consolidate in small groups. In all cases, the few end up with much, while the many are left with little. Whether it is social masses or energies at stake, there is a definite historical tendency of unequal distribution of social goods or values in all systems. When this happens, St. Mathew's Principle, Marx's aphorism and Acton's dictum come true.

Dynamics

Society, of course, is not simply a mechanical system. It also has important thermodynamic aspects expended in the transformation, distribution, and utilization of energy. The macrostatistical measures of heat, temperature, and pressure then apply to social as to physical systems.

Social heat is produced by energy conversion due to work. What kind of matter, energy, and information social systems extract, convert, and distribute; how they use their natural resources and why, reveal a lot about their culture or way of life. Obviously a society animated by nuclear power will evolve a different lifestyle than one subsisting on coal or solar energy.

Both biological and social systems share the same basic structures and functions involving an organic economy, informatic society, and cybernetic polity. Like organisms, societies process matter, energy, and information in order to preserve and propagate themselves in their particular environment. Social life exists at the edge of order and chaos, moving between one and the other; it needs a nutritive environment and a rich network of facilitating relationships to get up and keep going.

Like all life, society fights entropy as long as possible, by exploiting the matter and energy bounty of nature. An economy provides the metabolism by which societies counter entropy and maintain their collectively social as well as individually biological life. The more energy a system consumes, the more entropy it produces in its environment. The high level of human energy and ingenuity creates facts and artifacts by mental and physical work, which decrease the entropy of the social system by increasing the natural entropy of the environment.

Social order is a state of low entropy which requires high energy to maintain it. When such energy is not available, socioentropy sets in, manifested by systemic disintegration, disorientation, and disorder. An entropic society then is a system of deteriorating levels of potential in matter, energy, and form. The natural tendency of all systems is to degenerate from high energy potentials to random waste heat, so there is a social tropism towards enervated and disorderly states, unless continuous efforts are made to maintain their structure against the ravages of time and the forces of entropy. The arrow of time decrees that all things left to themselves naturally degrade and ultimately die: from the biological life cycle of birth and death of individuals to the historical rise and fall of civilizations.

Primitive economies maintain social life very close to naturally low levels, without too much environmental disturbances, therefore they are able to last a long time. Social development, however, like biological evolution, raises the potential energy levels of increasingly complex systems by sucking in and using up more and more environmental resources. Historical progress strives to climb up to higher peaks in the fitness landscape represented by improving chances for survival.

At the same time, the fitness landscape itself evolves as systems create new opportunities for their survival and progress. By doing so, however, most technological advances raise metabolic activity, burning more energy and using more materials, thus shortening their life span. In contrast to millennial agricultural economies, the centennial industrial revolution increased the energy throughput of modern societies, transforming them into high-temperature thermodynamic systems.

Economic development not only increases social temperature, but also pressure, by raising expectations and demands for higher standards of living. Due to systemic inertia, however, structural changes are hard to make and slow to bring about. Periodic social revolutions, like natural catastrophes, clean the slate somewhat, so that the underdogs of ancient regimes can get a chance to dominate for a while in a new setting. With changing environments, what was fit under certain conditions becomes a burden in others and vice versa. But since, per definition, revolutions are very rapid and radical changes, they require a great expenditure of effort or concentrations of energy, hence they occur seldom. When they do happen, random and chaotic events, such as wars or revolutions, are very costly in human and material terms. Since it is impossible to predict and control their outcome, even when successful, it is also impossible to calculate their net cost-benefit results.

More likely, organic and social systems alike struggle to maximize fitness and flexibility by an evolutionary manner. Social Darwinism applies its combination of random variation of inherent traits, and selection of the fittest by adaptation, for survival from biology and ecology to sociology and ideology. It thus equates social egalitarianism with communal primitivism and considers the development of social hierarchy as a sine qua non of evolutionary progress.

Simple Darwinism, however, underestimates social cooperation by emphasizing competition. Normally, organic and social systems are both cooperative and altruistic, competitive and egoistic, productive and destructive, playful and ponderous. So the Spencerian survival of the fittest does not occur only by dominating others, but also by cooperating with them and adapting to their environment.

Moreover, social evolution differs from natural evolution, in that it is more Lamarckian than Darwinian—a trait that makes social development more rapid than natural evolution, which, ironically, created an intelligent species whose collective actions affect the environment so much that humanity is now poised to accelerate the rate of natural evolution itself.

Dialectics

Societies, like organisms, are centers of autonomous activity and creativity. Beyond biological and social systems in general, however, human societies are characterized by the uniqueness of their membership. Man is the paragon of animals and the highest stage of organic evolution because of introspectivity, intellectuality, and intentionality. Thus human consciousness contains not only cognitive facts, but normative values, cultural symbols, and proactive plans. As a result, naive reductionist and quantitative sciences are insufficient to explain all social dimensions. The logic inherent to social life makes it meaningful at a deeper level than merely functional incident or historical accident.

Human societies have an added and unique character which simple organic or social systems do not. Since men possess self-consciousness, our societies partake of greater creativity and complexity than other collectivities. As such, information and communication play a major role in shaping their form and content. Unlike instinctive behavior then, intentional action is preceded by consideration, deliberation, and anticipation of its consequences.

Human behavior involves a symbolic interaction between subject and object, because self-consciousness makes subjective actors interpret and impact objective reality. Men are the only self-conscious and self-steering actors with multiple and contradictory goals; consequently, as human knowledge is the result of a mind-matter dialogue, political knowledge is the result of an I-thou dialectic.

Because of their high intelligence and self-consciousness, humans can be both more cooperative and competitive than other animals. Our societies then are both more communal and conflictual than those of other species. Most important, we are the only political animals because we can solve social conflicts by dialectical means.

Social evolution converges physics and politics by softening the former and hardening the latter. This dialectic convergence from confrontation to cooperation effects a synthesis of opposites and implies that not only are they interdependent, but also capable of fusing into a single entity. For that reason, traditional philosophies stress the dialectic quality of existence, as a play between opposites: yin-yang, creation-destruction, war-peace, life-death, all of which are equally necessary.

Societies are complex self-organizing adaptive systems which value creation and propagation. Since they are precariously balanced on the cosmos-chaos boundary, autopoietic systems evolve by selection and mutation, convergence and divergence. Thereby, order can emerge spontaneously by homeostatic convergence of various factors.

Between the Carlylean view of personal history as being made by great men and the opposite Marxian view of impersonal forces making history by deterministic processes, there is the intermediate view of combined factors operating interactively. Although historical explanations may not be directly deduced from physical laws or isolated phenomena, they can be indirectly factored from contingent chains of interdependent events. These contingencies follow from the interplay of natural, social and personal forces which are so numerous that they never combine in exactly the same way, making it impossible for history to repeat itself in precisely the same manner. For that reason, it is an *opera aperta*, something that makes drawing lessons from history an eclectic and dangerous occupation.

The evolution of social systems is chaotic because it is oversensitive to initial conditions. History does not repeat itself exactly because no matter how similar cases may be, their outcomes diverge significantly. Since they are complex and open systems of near-infinite degrees of freedom, societies seem to be much like quantum fields where each individual is subjected to the vector sum of forces exerted by all others.

As Poincaré's premise stressed a hundred years ago, chaotic phenomena are inherently unpredictable, because small arbitrary influences can have enormous unforeseen consequences. Thus a tiny initial mistake grows into a large final error. This peculiarity has by now been generalized by the new science of complexity, whose Mandelbrot thesis points out that since simple mathematical equations give rise to extremely complicated patterns, simple principles may underlie complex phenomena.

Human societies are perfect examples of complex systems. As such, they are more than the sum of their parts, because they possess an emergent sociality due to their dynamic morphogenetic field, which creates intersubjective consciousness into which individuals are socialized. Compared to animals who may show a tremendous intraspecies variation in their physical appearance, humans have only slight sex, size, and color differences.

Our marked physical homogeneity, however is more than made up for by our extreme cultural diversity due to differential socialization. Whereas other animals have no culture to speak of, humans have a plethora of language, art, religion, kinship (LARK) traits arising out of their different ways of thought and behavior, rather than size or shape.

Cultural traits are said to be propagated by memes who act like a colony of socialized viruses. Because of their similar functions, there is a profound parallelism between genes and memes. But memes, the units of cultural inheritance, unlike genes, do not have a single archival medium of propagation because they operate via various linguistic communicators.

The marked integrating trend of globalization contains and contradicts the memes of local traditional cultures, just as intermarriages combine genes into a common pool. Out of an increased genetic and memetic interpenetration, there is now forming a world superculture which increases human unity in both its biological and anthropological components.

Yet, rampant globalization has not yet effaced local cultures because cultural melting pots are asymptotic in their assimilating power. The more one trend acts, the more its opposite reacts, much like Newton's Third Law of motion. Rather than blending together, old cultures assert their differences and diverge further from one another. It seems that the more people know of each other, the more they want to retain their unique identities and accentuate their differences.

This conflict between centripetal modernization and centrifugal tradition have been going on since the dawn of urbanization and civilization. Intercultural contacts between so-called civilized and barbarian societies often resulted in conflict and violence, with the aggressor and defender roles reversing in many historical cases. Anyway, in spite or because of their conflictual character, intercultural contacts involve and evolve progress.

Nothing new can come out of highly ordered and controlled systems. Only those at the edge of chaos, between order and disorder, can create novelty as well as court catastrophe. The prime mover of social change then seems to be the dynamic tension between interacting cultures and the resulting struggle for survival or accommodation. Isolated cultures have a predictable lifetime of rise, stagnation, and fall.

On the contrary, vigorous interaction and competition bring about the necessary changes for prolonging and promoting a society, albeit with an altered culture. The alternative in any case is either intense interaction and evolution or isolation, decline, and death. That is the ultimate option of dynamic systems and above all human societies. The question is to what extent it is possible or desirable to balance stability and manage change by optimal social control.

SOCIOCYBERNETICS

Since the publication of Ross' *Social Control* (1901) at the beginning of the twentieth century, sociocybernetics became the study of social normality. In a somewhat different thrust, we look at sociocybernetics as a function of three sectors: economy, society, polity. In this focus, the tasks of social control may now be classified in the domains of impersonal impact of human activity upon natural processes and their preservation; interpersonal relations regulated by social institutions and cultural promotion; personal responsibility versus inalienable human rights and individual protection.

Accordingly, social control revolves around three essential poles: substantial (determining the transformation and transportation of matter and energy); behavioral (restricting human expression into socially acceptable activities); formational (regulating the flow of symbolic information and communication). On the basis of these salient points, we have to consider sociocybernetics: factual necessity (need of social control in present economic-ecologic circumstances); functional possibility (extent of human behavioral control within the social system); formal desirability (preference of political control over governmental fiat).

This section interposes these multiple dimensions in order to inscribe the necessity, describe the possibility and prescribe the desirability of social control for each of the above contents and contexts in three critical sections concerning:

- Macrounsustainability of nature by increased external human economic activity
- Microungovernability of society by increased internal cultural entropy and complexity
- Metaunaccountability of government by increased central technopolitical autonomy.

Macrocybernetic Factualism and Natural Realism

The necessity of behavioral control manifests itself in many realms. Order informs living systems by bits or genes, whose information is another way of countering entropic chaos. It is the morphogenetic field generated by inherited traits and environmental influences that shapes the behavior of a system in space and time.

Potential fields naturally self-organize and generate new patterns without needing any preconceived plan or program. Natural selection thus operates in a random way to maintain the dynamic stability of ecosystems. Organisms, from amoeba to man, may behave randomly or independently in plentiful or pleasant conditions, but collectively or purposely under scarce, dense, or critical ones. Thus emergent behavior is due more to incident fields than inherent traits.

Unless we presume the existence of God, the architecture of most natural systems has no supreme governor in absolute control, so a great deal of activity goes on autonomously. Overall order may then be created without a totalitarian organizer. Such naturally emergent order is much more robust, flexible, and viable than that constructed arbitrarily by a complete controller. In this way, natural systems have evolved under conditions unfavorable to central control.

In contrast, human systems are not natural creations but artificial constructs, so control is moot in all its aspects. As the first and primary sector of the social system, the economy provides the metabolic functions of society, thereby extracting, converting, manipulating, exchanging, and distributing raw materials and brute energies into the social system. By increasing the capacity of social metabolism, industrial economy has created serious depletion, erosion, and pollution in many regions of the global ecology. Widespread problems of natural resource scarcity, declining food supply, shrinking crop land, global warming, ozone depletion, unstable weather, and swelling population are interacting by positive feedbacks to overshoot Gaia's natural carrying capacity.

Thus, as technological progress has done away with many existential problems for civilized life, it has created many environmental problems for wildlife. While increasing human power has gradually reduced the impact of natural forces upon us, it has also increased the impact of social forces upon nature. As a result nature is now threatened by humanity, much more than humanity was ever threatened by nature.

Our looming environmental problems stem mainly from excessive material transforms and transfers between culture and nature, brought about by overheated industrial economies. In this case, either economic depression or dematerialization seem to be the alternatives of slowing down the throughputs between our systems and the environment. Postindustrial reengineering has already began this process of social intangification and informatization.

However, the invisible hand of free market forces in supply and demand is not sufficient by itself to control collective economic activities, so that they can harmonize the countless contradictory individual actions. Although conservative thinking believes that such balance can eventually and inevitably be established, a considerable time lag creates great systemic instability which must be addressed by other social means.

In this respect, natural law as the basis of social morality is now more urgent than ever before. Already, along with planetary globalization, certain uniform ethical principles are becoming widely legitimized. These new global standards are now spreading around the world as constant and universal natural law infrastructures, on the basis of which different or variable local custom superstructures may exist and flourish. Ethical relativism and cultural particularism can thereby exist on the surface, if they do not violate these deep underlying fundamental canonic human values.

In any case, whatever solutions may be considered appropriate, they should be assessed and applied carefully. Since social experimentation is dangerous and difficult or risky and costly, most social evidence is open to wide differences of interpretation and confirmation. Reality cannot be grasped entirely or accurately by anybody because of the limitations of of our sensory and mental apparatus, the prejudices of our ideologies and the restrictions of our language.

Moreover, social complexity makes it impossible to single out monocausality as an explanation for equifinality. These constraints impose limits to human control, due to a multitude and complexity of site- and time-specific factors: ecologic givens, demographic imperatives, technologic inadequacies, socioeconomic constraints.

Vying for complete control of complex systems is hopeless, as various externalities, such as incomplete information, imperfect rationality, and unintended consequences, can never be completely taken into account. Even if each link in the causal chain could be explained, their concatenations cannot; since that would require measuring initial conditions with infinite precision and then deducing all their effects: something impossible in practice as well as in principle.

Taking all these things into account, we could apply Heisenberg's uncertainty principle to politics as well as to physics. Some measure of uncertainty underlies all human thought and action. This situation faces us with a vengeance in sociocybernetics, where the impossibility of pinpointing existential states means a loss of control and information. We must then accept these limitations is a strength, rather than weakness, because it makes us more realistic, humble and prudent.

Microcybernetic Functionalism and Moral Humanism

Above and beyond economic infrastructures, there are cultural structures in all social systems. Culture serves consumptive and reproductive, creative and recreative, purposive and evaluative, cognitive and imaginative functions, by its familial, educational, religious, artistic, and scientific institutions. These complex structures and functions obviously require some measure of control, which is not always forthcoming. When this happens, the loss of control and breakdown of order with its accompanying threat of social chaos becomes the ultimate problem of sociocybernetics.

The probability of social disorder and chaotic activity increases along with systemic potency, complexity, and fragility. Powerful, sophisticated, nonlinear systems are prone to abrupt discontinuities due to random disturbances which, although they could be either constructive or destructive, are anyhow unsettling. Weighing the import of such hazards requires multiplying the probability of their occurrence by the severity of their outcome, both of which increase along with accelerating social change.

The ever-present tendency of social entropy erodes social order, producing anomie, atomization, and alienation, primarily due to the loosening of human control over both internal passions and external actions. The socialization which keeps behavior within certain bounds loses its legitimacy and unleashes brutal instincts belonging to the law of the jungle. It is this degradation that sociocybernetics tries to prevent or correct, as the loss of civility eventually leads to the fall of civilization.

Technological progress has done away with a lot of existential problems, but it has also exacerbated many social issues. While increasing industrial power has gradually reduced the impact of natural forces, it has also necessitated the tightening of social controls, thus reducing people's freedom of action. At the same time, the increase of social options brought about by technology and industry has also increased choices and therefore people's freedom. The individual must now constantly make economic, political, and social choices which did not exist before when either the necessity of nature or the authority of culture made them automatically.

A system that does not offer choices does not need control. Determinism being noncybernetic, control is a function of option. The greater the freedom of the components in a system, the more control each one must exert in order to choose responsibly. As the increase of individual freedom releases man from traditional ties, it also compels him to bear individual responsibility for the consequences of his decisions. It thus becomes increasingly difficult to blame society for one's failures, so what seems an opportunity for the strong becomes a risk for the weak.

Human predilection for power and control are incentives for both liberty and tragedy. Our inquisitiveness and curiosity are great incentives for innovation and progress, but also imply grave dangers of getting out of control and going over the limits of viability. Now that we have been freed from many natural controls, it is incumbent upon us to replace them with either self- or social-control, in order not to fall into indulgence or inertia.

Individual self-control, however, is constrained by the inherent limits of mental and physical capability, as well as love of adventure and mischief. Since the very idea of system implies a certain structural-functional order, any society requires some control to regulate its institutions and activities. The need for such control arises whenever the members of a group realize that they are interdependent. The higher their interdependence, the greater the need for some regulation of individual behavior for the benefit of collective coexistence. Consequently, it seems that control becomes increasingly necessary in modern societies, since they need some servomechanism to regulate behavior, lest they run amok and either implode or explode.

Yet, even if some social control may be necessary, it is not evident how to bring it about. In this quandary, two polar positions represent the ideal alternatives. On the one end, libertarianism believes that cultural as well as natural evolution can neither be stopped nor controlled. Things happen according to their own dynamic and agenda, so it is better to let them develop naturally, than try to control them inadequately. On the contrary, totalitarianism expects that social control is quite possible and desirable. At its extreme, this technocratic optimism seeks to impose controls on all social activities and thus attain complete social order. Thus, although individuals are imperfect, the collectivity can be perfected, given strong and wise leadership.

While the first position assumes the impossibility and undesirability of social control, the second assumes its need or necessity. Reality most likely lies between these two extremes. The notorious lack of human self-control supports one side and illustrates some need of social control, but sociocybernetics also shows the difficulty, if not ungovernability, of human institutions. Since humans are prone to err and sin, social policies will often be unrealistic and incorrect, so both theory and history show that perfect central control is impossible and its search is illusory.

Moreover, increasing collective social control may be undesirable because it necessarily decreases individual self-control and delimits human free will. Replacing the declining instinctive natural controls, strong mores and morals have traditionally served as cultural straightjackets, guiding social behavior within narrow channels of acceptable performance. Modern societies, however, have destroyed these age-old traditions, thus creating a value vacuum where trial and error are now taking place.

At the most general level, social control or governance involves institutions (rules and roles) capable of conflict resolution and collective action. Effective governance channels behavior in such a way as to minimize social problems, facilitate public policy-making, and maximize collective action. The rise of the third sector of civic society (association) after the first (government) and second (corporation) points to the necessity of a balanced, horizontal, flexible order in a complex world. Thus governing complexity requires a high degree of flexible organization, balancing social responsibility and individual duty.

Nevertheless, permanent social stability is neither possible nor desirable because it leads to the rigidity of socioclerosis. Much more probable and preferable is a dynamic equilibrium which can sustain cultural development and advance natural evolution through light and flexible control.

Metacybernetic Formalism and Practical Rationalism

Although it is impossible to attain complete knowledge of chaotic systems, it is possible to control them somewhat. The behavior of nonlinear, nonequilibrium, nondeterministic systems can be so controlled, if the controller is a conscious part of the system, as is the case of man and society. This may be done by discovering the laws of chaos which reveal a hidden higher order. In this way, some social management is feasible even in chaotic social systems.

If a modicum of social control is both necessary and possible, political institutions are the usual candidates for effecting it, since voluntary social associations and profitable economic corporations do not suffice to provide such control. Liberty and prosperity are not enough to satisfy the human will to power and control, thus we shall forever struggle to find an optimal social system somewhere, sometime.

Actually, political structures are epiphenomena of the underlying configuration of power in society, confirming that control is a function of power. The more power technology concentrates in human hands, the greater the danger of calamity or catastrophe if control is lax or lost. At the same time, the more power one has, the greater skill, nerve and foresight are necessary to handle it. Powerful societies then need relatively powerful governments.

On this matter, anarchy, monarchy, and polyarchy, along with centralist and federalist models, provide different controls to power. We cannot go here into the pros and cons of all these political options other than to say that sociophysics suggests a flexible and multiple combination where policy-making is shared among as many centers of power as possible by a constitutional regime of checks and balances.

Governance becomes much more difficult when both codes and facts or programs and data keep changing, as they do now. But since collective behavior emerges predictably out of myriad unpredictable individual acts, most of which stem from human habits and social memes, it is possible for sociocybernetics to be applied in political regulation, as in economic production and social reproduction.

For this to happen, the permanent coexistence of historical routine-forming and unexpected routine-breaking novelties should be modeled in more sophisticated computer programs which take into account the probability of optimizing a priori norms against a posteriori facts, depending on a combination of actor gestures, system structures and event conjunctures.

Although human control varies from little to nil in these three categories, necessity being the mother of invention, it behooves us to probe and find the limits of sociocybernetics in each. Recognizing different approaches to common problems may yield equally appropriate solutions. The aim is not seeking a single answer to complex questions but a range of available options for optimal selection.

Choosing between competing options is rationalized by Bohr's Complementarity Principle, which resolves the wave-particle duality paradox as a metaphor to language, wherein we are doomed to speak words best suited to describing simple and distinct large-scale objects, rather than complex and contradictory abstractions. To the simplistic and deterministic true-false dichotomy of ordinary logic, we must then add a third option of indeterminacy. Social logic, like quantum logic, is thus trivalued: instead of things being either-or, they may also be both and neither.

As Bohrian probability replaces Laplacian certainty, it is evident that no model containing the complete picture of the world can possibly exist. All measurements are imprecise and uncertain, thus all knowledge must be imperfect. In social terms, complementarity explains the dual nature of man as both individualist and collectivist, egoist and altruist. These growing limits to the role of classic governance indicate that Newtonian cybernetics are superseded by chaotic cybertechnics.

Given incomplete information and imperfect rationalization, sociocybernetics must bow to the Law of Unintended Consequences, which warns of the unwanted by-products of uncontrolled or unforeseen causes, as is often the case in chaotic systems. Since no cause can be controlled to such an extent that all its effects can be foreseen, caution must be the name of our political game.

This does not always mean tepid policies. Moderation to toleration compares as modesty to mediocrity, so prudent policies need not be synonymous to pedestrian politics.

In summarizing the assessments of this section, we can state that as necessary as it is to impose strict controls of the social impacts on the natural environment, it is not so upon the social system itself. Similarly, it is more possible to control culture than nature, while it is most desirable to control the controllers than it is possible to do so. These differentials make sociocybernetics a difficult and diffident undertaking, not to be taken lightly or hastily.

In spite of that, sociocybernetics is as necessary as it is difficult, especially in our advanced societies entering their postmodern era; where scientism, objectivism, positivism, or progressivism are no longer taken for granted and neoskepticism based on the ambiguity, uncertainty, and absurdity of life becomes the order of the day. Our thesis then concludes that sociophysics provides the only objective standards for sociocybernetics, thus helping humanity avoid the self-contradictions which lead to excess and hubris.

CONCLUSION

Sociocybernetics involves a hierarchy of mechanic, organic, and symbolic systems, so a temporal descriptive-explicative-predictive theory of social control must strive for a selective simplicity, combining static, dynamic, and dialectic processes. Operating in all spheres of life (personal, cultural, natural), physics, politics, and cybernetics combine deterministic, randomistic, and voluntaristic factors to give us a systemic and systematic understanding of reality. In this respect, here is an apt analogy: as a successful airplane flight must abide with the laws of aerodynamics, an effective sociocybernetic exercise must abide by the laws of sociophysics.

Prefering Occam's razor to Hume's guillotine, sociophysics combines a simple naturalist-moralist position. Like Zen, it strives to make sense of the human condition by recognizing that it may do so in vain and transcends the absurdity of life by living it as if it were worthwhile. Consequently, our paradigm proposes that doing what comes naturally means riding the powerful forces of nature and going along with the flow of evolution. Adapt or die is thus the natural imperative which we can only ignore at our peril.

In summary, the contribution of sociophysics to sociocybernetics may be said to emphasize social constraint, moderate behavior, and prudent policy, reflected in three fundamental principles: factualism—basic dependency of culture on nature (Natural Realism); functionalism: behavioral interdependence of individuals (Moral Humanism); formalism: checks and balances of responsible government (Practical Rationalism).

Weaving these strands together, we have arrived at some provisional theses regarding the essence of sociocybernetics in the context of nature and culture. Accordingly, social control becomes a function of the human capability to influence its internal nurture, as well as external culture and nature. The level of such control is directly proportional to cultural dynamics and its natural impacts, but inversely proportional to individual introspection and self-control.

Social and personal control are thus negatively correlated, because wherever there is an adequate amount of the latter, there is no need of the former. Conversely, personal impotence and social irresponsibility, as is the case in large and complex societies, demand strong collective controls. But since practical applications always lag behind ideal declarations, social control can never be complete. Although such control is increasingly necessary, it does not mean that more bureaucracy is desirable. The difficult trick is to bring about better governance (functional control) without more government (structural center).

At present, sophisticated global computer models show the way to better data gathering and overall planning by proper accounting of the costs and risks of socioeconomic activity, thus helping governments make more enlightened decisions. As indicated here, increased knowledge of the laws of chaos should help us understand the behavior of large collectivities, thereby improving rather than increasing human control of its cultural and natural environment.

Since social development is still a long way from sophisticated centralized control, it would be more efficient and effective to promote it in conjunction with socially and economically decentralized associations and corporations. Because of social complexity, chaotic causality, and human incapacity, all efforts for social control must then be sensitive, relative, and tentative.

Our syllogism then proceeds from the main premise or thesis that some control is necessary in all complex systems; it encounters the minor premise or antithesis that perfect control is impossible in reality; and finally ends with the conclusion or synthesis that a modicum of control is both feasible and desirable or optimal and sufficient. Just as complete control is impossible and some control is inevitable, it behooves us to find the optimal conjunction in any particular place or time.

Although we are gene organisms by nature and meme machines by culture, we can rise above both by a conscious sociocybernetic control of human nurture. Even if humans have an innate tendency for the sin of egoism (major premise) and are condemned to a life of conflict and toil (minor premise), we can redeem ourselves by mentality and morality (conclusion).

On that argument, the hypothesis defended was that: due to systemic complexity, social control is necessary; due to scientific progress, such control is possible; and due to human imperfection, it is desirable. Having said that, we were also careful to admit that perfect control is unnecessary, impossible and undesirable. Thus we conclude that the most important and difficult task of sociocybernetics is to find the point of "cyberoptimality".

In response to this challenge, we must recognize these symptoms, assess their seriousness, and resolve to change our course of action by imposing some rational control on our wayward ways. The third and best way can be found between the rigid order of complete control in closed crystalline systems and the random disorder of uncontrolled anarchic chaos in the thin edge of probabilistic dynamic, quasicontrolled, open systems. Given the great need for social control and the constraints of Bohrian complimentarity, Heisenbergian uncertainty, and Gödelian incapacity, sociocybernetics has a heavy task which sociophysics can enlighten. This chapter was an initial attempt to do so.

REFERENCES

Abell, P. (1989) *The Syntax of Social Life*. Oxford: Oxford University Press.
Adams, R.N. (1975) *Energy & Power*. Austin: University of Texas Press.
Ahmavara, A.Y. (1974). *The Cybernetic Theory of Development*. Helsinki: Tammi.
Arnopoulos, P.J. (1993a). *Sociophysics*. New York: Nova Science.
Arnopoulos, P.J. (1993b). Dialectics-Politics-Cybernetics. *Cybernetica, 36*, 345-353.
Arnopoulos, P.J. (1993c). Ideal-Real Links. *Kybernetes, 27*, 20-34.
Arnopoulos, P.J. (1995a). *Sociopolitics*. Toronto: Guernica.
Arnopoulos, P.J. (1995b). Social Development. *Sociology & Social Policy, 15*, 42-69.
Arnopoulos, P.J. (1997). *Cosmopolitics*. Toronto: Guernica.
Arnopoulos, P.J. (1999). *Exopolitics*. New York: Nova Science.
Ashby, W.R. (1956). *Introduction to Cybernetics*. London: Chapman & Hall.
Aulin, A. (1982). *The Cybernetic Laws of Social Progress*. Oxford: Pergamon.
Bailey, K.D. (1990). *Social Entropy Theory*. Albany: SUNY Press.
Baldacci, D. (1996). *Absolute Power*. New York: Warner Books.
Baldacci, D. (1997). *Total Control*. New York: Thorndike Press.
Beniger, J.R. (1986). *The Control Revolution*. Cambridge, MA: Harvard University Press.
Black, D. (1984). *Towards a General Theory of Social Control*. New York: Academic Press.
Boyarsky, A. & Gora, P. (1997). *The Laws of Chaos*. Boston: Birkhauser.
Burns, T. & Buckley, W. (Eds.). (1976). *Power and Control*. London: Sage.
Cohen, S. (1985). *Visions of Social Control*. Oxford: Polity Press.
Dunsire, A. (1978). *Control in a Bureaucracy*. New York: St. Martin's Press.
Eccles, J. (1994). *How the Self Controls Its Brain*. Berlin: Springer.
Evernden, N. (1992). *The Social Creation of Nature*. Baltimore: Johns Hopkins University Press.
Falk, R.A. (1995). *Humane Governance*. Oxford: Polity Press.
Geyer, F. & van der Zouwen, J. (Eds.). (1986). *Sociocybernetic Paradoxes*. Beverly Hills, CA: Sage.
Gibbs, J.P. (1989). *Control: Sociology's Central Notion*. Urbana: University of Illinois Press.
Glasser, W. (1996). *Control Theory*. New York: HarperCollins.
Hagge, J. (Ed.). (1994). *Formal Theory in Sociology*. New York: SUNY Press.
Kaye, H.L. (1986). *The Social Meaning of Modern Biology*. New Haven, CT: Yale University Press.
Kelly, K. (1994). *Out of Control*. Reading, MA: Addison-Wesley.
Klausner, S.Z. (Ed.). (1965). *The Quest for Self-Control*. New York: Free Press.

Lasker, G.E. (Ed.). (1994). *Sociocybernetics.* Windsor, ONT.: International Federation for Advanced Studies in Systems Research and Cybernetics.
Lewin, K. (1951). *Field Theory in Social Science.* New York: Harper & Row.
Mee, C.L. (1993). *Playing God.* New York: Simon & Schuster.
Nagel, S.N. (1997). *The Super-Optimum Society.* New York: Nova Science.
Nicolis, G., & Progogine. I. (1989). *Exploring Complexity.* New York: Freeman.
Powers, J. (1991). *Philosophy and the New Physics.* London: Routledge.
Powers, W.T. (1989). *Living Control Systems.* Gravel Switch, KY: Control Systems.
Rosenau, J. & Czempiel, E. (Eds.). (1992). *Governance Without Government.* Cambridge, MA: Harvard University Press.
Ross, E.A. (1901). *Social Control.* New York: Macmillan.
Sardar, Z., & Ravetz, J. (Eds.). (1996). *Cyberfutures.* London: Pluto Press.
Searle, J.R. (1995). *The Construction of Social Reality.* New York: Free Press.
Thoresen, C.E. & Mahoney, M.J. (1974). *Behavioral Self-Control.* New York: Holt, Rinehart & Winston.
Wilson, E.O. (1997). *Consilience: The Unity of Knowledge.* New York: Knopf.
Young, A.M. (1976). *The Geometry of Meaning.* Mill Valley, CA: Robert Briggs.

Chapter 2

MIND AND BRAIN: A DYNAMIC SYSTEM MODEL

Walter Buckley

INTRODUCTION

In this chapter I outline a model of mind-brain interaction and the continuous real-time generation and maintenance of consciousness and mental events in terms of the organism-environment interaction, or recursive loop, characteristic of organisms pursuing everyday life needs. It is presented as a scientific approach utilizing concepts of modern science and technology, rather than traditional mainstream philosophical speculation. A reductionist brain-alone theory is questioned but the nervous system is given its important place within the broader dynamic loop. Put in other terms, the brain is a "necessary" but not "sufficient" condition for mind and consciousness. This avoids a dualism as the only alternative to brain physicalism, neither of which is scientifically viable. Consciousness and mentality are seen as dynamic system processes, not entities with a spatial or temporal locus, which means that it is useless to search the brain for the locus of these processes.

    The main phases of this organism-environment loop, within which conscious events are generated, are discussed: sensory input, perception and cognition, decision, and motor output back onto the environment. It is not merely argued, as many have in the past, that consciousness and the mental have something to do with the interaction of the organism, its brain and bodily processes, and the environment. Rather, it is specifically argued that conscious awareness emerges second by second from the continual organism-environment looping. This means that if this cycling is cut off for long within the loop, consciousness is impaired or ceases. Some empirical evidence for this is given. During the discussion a number of conceptual stumbling blocks to a scientific theory, many deriving from centuries-old philosophy, are addressed and resolutions suggested.

A MODEL: THE RECURSIVE DYNAMICAL ORGANISM-ENVIRONMENT LOOP

We focus here on the generation of consciousness as based on the outcome of processes involving the organism's control of its actions in pursuit of life needs in a complex environment. Reductionist models assume that the relevant causal system lies strictly within the central nervous system—that is, brain physiology alone accounts for consciousness and the mental. The view here is a broader one, arguing that conscious mental processes are generated by the ongoing second-by-second process of (1) environmental inputs to the sensory apparatus; (2) the sensory, perceptual, and cognitive processing of this input; leading often to (3) motor processes back out onto the environment (or to further internal mental processing), all occurring with many levels of recursion and feedback in a continuous dynamical, self-referential, control system cycle. The continuous flow of time (there is no "now") is overcome or caught momentarily by working memory, and careful temporal study would be required to distinguish the time phases in the loop. It is conceivable, though I will not pursue it here, that the oscillating circuits recently found in parts of the brain have something to do with the cycling of the loop.

Such a view resolves the fact that the brain by itself does not have consciousness. It is the whole organism, complete with its emotive, hormonal, endocrine, and motor systems, as well as its total nervous system, interacting with its environment, that generates consciousness and the mental. It is argued that if this organism-environment loop is cut at any point for too long, conscious mental activity deteriorates and may cease completely. Evidential support for such a model comes from a number of sources, including neurophysiological research, earlier studies of sensory (and motor) deprivation, experiments with vision-inverting goggles (these are discussed later), and possibly from the study of the phenomenon of high-G blackout and unconsciousness of fighter pilots undergoing high-speed turns. The fact that we try to shut off consciousness when going to sleep by insulating ourselves from environmental inputs (as well as from inner mental activity) seems all too obvious but pertinent to our argument. There is also the fact that many birds and animals enter into a quiescent, reduced state of consciousness when their heads or whole bodies are enclosed or covered over, thus cutting off environmental input at the sensory input stage. Further support from recent neurophysiological studies will be discussed soon.

This model is based on something like the paradigm shift in psychology in the early 1970s that began to replace Behaviorism. This shift recognized a higher-level emergent system of cognitive processing, based also on the rise of wholism or emergentism over reductionism. Both cognitivism and wholism depend on irreducible emergent phenomena that interact as wholes.

Life itself is a dynamic process, not a material entity based on "entelechy" or "vital force," and is a good example of this top-down causal control that Sperry

(1995) spoke of. Imagine a great beast—a rhino or elephant—lying quietly in a field. Suddenly, spotting a human coming near, the great bulk rises to its feet and begins to move at good speed. But how could this happen? No external forces were applied to this heavy object; clearly, on the face of it, it must violate the laws of mechanics, gravitation, and thermodynamics, since our physics texts tell us that objects at rest remain at rest unless acted upon by an external force. A mere visual input with negligible energy has led to the enormous energy required to move that bulk. Now that's top-down control! If only we knew all the stages of processing required for this organism-environment loop to happen.

To establish the full nature of the problem addressed here, a recent neurophysiological study of mind-brain interaction will be discussed, before we outline more fully the dynamic recursive organism-environment model to be presented for consideration as a possible resolution. Just et al. (1996), using Magnetic Resonance Imaging (MRI) technique, which through electrodes attached to the head show images of active brain areas, found an increase in brain activity in language areas of human subjects as a function of their cognitive processing of increasingly complex sentence structures. In their introductory summary they say, "The comprehension of visually presented sentences produces brain activation that increases with the linguistic complexity of the sentence. These findings generally indicate that the amount of neural activity that a given cognitive process engenders is dependent on the computational demand that the task imposes" (p. 114). In the body of the report they state: "One of the challenges of brain science is to relate the dynamics of higher level cognition to the equally dynamic activity of brain-level events" (p. 114). They go on to suggest that their study represents a possible meeting ground between these two levels.

The experimental setup involved subjects reading sets of increasingly complex sentences and answering true or false experimenter probe questions (to assure that they were comprehending the meanings of the sentences), as their brain activity was being measured. Just et al. saw this as a complex cognitive level syntactic and semantic task imposing a varying amount of computational demands on the subjects as sentence complexity increased. From our point of view, then, the cognitive process (the comprehension of sentences) is presented as the independent variable, but is a matter of the wider organism-environment dynamics: subjects in an experimental setting reading sentences and responding to questions with true or false. This larger system is what makes up the "higher level" cognitive system, and engenders (to use their term) the lower level brain activity (as the dependent variable being measured). Important for our view, then, is that it is not the brain generating conscious activity that is the focus here, but rather organism-environment dynamics, generating cognition, which in turn generates further brain activity.

Clearly, what is going on here is more than simply a stimulus-response kind of brain response to sentence stimuli: there is a continuous dynamic, probably recursive, interaction involving:

a) attention of the subject to the environmental situation of word symbols in the experimental setup;
b) subjects perceiving these symbols—their brains processing the retinal input to produce subjective (mental) visual awareness of the sentences;
c) further cognitive/brain activity reading and determining the meaning of the sentences;
d) experimenter probe questioning to verify the higher cognitive nature of the subject's mental treatment of the sentences;
e) the brain scanned for level of cognitive activity;
f) the subject's attention to the next more complex sentences, perceiving and reading them...and so on throughout the experiment.

There is ample room, it would seem, for maintaining the distinction between brain activity and mental activity, although the latter must involve brain activity. To get at the distinction, however, we argue that a rather complex dynamic model of total organism-environment interaction is necessary.

To explicate this organism-environment loop model we will discuss in turn (briefly) the main phases of the loop: (1) the environment; (2) sensory input, perception, and cognition (i. e., the brain part of the loop); and (3) the motor side-behavior (external or internal) back onto the (external or internal) environment, thus completing the loop. Before doing so we will make two observations that might be helpful in orienting the reader to our point of view.

First, it can be noted that, very roughly speaking, the history of philosophical theories of epistemology is the story of arguments that select, in turn, a particular section of our loop and locate the source of knowledge and sometimes the real data of the world within that section. Thus the Empiricists focused on the sensory input section; the Phenomenalists (e. g., Ernst Mach) even more narrowly on raw sense data (whatever those are); the Phenomenologists on the perceptual and cognitive processing of input data; the Instrumentalists and Pragmatists on the motor and environmental behavior section. Thus, from the perspective of our model, we could say that each was correct, but incomplete: the whole loop must be considered.

Our second comment suggests an analogy that may highlight some problems in a number of current theories of consciousness and the salience of aspects of our present model. We are arguing that consciousness and mentality are dynamical processes, not things to be located somewhere in space or in the brain. "Process" refers here to the interactions of the parts of a larger structure or system (for example, the life process), such that it would be incorrect to identify and explain the process in terms of just one of the parts. Thus, consider self-regulation or feedback control. This is a process of component relations well understood by engineers, and realizable in physical or electronic systems (e.g., the Watts steam engine or the common room thermostat), biological systems (homeostasis), psychological systems (e.g., rational thought), or social systems (organizational control subgroups). Famous discussions of feedback control in the 1940s by Norbert Wiener and others led to our fuller understanding of the nature of purposive behavior, self-regulation, and automatic control in general. A process, then, may be independent of the particular material of which it is constructed; it is the dynamic arrangement of the components and the consequent emergent functions of the whole that define it. It is this kind of matter-independent consideration that seems to underpin the cognitive or computer scientists' silicon model of the brain and software view of consciousness.

Another common phenomenon that is neither a material object nor a disembodied spirit is the phenomenon of motion. It is also a process or relational entity, referring to the change of position in space of an object over time. Thus, process, or dynamic relations among parts, is unexceptional as a subject of everyday observation or study. But somehow it is not given at least equal ontological status in modern Western societies on a par with material objects, despite the fact that ongoing process is a large part of our experiences of the world. Western materialist ontology with its dominant orientation to static, physical things contrasts with the earlier traditional Eastern view of the world in terms of continual change, relations, process. And as A.N. Whitehead (and others) argued, the world is Process.

Our point here, then, is that it is inept to take the physical as the only alternative to the Cartesian mental. We do not have to turn to a mysterious dualism if we reject the view that consciousness and the mental are identical to the workings of the brain—nor do we need to "supervene" our way out of it. Conscious mental activity viewed as an organism-environment process is a scientifically respectable alternative.

Consider a particular kind of motion: the process of automobile travel. It involves the operation and interaction of the whole automobile with its engine, transmission, wheels, the roads, the fuel driving the engine, and so on. Thus, travel is a process, not a thing that cannot be identified with the engine of the car, no matter how important the latter. It is a process of ongoing interaction of objects with their environment involving all parts of the system. If some part of the motor fails, travel falters or ceases, but this does not prove an identity of motor and motion or travel. Likewise, just because bilateral damage to the intralaminar nucleus of the brain causes loss of consciousness does not mean that the former is a sufficient cause of the latter, or that consciousness does not involve much more of the central nervous system (CNS) and other parts of the body—especially in interaction with the environment, extenal or internal.

This admittedly less than perfect analogy between the process of travel and the process of mentality may help nevertheless to bring out the sense in which we argue that mind and consciousness cannot be reduced simply to brain processes. Other parts of the body and its chemistry certainly contribute, along with important aspects of the physical, biological, and sociocultural environment—at least in accounting for human mentality.[1] A recent article in Science magazine (Glanz, 1997) entitled "Tracing Molecules that Make the Brain-Body Connection" points out that, contrary to the previous beliefs of researchers, over the last fifteen years they have learned that the body's network of immune defenses is not an independent system but is intimately intertwined with the nervous and endocrine systems. There are direct physical links, neurons that innervate immune organs such as the spleen and lymph nodes, for example. And now, researchers are unraveling the molecular links, which include the interleukins, originally viewed only as regulators of immune cells; neurotransmitters, once thought to act only between nerve cells; and hormones, the endocrine messengers.

This helps to explain, the article suggests, "some of the previously mysterious correlations between mental and hormonal states and the immune system," for example "how the immune system triggers specific pathways in the brain to produce the fever and fatigue that accompany infections."

We should take note of, but cannot take space to document, the fact that more and more studies of the important role of emotions in cognition and perception have been appearing lately. An implication of all this, also, is that a brain if it could be kept alive in a jar (shades of Dr. Who) could have no consciousness or mental activity without inputs and outputs. It is important in the current debate to keep in mind that, just because brain activity or breakdown correlates highly with cognition (just as automobile engine activity and malfunction correlate highly with motion) does not logically entail that the latter is an epiphenomenon of, or identical to, the former. It is also necessary to keep in mind that it has seldom been shown that the brain initiates mental states and behavior, whereas cognitive states and environmental context do the main work of initiating further mental activity and action—the latter term, "action," coming more and more to be preferred over the mechanical connotation of behavior. From this point of view, the brain acts as an intermediate input signal and information processor and output enabler within the larger organism-environment loop, although this computational computer analogy is relatively arbitrary and probably not too cogent in the face of the fundamental differences between brain function and physiology and current computers.

MAKING SENSE OF THE EXTERNAL WORLD: THE INPUT INTERFACE

The organism-environment model applies to the broad view of consciousness as a general subjective awareness of the organism facing a contingent and often problematic external world, as opposed to being unconscious. We will not be concerned to any great extent here with lower levels of attention or awareness such as failure to notice some things going on around us, nor with implicit (or nonconscious) learning or behavior, nor with the many intermediate levels, or altered states, of consciousness as in daydreaming, sleeping, hypnosis, meditation, or drug/alcohol-induced states.

If we place consciousness and mentality squarely into an evolutionary framework where they belong, we may see more clearly the close integration of environment, body, and brain processes making possible these former phenomena. The early twentieth century Chicago philosopher and social psychologist George Herbert Mead, whose brilliant study of *Mind, Self and Society* (Mead, 1934) has been universally ignored or unknown in the recent surge of writing on mind and consciousness, founded his work concerning language, self, mind, and social processes squarely on evolutionary theory and Pragmatism[2] (Buckley, 1996). If we try to answer the question, "What is the main adaptive function of consciousness that promoted its evolution?" then a reasonable answer is that it brought together in real time all the environmental features relevant to a decision about the organism's next action—for example, to capture prey or avoid a predator, and directs its implementation.

If one asks what the external world is really like, the only reasonable answer for the scientific observer is: It is all those things that well-verified scientific research has found it to be, at any size scale that one wishes to select. That is, it is really elementary particles (so called), organizations of atoms, molecules, macro objects, biological systems, astronomical systems, and such. It would be anthropocentric to say that the world is "really" made up of objects we are familiar with on a human scale. And this brings us to our model and the epistemological question of how the world is sensed by us and how a veridical view of it could be generated by the apparatus that has evolved, presumably for that purpose (i. e., via natural selection).

To pursue our conception of this issue, we must introduce the simple notion of mapping, along with that of transformations and structural invariance. To take a familiar example (that is probably taken for granted by most of us), consider an audio recording (a cassette tape, CD, or the ancient phonograph record, for example) and imagine the many stages of production it went through so that one could hear sound (let's say music) almost indistinguishable from the original. There is a mapping or correspondence of the musical instrument vibrations to air vibrations, to microphone elements; then from the latter a series of transformations via transducers to electrical signals, and eventually to electromagnetic pulses on a master audio tape, for example. When we play our copy of the tape on our hifi, a similar set of transformations occur in the opposite direction, leading to the eventual vibrations of the speaker cones and finally the airwaves and our eardrums. How, we ask, can the original musical signals be preserved through all of these physical transformations, to give us such high fidelity at the receiving end? At each stage there is something that is preserved of the original signals despite all the physical changes: the only thing invariant from one transformational mapping to the next is the consistent variation in structure of the signal regardless of its particular material form.

In a broadly similar way (though certainly very different in detail), the neural mappings of some aspect or representation of the external world occur through the many stages of sensory input and brain processing, and may be relatively arbitrary for different species of animal but with similar veridical results as long as invariant structure is maintained. In the case of the sound recording system we may ask, Where is the "real" representation of the music? The answer is relatively arbitrary and depends on what stage of the many mappings one wants to select. It is a matter of evolutionary contingencies that the human auditory sensory apparatus cannot respond directly to electrical or electromagnetic signals, so we must depend on their transformation to air vibrations in order to sense, to hear, the signals.

In a comparable way, there is no one correct answer to the question: "What or where in the organism-environment mappings is the real representation of the external world?" and in no case are the mappings error-free and complete: only of varying degrees of fidelity. The picture we get from neurophysiological studies of brain processes in perception is a fairly large set of separate neural subassemblies that process (map) different features of the external input, which leads eventually to a unified, usually quite veridical conscious experience of the world. It is still an open question, from lack of data, just whether and how the higher, yet unstudied, levels of cortical processing perform the binding together of the different mappings into that unity.

My (nonexpert) reading of the neurophysiology of sensation and perception leads to the following conclusions. Focusing on vision as the most intensively and extensively studied sensory system, it is found that the retina of the eye is a very complex biochemical transducer of electromagnetic signals in the visible light range, with sensitivity to three color ranges (closer to red, yellow, blue rather than the popular red-green-blue of the computer tube.) Irvin Rock, the late senior researcher on perception, stated that the central question of the science of visual perception is: how do we come to construct a more or less veridical world when the source of the information from it is filtered through a distorted and highly variable retinal image? The "distorted" retinal image refers to such facts as the oval image given by a round object seen at an angle, or the illusion of parallel lines, like railroad tracks, seeming to converge in the distance. By veridical Rock means "that our perceptions correspond with the properties of things considered objectively and independent of viewing conditions, such as can be ascertained by measurement" (Rock, 1995, p. 5).

Neurophysiological studies of sensation show that a good deal of processing of the signals occurs at and just beyond the retina (before reaching the cortex), with much of the signals being discarded.[3] Remaining signals from the retinas pass along the optic nerve from each eye through the crossover or chiasma to a way station just before the main cortex (the lateral geniculate bodies just beyond the chiasma). After more processing the signals pass into the cortex proper and go through several more stages of processing. Several subsets of the retinal signals are responded to by separate feature detector cortical subassemblies for detecting such aspects of the retinal scene as spots, edges, lightness, vertical lines, horizontal or diagonal lines, contours, and the like. These are the various "mappings" we referred to above.

But beyond these earlier stages of cortical processing, we know nothing. One researcher tells us that there are at least seven later stages of processing of the retinal input, but we haven't the slightest idea what they do with the signals. Hence, whether or not these higher centers may integrate the various pieces of the processing into a more unified scene (and hence resolve the binding problem) we just do not know. To pass judgment one way or the other is premature (see S. C. Rao et al., 1997). One thing that is quite clear is that we would have to believe in some kind of "extrasensory perception" to reject the view that it is the quite faithful mapping of the sensed features of environmental objects that makes possible a veridical cognitive construction of them. Very recent study of neural processing provides support for our broader view.

Thus, Amos Arieli et al. (1996) measured the evoked responses of sets of neurons in the visual cortex of mammals (cats) responding to repeated presentation of the same visual stimulus. It has often been found in the past that neural responses to the same stimulus are never the same from trial to trial, and "noise" was taken as the culprit. In this new set of experiments an answer to this puzzle was found in "the dynamics of ongoing activity": the variability of neural response to the same stimulus was due, not to noise, but to other neural activity going on at the same time, which continually varied, and could be due to ongoing cognitive and behavioral activity. It was found that if the neural response to the stimulus was summed to the previous ongoing activity signal, the evoked response to a single trial could be predicted. The authors conclude that ongoing activity must play an important role in cortical function and cannot be ignored in "exploration of cognitive processes. Not only must the notion of "noise" in the brain be revised," but ongoing activity "may provide the neuronal substrate for the dependence of sensory information processing on context and on behavioral and conscious states" (Arieli et al., 1996, pp. 1868-1871). With benefit of hindsight it might seem curious that a researcher studying cortical response to a stimulus he applies would assume total quiescence of a conscious animal during the recording, but such simplifying assumptions have to be made all the time in complex research. Such a study as that of Arieli et al. at least implicates consciousness or cognition with current ongoing behavior and background neural activity, thus alerting us to a wider system dynamics.

Irvin Rock concludes his study of perception by offering a "cognitively oriented theory," that perception is "stimulus bound"—and hence independent of what we know on the one hand, thus we still perceive visual illusions despite knowing that they are such—but is a "mental construction" on the other, though it is autonomous in respect to cognitive processing on a conceptual or linguistic level. His concluding answer to the question, "Why do things look as they do?" is: "because of the cognitive operations performed on the information contained within the stimulus" (Rock, 1995, pp. 228-231). From the point of view of our model, we can rephrase the answer: Because, despite (or because of) the various neural transformations and mappings of the input signals, there is a high degree of structural invariance maintained (line orientations, edges, contours, light shades, reflected color frequencies, etc.), and the consequences for the organism are what we call "subjective experience" of the world that has substantial veridicality. As Rock points out, adapting organisms and evolving species would not have survived long without this close mapping.

Although, in my reading, evolutionary biologists don't usually like to acknowledge trends in evolution, the evidence suggests that, with many ups and downs, some living species have developed closer and more refined mappings to their environments, at first in terms of their genotypes, phenotypes, and genetically based behaviors; then by way of greater and greater learning capabilities, with behavior necessarily becoming more and more uncoupled from the genes so that it could follow instead the more flexible and adaptive learning; and then through sociocultural group processes of concerted study, learning, organized science, and social inheritance (the sociotype, if you will).

We have complained above about the loose use of the term "information" for the environmental signals that impinge on the senses, although we usually know what the authors mean and little harm is done. Sometimes, however, serious confusion and bad theory can result. After publishing his seminal work on the mathematical theory of communication, Claude Shannon (1948) admitted that his study, based on research to improve the quality of telephone line performance, was not about information in the sense of meaning at all, but might have been called "signal theory." Information is what goes into one end of the line by a meaning-laden caller and is received after leaving the other end by a linguistically knowledgeable person who can interpret the meaning of the signals transduced by the telephone equipment. Information is not a thing moving along a telephone wire but a mapping relation between two or more communicants with more or less common understandings of the mapping of symbols to aspects of the world.

Thus, if we (incorrectly) say that computers are processing information rather than signals, we are implying that they might somehow come to "understand" what they are doing—that the signals are symbols with meaning for them. This helps perpetuate the view that computers are intelligent, someday sentient, machines.[4] In the middle are only varying voltages, just as in the middle of the organism-environment system are varying rates of neural pulses that must be put together into cognitive events meaningful to the whole organism in its environment.

All of this leads us to question the wisdom of attempting to localize the "really primitive or fundamental data of experience" as did the empiricists, idealists, and others. To localize such data in "immediate sense data," "percepts," "phenomenal mental configurations," language symbols, computed "representations," or other cognitive constructions, is probably not by itself of any greater significance than to ask whether, in reproducing music via a phonograph or tape player, any one transformation of the signals—mechanical, magnetic, electrical—provides the more "fundamental or primitive" data about the original acoustic input signals (which, themselves, are only vibrating air molecules; it's the larger patterning that is of interest to us). Theoretically, the question is not meaningful. If the invariant signal pattern is well preserved in each case, then the potential mapping or information coding is as "fundamental" in any form because it is fully equivalent (as long as there is a good transducer to extract the invariance). And just because the substantive form of the signals has changed, the potential information about the external world is no less direct or indirect, and is just as good for knowledge purposes regardless of the transformation, as long as the fidelity of pattern is maintained and reproduced.

In sum, since the information, hence meaning, in signals mapped by organisms through experience is inherently relational, it becomes meaningless to ask what the "real world" is like in and of itself, apart from a knower. And given the notion of information transmission as the preservation of pattern despite transformations, there is no question, in principle, about how we can experience and know the external world. That we "only" know it through its effects on our senses is no block at all to our experiencing and knowing it in the fullest veridical sense. There is little sense to the notion of experiencing or knowing the external world "directly," rather than through the sensory and cognitive systems. What would it mean to ask what a violin, say, "really" sounds like, or a rainbow "really" looks like, if they could be experienced "directly"?

The notion of "directly experiencing" is an oxymoron. The prejudice here is the long-held belief that the sensory or perceptual system of a normal organism cannot provide a veridical mapping of the world (within the limitations of the sensory apparatus, of course), and consequently that there is no structural invariance extracted and thus no necessary relation at all between the world and what is experienced. This belief, based earlier on lack of, or ignorance of, appropriate scientific knowledge, cannot now be reasonably maintained. Hence, distinctions such as that between "noumena" and "phenomena" can be seen to have little merit. We can even arrange to see what sound (air vibrations) looks like on a computer screen or oscilloscope and gain new knowledge, new mappings of its invariant structure, from it.

In general, the scientist can analyze the physical nature of external signals such as air vibrations (the "noumena" if you will) before they interact with the organism; after the interaction, the resulting sounds become "phenomena." Sight, sound, and smells are interactions of external phenomena (light waves, air vibrations, chemicals) with organisms' sensory apparatus, they are not part of the external world in itself. Hence it is otiose to ask whether a falling tree makes a "sound" when no one is there to hear it: it makes air vibrations but not perceived sound. Much of the confusion here can be traced to the often prolix philosophical debates of earlier centuries over "primary and secondary qualities" and the like, which did not have the benefit of modern scientific understanding.

ACTING BACK ON THE WORLD: THE OUTPUT INTERFACE

The dynamic organism-environment model argues for a continuous recursive cycling between input signals from the environment, bodily processing of those inputs, and actual or virtual output behaviors back onto it as necessary for the maintenance of conscious awareness of the world. This continuous looping is important, for it seems generally the case that biological systems, especially nervous systems, dislike stasis. If something doesn't vibrate, oscillate, move in some way, then it ceases to register. For example, the eye oscillates very rapidly so as to maintain an active record of the external scene and keep it from fading.

We cease to feel something that touches us if it doesn't move for a period of time. (And writers pace the floor to keep ideas from fading.)

Some time ago a number of experiments were undertaken to ascertain the effects of sensory (and motor) deprivation. A useful summary is given in G. F. Reed (1979). Although these were not very comparable or cumulative, and often poorly conceived and executed, some generalization seems possible. Usually the subject was enclosed in an isolation booth or tube with breathing apparatus, sometimes submerged under water such that all of the senses, including touch, were shut off from any inputs. Mental behavior was about all the subjects could engage in, and this very likely reduced the seriousness of the consequences for them. It provided a substitute kind of interaction with an environment, in this case internal. In a matter of hours or even minutes the subject typically began to experience disturbances of cognition and consciousness that built up rapidly, such as hallucinations, mental confusion, panic, and loss of consciousness. Even when we ourselves are quietly concentrating or meditating, small body movements or muscle twitches continue to occur unnoticed, so that we are not entirely without environmental contact. When somewhat tired, we might sense the fading of conscious awareness as sleep begins to take hold, and can with mental and physical effort bring ourselves back to full contact with the world. There certainly are degrees of consciousness, and much study needs to be done on partial, intermediate, or altered states. Such research may support further my view that the total organism engaged with the environment (including the internal environment) is the proper frame to enclose consciousness and mentality.

Just how the brain maps to mental processes and events is partly a matter of the internal and external context of the larger system dynamics. As Calvin and Ojemann (1994, p. 269) put it:

The disembodied mind? But the brain is intimately a part of the body evolved to be the ultimate hand-in-glove combination. You might be able to design a thinking machine with minimal sense organs and output devices, but it's hard to imagine a human mind perking along without at least a head and a hand. Remember all those sensory isolation experiments that caused hallucinations after a little while? External reality is what keeps chaos in check, the brain has a perpetual battle between stability and flexibility, and external reality is a major arbiter.

Another set of possibly relevant experiments are the often-cited ones involving subjects wearing prismatic goggles that caused the world to appear inverted relative to its normal appearance. (Rock, 1995, Chaps. 7, 8) Although there appears to be some controversy concerning the detailed results of these experiments, there seems little doubt that after a few days of constant wearing of the goggles during waking hours, the subjects reported that the world suddenly began to appear as if in a normal upright position. In some cases the subject could then ride a bicycle, for example, with no difficulty, removing or putting on the goggles at will with no noticeable effect, something that would have meant disaster in the first days of the experiment. However, this result is less important for our model than an additional observation often not given sufficient attention. The experience of the world eventually reverting to its normal appearance did not occur if the subjects did not actively work at adapting their behavior through continual correction of the many errors of movement occurring especially in the early stages of the experiment. A subject just sitting and looking at the world through the goggles, without acting toward it, did not experience any reinversion.

Although this set of experiments may not speak directly to the question of consciousness maintenance, it does point to the important role of conscious attention to and motor action onto the world to generate a veridical picture of it. It is insufficient to merely perceive or cognize it. This would be like our trying to perfect our golf swing by just watching an expert.

COGNITION: THE CAUSAL LINK BETWEEN ENVIRONMENT AND BEHAVIOR

It makes good evolutionary sense, we have argued, to view conscious mental activity as a stage in the organism-environment loop in which perceived environmental contingencies are assessed and appropriate action decided upon. We cannot take the space here to develop and argue this view in any depth, but it does imply that mental processes (themselves involving neural activity) evolved because they can act as causal forces directing further neural processes leading to muscle action and behavior, and sometimes (for humans) further mental behavior. It is not clear why this is problematic for some, since it seems intuitively obvious that humans, and quite clear that higher animals, consciously direct their behaviors in certain ways rather than others. It seems certain that brain processes are involved, but to argue that it is the neurons of the brain alone that do this is problematic, implying an epiphenomenalist theory of consciousness. This calls for continued empirical and theoretical work toward figuring out the flow chart of recursive processes involved in the organism-environment loop.

Our emphasis in this chapter has been on sensation and perception, the sensory experience facet of consciousness, the interface of the organism with the external environment. For the human organism, however, the inner cognitive processes—thought, problem solving, self-reflecting, and the like—are central: some physically challenged individuals have very limited sensory contact with the external world but nevertheless live rich and productive lives. These higher cognitive capabilities are made possible by sociolinguistic processes that began at least with early homo sapiens, and generate through the developmental socialization process a sociocultural human being. Any complete theory of consciousness will have to take into account this organism-social environment dynamic loop, and show how higher cognition and a sense of self is made possible by the intimate interaction of the organism with its sociocultural linguistic community. Such a theory exists in fundamental outline based on the work of George Herbert Mead, Chicago pragmatist and social psychologist, in the first third of the twentieth century, as we mentioned earlier.

If we focus on human consciousness and cognitive processes, we must implicate social and cultural processes. Social interaction of early humans adapting to a harsh environment generated language, which made possible a richer culture, a more complex social organization, and the higher human cognitive functions of rational thought and self-reference (Cf. Mead, 1934). This was not simply a biological adaptation but a sociocultural one, representing a quantum leap in evolution involving a qualitative as well as quantitative increase in cortical and hence cognitive growth. Unless we revert to Behaviorism and throw out the mental entirely, the causal efficacy of human thought and decision seems undebatable.

The stages of metaevolution, if we can call it that, proceed from lower levels of biological organization such as single-celled, multicelled, organs and organisms, and so forth, up to herds and flocks, and to nonlinguistic family groups (e.g., higher apes) and populations. This is as far as most biologists seem mentally prepared to go in recognizing levels of biological organization, unaware, it seems, that there is the more highly evolved sociocultural level of organization with its normative structures and symbolic intersubjective communal dynamics (usually referred to as human societies) that is not explainable in terms of lower psychological or biological concepts alone, any more than these latter are fully explainable in terms of chemical or physical concepts alone. But the role of language and the sociocultural system in the development of higher human cognition and self consciousness is another story too long to develop further here (see Buckley, 1996).

In essence, the model of the real-time generation and maintenance of mind and consciousness presented here pictures a flow of signals from the physical—and symbols from the social—environment through the various transformations, codings, and processings of the human sensory, linguistic, cognitive, and other mental or neurophysiological mechanisms, to the decision-making and consequent motor output apparatus, and thus to actions or behaviors that constitute transactions back again on aspects of the physical and social environment often changing the latter and hence the nature of its later inputs into the system. Yes, for those who noticed: this is reminiscent of Hegel's and Marx's "Dialectical Process," but no political overtones need apply. This constitutes a circular, recursive, causal flow, within which consciousness is generated and maintained. At various stages around this loop there are complex recursive feedback processes which can result in later stages of the loop influencing earlier stages. As long as the system is active, with the brain and body in normal operation *vis a vis* an environment, the flow of consciousness continues. A serious break in any part of the loop, whether on the sensory input side, the inner physiological center, the cognitive focus, or the motor output side, for any length of time could dampen, distort, or cut off consciousness.

CONCLUSION

By way of conclusion, the main points of the model may be summarized as follows:

1. Adequate analysis must focus on the *total system of organism and environment as a complex on-going dynamic whole*. And it is the whole organism that relates to the environment and to consciousness, which suggests that more consideration be given to the interaction of parts of the nervous system that involve the body: the limbic system involving emotions and motivation, and the autonomic system which plays a role in regulating such parts of the body as the heart, intestines, glands, and hormones. These are all interrelated in a systemic manner and can affect conscious processes as well as the brain and behavior.

The signal or information selection, transformations, or codings that occur at any stage in the ongoing system loop depend not only on prior events and processes in the system, but also on feedbacks from latent endpoints. As is well known in behavioral sciences, information attended to, or selected for, processing during activity is continually changing as a function of the ongoing intentions, decisions, and actions of the individual. Perception, as well as conception, is at best a continual sampling out of the extensive potential informational cues available in the external (or internal) environment. To include such things as emotions or felt needs, we need to emphasize the extensive network of efferent or proprioceptive nerves throughout the body, those that send signals back to the CNS about the states of different parts of the body, both external and internal. We could not even walk without constant feedback about the current states of the legs, body balance, and so on. This network is a necessary part of the larger dynamical system making up our sense of self, of others, and of the external world—that is, our consciousness.

2. Thus *the total system*, when operating fully (sometimes parts of it are bypassed or truncated), *is* what can be referred to as *a transactional system*, with structure-changing (or morphogenic) as well as structure-preserving (morphostatic) capabilities (Buckley, 1967, 1968). What this means, among other things, is that knowledge is not passively and finally given merely through information input to the sensory apparatus, but rather is actively constructed and reconstructed through continual interchange between the individual and his or her physical and social environment. Cognitive, emotive, decision-making, and instrumental motor energy are also required to drive the system. Each of these subsystems contributes to the structuring and operation of the others.

3. Consequently, the *classical philosophical approaches to epistemology*, which are often tacitly accepted, *are seriously incomplete and deficient*, focusing as each does on only one or two links and transformations of the total epistemic system outlined above.

Since the information, hence meaning, in mapped signals is inherently relational, it becomes meaningless to ask what the "real world" is like in and of itself, apart from a knower. Hence, different types of knowers (e.g., aliens and higher animals with different mappings and relations to the world) would experience a very different "real world." And given the notion of information transmission as the preservation of pattern despite transformations, there is no question, in principle, about whether endowed organisms can experience and know the external world with some degree of fidelity.

4. *The mind* is not simply a passive receiver and recorder of incoming signals and sense data, but *actively contributes additional information and control* as well as helps to construct the particular framework or organization of the internal knowledge reference set that alone gives meaning to additional signals generated from without or from within (e.g., by thought or emotion). Additional information and knowledge structure are no doubt added, then, by the basic physiological structure of the organism, especially its peripheral, central, and autonomic nervous systems; by on-going feedback from various phases of the total transaction of the organism as an open system adapting to or goal-seeking in its environment; and by the sociocultural processes, including language and other symboling, in which individuals and their information-processing activities are constantly embedded.

The model we have outlined certainly does not solve in any detail the central problem of the basic "mechanisms" underlying consciousness: just how it is that the components of the total process interrelate and help maintain subjective awareness and mental processes. The model does however suggest the organism-environment loop as fundamental to this mechanism. The job ahead is to map out the self-organizing structure and dynamic flow of those recursive processes in conjunction with continued progress in tracing the brain processes proper that take their place within the broader loop. It is essential to face up to the fact that our knowledge of the brain and the rest of the nervous system organization and dynamics and the way it functions is still meager, despite the dedicated years and decades spent by neuroscientists and neuropsychologists to map it out. In light of this fact, it seems prudent to keep an open mind about it; one should be prepared for serious surprises in the years ahead. The orientation needed is in the direction of the current movement toward a science of consciousness.

NOTES

1. It is unfortunate that so many studies of the impact of brain damage on behavior and cognitive performance imply or claim that it is the brain alone that causes consciousness and the mental.

2. One could say that Pragmatism is a natural philosophical offshoot of evolutionary theory: the meaning of an object or event to the organism is the adaptive consequences of that object or event for the organism, including the latter's possible behavior toward it. It also comes much closer than Positivism, it can be argued, to capturing the day-to-day practice of contemporary scientists.

3. I must comment later on the inappropriateness of the widespread use of the term "information" for these signals, since "information" with its possible meanings is a matter of interpretation at the cognitive mental level.

4. Computer engineers will tell us that a computer only processes varying voltages; if you study its inner workings very carefully that's all you'll find, not symbols or information. These latter are interpretations that are input by programmers, transduced as signals by the hardware, and output in a physical form designed by the programmers to be meaningful to users (with varying degrees of success). In the middle are only varying voltages, just as in the middle of the organism-environment system are varying rates of neural pulses that must be put together into cognitive events meaningful to the whole organism in its environment.

REFERENCES

Arieli, A. et al. (1996). Dynamics of Ongoing Activity. *Science, 273*, September 27.

Buckley, W. (1967). *Sociology and Modern Systems Theory*. Englewood Cliffs, NJ: Prentice Hall.

Buckley, W. (1968). Society as a Complex Adaptive System. In W. Buckley (Ed.), *Modern Systems Research for the Behavioral Scientist*. Chicago: Aldine.

Buckley, W. (1996). Mind, Mead and Mental Behaviorism. In W.K. Kwan (Ed.), *Individuality and Social Control*. Hartford: JAI Press.

Calvin, W., & Ojemann, G.A. (1994). *Conversations with Neil's Brain: The Neural Nature of Thought and Language*. Reading, MA: Addison-Wesley.

Glanz, J. (1997). Tracing Molecules that Make the Brain-Body Connection. *Science, 275*, February 14, 930-931.

Just, M.A. et al. (1996). Brain Activation Modulated by Sentence Comprehension. *Science, 274*, October 4, 114-116.

Mead, G.H. (1934). *Mind, Self and Society*. Chicago: University of Chicago Press.

Rao, S. Chenchal et al. (1997). Integration of What and Where in the Primate Prefrontal Cortex. *Science, 276*, May 2.

Reed, G.F. (1979). In G. Underwood & R. Stevens (Eds.). *Aspects of Consciousness (Vol. 1)* (pp. 167-181). London: Academic Press.

Rock, I. (1995). *Perception*. New York: Scientific American Library.

Shannon, C.E. (1948). A Mathematical Theory of Communication. *Bell System Technical Journal*.

Sperry, R. (1995). The Impact and Promises of the Cognitive Revolution. In R.L. Solso & D.W. Massaro (Eds.), *The Science of the Mind: 2001 and Beyond* (pp. 23-46). New York: Oxford University Press.

Chapter 3

MANAGEMENT BY COMPLEXITY: REDUNDANCY AND VARIETY IN ORGANIZATIONS

Heinrich W. Ahlemeyer

INTRODUCTION

There are two ways of approaching the topic of complexity (Baecker, 1998). One can describe complexity as the problem, and then look for solutions. Complexity, after all, makes things complicated, and it may easily get out of control. In this perspective, nothing is more welcome than an effective technique of reducing complexity. Or one can conceive of complexity as a solution, a solution for a problem yet to be described. Complexity then is not an unintended side effect of an otherwise orderly world, but a form of the world itself, a mode in which the world deals with itself. In this perspective, a simple reduction of complexity which does not at the same time refer to new complexity is to be avoided. This second approach is in line with the objections of cybernetics and sociology against all too sudden endeavors to control complexity. W. Ross Ashby stated in his Law of Requisite Variety that only variety can destroy variety. If one wants to construct a system able to deal with a high level of environmental variety, one has to provide a sufficiently high level of system variety (Ashby, 1956).

In this chapter, we shall not contribute to the techniques of complexity reduction. Instead, we shall look at organizations and ask how they use complexity. After clarifying the term complexity, our observation of organizations and their complexity management will use two perspectives: one which focuses on organizational redundancies (in the second section) and one which focuses on variety (third section). In the concluding section we shall delineate some practical consequences of this analysis for management.

THE NOTION OF COMPLEXITY

The notion of complexity offers itself more than any other to bring our professional and everyday life experience with intransparency, uncontrollability, and uncalculability on a common denominator. In spite of its particular vagueness, the notion combines high plausibility with a reference to common experience. As an expression of a widespread general attitude, it presupposes an unspoken consent in communication.

For systems theory, both the notion and the phenomenon of complexity are nothing new. To the extent that systems were conceived of as the selective combination of numerous single system elements, which also could have been combined differently, system researchers hit upon the phenomenon of complexity.

What exactly does the notion of complexity denote? Complexity is not a system operation—nothing a system does or what happens to it. It is rather a notion of observation and description including self-observation and self-description. Complexity in itself is not a simple, but a complex notion for which we propose four central features:

1. A system is complex for an observer when it is neither in a state of complete order nor of complete disorder, that is to say: when it represents a mixture of redundancy and variety. Redundancy refers to structural limitations of the ongoing production of system elements—for instance, of decisions by decision premises in organized social systems. The redundancy is high, if little information suffices for an observer to anticipate future decisions of the system (Luhmann, 1988b, p. 174). The counterterm to redundancy is variety. The variety of an organization grows by increasing the range and heterogeneity of decisions. Take, for example, hospitals which no longer limit themselves to treating existing diseases, but strive to prevent future ones by influencing their communities. The notion of complexity is paradoxically constituted: multiple phenomena are grasped with a notion which presupposes a unity. Complexity denotes the unity of a multiplicity (Luhmann, I, 1997, pp. 134-144).

2. To unfold this paradox, one may use the distinction of element and relation. A system is observed as complex when it contains more elements than can be connected completely. This implies that only some elements can be bound to some other elements by specific relations. The important point here is less the absolute number of elements, but the necessity of a selective connection. Complexity unfolds with the difference between a complete and a selective connectivity of elements. All the selected relations have one thing in common: they are contingent. They would have been possible differently. Take, for example, the founding decision of an organization, the decision for a particular legal form of an enterprise, the selection of particular markets, the product policy, the creation of positions, the hiring of certain persons—there is always a selection from a range of possibilities, and this selection is made by decision. Complexity enforces a selective connection. One has to make a decision, and the selection could have been different (Ahlemeyer & Königswieser, 1998).

3. Complexity is a notion without a difference (Luhmann, 1990). There is no longer a counternotion to complexity, such as simplicity or transparency. Today, everything may be recognized as complex. You only have to look close enough. Without a counternotion, tautologies may be tried out as second-best solutions: complex is what is complex for an observer. Complexity is by necessity bound to an observer. Without an observer, there is no complexity. The observer is defined by the sort of scheme that he uses for his observation (i.e., by the distinctions that he uses). There are many various descriptions of complexity depending on the distinction an observer uses to decompose the unity of a multiplicity into elements and relations. After all, a system may describe itself as complex in various different ways (Löfgren, 1977).

4. Although the notion of complexity has left behind the distinction of complex and simple, Baecker has recently proposed reintroducing this distinction to characterize a particular way of dealing with complexity in organizations. He speaks of "simple complexity" in order to indicate that the contingency of actual selections is bracketed and, instead, the system gains an understanding both of the necessity and the impossibility to limit complexity (Baecker, 1998, p. 28).

Baecker's notion of "simple complexity" is in itself anything but simple. His vantage point is the necessity of selection and contingency. Both negations which define contingency, the negation of impossibility and the negation of necessity are themselves negated. In doing so, the system gains a structure which allows controlling its own complexity with its own complexity. Simple complexity is thus both a reduction and an increase of complexity at the same time. It is a method of temporarily accepting constellations of necessity and impossibility, because one reckons being able at any moment to remobilize the contingency of the system and to return to complex complexity. Baecker considers simple complexity to be predominant in management and organization. One accepts the decision for a particular production method and at the same time continues looking out for a better alternative. One accepts the complexity reduction knowing one commits oneself, but also knowing that depending on the circumstances, the commitment may be cancelled and complex complexity may be reintroduced (Baecker, 1998).

Just as any other social system, organizations can neither put a claim on necessity nor on a natural impossibility. They are always contingent, in their existence and in their particular selections. They would have been possible differently, just as any other social system. The contingency of their selections is negated and faded out in a typically organized way. The reduction of complexity takes place by producing redundancy. Complexity reductions, as a consequence, are no longer visible as reductions, but taken as downright necessary. In the everyday observation of the organization, contingency—the possibility of alternative possibilities—is typically no longer available, but faded out.

MORE OF THE SAME: REDUNDANCY

Organizational systems have long been characterized as frozen, preserved problem solutions. It is this relative stability and duration which Paul Watzlawick has described with the principle of "more of the same." By this, he means the tendency of each organizational system to reject changes—changes of its structure, of its rules, of its identity. "Even or particularly in cases of severe disturbances, systems tend to resort to the counterproductive cure of "more of the same" thus reproducing inevitably more of the same underlying problem" (Watzlawick, 1985, p. 366).

Organizational systems have a strong preference for redundancy and, as a consequence, difficulties in dealing with change. They have found a problem solution and thus made a selection; they have stabilized it in time and tend to stick to it. Alternative selections are faded out. After all, nobody can afford to re-invent the world on a daily basis. In an organization, there is no reason to question a solution discovered—often under great difficulties—in the past which has demonstrated its worth many times since.

The same thought can be found with Niklas Luhmann, who has proposed to conceive of organizations as sytems which recursively produce decisions (Luhmann, 1988b). In this theoretical perspective, systems consist of decisions, and they produce the decisions they consist of, by the very decisions they consist of. These decisions must be imagined as events. In the very moment of their coming into being, they already fade away. That is why—according to Luhmann—so little can be changed in organizations. As decisions disappear with their appearance, they cannot be altered, but only give cause for the production of new decisions which, however, are subject to the same mechanism.

That organizations have difficulties with change, that they reject learning, flexibility, and innovation, that they prefer the old tracks instead of trying new paths—this hypothesis is not new, but still plausible and supported by vast empirical evidence in adminstrations, companies, maybe also universities. Let me briefly summarize in five points the reasons that have been proposed why change and innovation are unlikely to occur in organizations (Ahlemeyer, 1994):

1. *Structure*: No system finds itself in an entropic state of a complete indeterminacy of the next moment (cf. Luhmann, 1988b, p. 172). This is also true for systems which have a very large range of possibilities (i.e. for systems with a high structural complexity). Any system has to build structures in order to limit the range of consecutive events which follow one event. Organizational systems constitute themselves by decisions, and in their ongoing decision-making they recursively make use of previous decisions. These decisions secure redundancy: they have the very function to make the ongoing production of decisions possible, to ensure it, to ease it, and make future decisions expectable.

2. *More of the Same*: If system structures may be viewed as a condensation of successful problem solutions, there is initially no reason visible within the system why existent solution patterns should not be continuously used. This can

also and particularly be observed for new problems which the system will typically try to tackle by multiplying or enlarging existent structures which function satisfactorily. In spite of a vast amount of historical evidence which shows that seemingly insignificant quantitative increases may trigger enormous qualitative discontinuities, we still find a dominance of quantitative, linearly organized thinking not only in organizations, but particularly there.

3. *The Social Dimension*: In the social dimension, sticking to existing structures promises consent and security. Questioning or even leaving them means to proceed into uncertainty, possibly even to be held responsible for structureless situations in which one does not know anymore how to act and decide. Others are disrupted in their security, and one risks being identified as a troublemaker.

4. *The Observation of the Environment*: As do all systems, organizations too observe their complex environments selectively and system-specifically. Information about the environment is always self-produced by the system and not simply a fact of the environment which existed independently of the observation and judgment of the system. Only that information appears on the monitors of the system which its sensors get from the environment. For the system, information is a difference in the environment which makes a difference for itself, to allude to Bateson's famous definition that information is a difference that makes a difference (1972). The system is continuously disturbed by its environment, and with its network of decisions, it virtually seeks disturbances to transform them into information.

When all the antennas of the organization are tuned towards program execution, critical and program-adverse events appear as unconnectable disturbances, or one might also say as noise. They produce no information, and that is why organizations tend to either entirely ignore them or to assimilate them by corresponding interpretations. When, for instance, the bad image with the customer is viewed as an expression of his envy, the routines of the organization may remain unquestioned.

5. *Responsibility*: The decision premises of competence and responsibility lead to the distinction between decisions *within* decision premises and decisions *about* decision premises. This distinction usually goes along with differences in power and hierarchical position. Employees in direct contact with the customer are expected to execute decision programs, not to change them. At the same time, however, it is at the periphery that structure-critical information appears which is capable of questioning a mere continuation of "more of the same" within given structures. To put it differently: just because of the internal structure, structure-critical information occurs typically at places not entitled to decide on changing the structure.

One may add, though, that in reality organizations are indeed less inhibited in recognizing the necessity of their decision premises than it may seem in the light of these reflections. They have learned to install secondary flexibilities, such as generalizations, latitudes, far-reaching authorizations, and situational ad hoc decisions, thus allowing for flexibility with regard to unknown futures, unanticipated conditions, and uncalculable eigenstates beneath a level of structural adaptations (Luhmann, 1971).

In spite of these endeavors for more variety, however, the ongoing operation of producing decisions inevitably leads to the condensation of structures which again increase the system's redundancy. The gain of stability in the time dimension inevitably leads to the condensation of expectation structures and the often-noted crystallization of aging organizations.

To sum up: If complexity enforces a decision by making a selection, organized social systems themselves are a solution of the problem of complexity as both their existence and their elementary operations are based on decision-making. Only by drastically limiting the range of alternative possibilities, can organizations come into existence. Their continued operation demands the recursive production of decisions with an ongoing reference to former decisions. Redundancy as the typical mode of organizations to reduce complexity tends to deny the underlying contingency and to overestimate the stability of organizations. Until recently, organizational science has widely followed the self-observation of organizations emphasizing their reluctance to change.

MORE OF THE NEW: VARIETY

With so much evidence for the redundancy and stability of organizations, it is tempting to jump to the opposite hypothesis and contend that organizations are quite easily capable of dealing with innovation and radical change. That organizations reject change and prefer stability, is it not a reflection and projection of a widely stable past? Does it still describe our present social reality adequately? Do we not witness on the contrary an enormously accelerated social change propelled in the first instance by organizations within the economic system? Should we not rather emphasize that organizations need sufficient variety and are easily capable of dealing with change and innovation?

If organizations are social systems which recursively produce decisions, this not only implies routine and selective rigidity, but it also emphasizes principally the possibility of making decisions and of changing their very premises. Organizations no doubt need structure-providing premises, and they gain them by making decisions. It is by this basic mechanism, however, that they remain primarily open to change and innovation. Programs can be changed; responsibilities and processes can be reengineered; new persons can be hired; blockheads can be fired or sent into retirement; positions can be eliminated, redefined, and newly created. Compared to nondecidable decision-premises— emotional, religious, or fundamentalist—organizations whose premises are fundamentally open to decision are more flexible and more elastic.

An observer using the distinction of redundancy and variety cannot but notice how fast and radically large organizations have changed since the mid-1990s, particularly in the economic system. Former state-owned companies have turned into modern, highly flexible private-owned stock corporations. Large, formerly established, and seemingly stable enterprises have disappeared practically overnight; and equally rapidly and surprisingly new companies have emerged. The speed of innovation in the enterprises is enormous, as far as new products and a larger product variety is concerned. Just think of the car industry, the computer industry, the software industry, and the news media. A closer look, however, shows the dynamics of the process originate less from the organizations themselves than from the functional social subsystems, the economic system in particular. Using the fast and highly effective feedback mechanism of profit and loss, the economic functional subsystem of society has created itself, with the market an environment which is out for dynamic development and change.

The market is less a system than an environment. It is the environment of systems which participate in the economic system—that is, of enterprises and households. The market is furthermore a border: the perception of consumption in the perspective of production, distribution, and service. The efforts of cocompetitors also appear as the market. The border functions like a mirror in which each enterprise comes to view the competitors as well as itself as a competitor of the competitors (Luhmann, 1988a, p. 73). In financial markets, both buyers and sellers try to calculate a future which depends on their own decisions.

To put it differently: the market marks the difference between definite and indefinite complexity, the complexity of the organization itself and that of its environment. To the organization, its own complexity looks controllable, however inappropriate this notion may be. The complexity of the environment in contrast is acknowledged and accepted as uncontrollable. It encompasses a multitude of competitors and its own activities as competitor of the competitors. The market is thus based on the intransparency of indefinite complexity. With its own code of prices, it offers, however, a highly effective mechanism to substantially reduce the inextricable complexity of resources, motives, needs, decisions, and products. Far from being perfect, the market as a system environment offers an effective mechanism to observe the results of decisions and learn from past mistakes.

The economic system communicates exclusively in the language of prices. It encodes everything into a price. With the instability of prices, which at any time may be increased or decreased, it creates at the same time the possibility to react to changing conditions sufficiently fast. Take for instance the falling price of bananas at the end of the market day or rising flower prices in the wake of Mother's Day. With its variable prices, the market is all oriented towards instability. The market participants, the organizations, observe and calculate primarily connections for their own decision-making. They cope with the complexity of the environment by transforming uncertainty into risk: as investment risk, employment risk, payment risk, purchase risk, credit risk, and so on.

Even if the pressure for change and variety comes from the environment of the economic subsystem, the organizations prove quite easily capable to cope with it. An observer who has had an opportunity to look into various organizations will notice almost everywhere strong endeavors to increase variety and thus to increase complexity. Until recently, these radical changes were deemed almost unthinkable. We observe far-reaching transformations of historically grown organizational structures long held to be unchangeable. Entirely different construction principles of organizations are now emerging, and they have widely reintroduced new contingencies.

1. *Structure*: Many companies have increasingly given up traditional function-oriented organizational structures (such as accountancy, sales, production, human resources) and have organized themselves into smaller units which act as self-reliant enterprises within the enterprise. These units or centers are usually fully vested with decision powers, such as budgetary responsibility, commissioning powers, and full responsibility for their internal organization. These centers are also responsible for contributing their share in the overall profit of the company. At many places, numerous smaller units have thus emerged, operating closer to the market and reacting faster and more flexibly to their relevant environment, the customer. With this, former restrictions and complexity reductions have been sharply questioned and given way to a return of autonomy and complexity. The emergence of enterprises within the enterprise has reintroduced increased decision possibilities, but also increased decision requirements into the organization (Wimmer, 1996).

2. *Hierarchies*: In recent years, many large organizations have undergone drastic changes in their hierarchical structure, a strong decrease in the number of management levels, and a dramatic thinning out of middle management. More importantly, hierarchy itself has assumed a different function.

Hierarchy used to be an organizational communication technique for reducing the complexity of an organization to simple complexity. A hierarchy restrains communication among the members of an organization. Communicating on the same level is optional, but remains widely without consequences; communication between superiors and subordinates, in contrast, is sharply restricted. It occurs rarely, but usually produces immediate consequences. With its distinction between unrestricted communication in the horizontal dimension and restricted communication in the vertical dimension, hierarchy enforces that the communication of decisions remains within the prescribed structures of the organization (Baecker, 1998, pp. 33-36).

Today, with the extensive introduction of autonomous, self-organized units, the undercomplexity of vertical communication—which has always been observed and known about in the organization—has become evident. It is observed as too selective, too rigid, and too far away from both the customer and the employee. Hierarchy is replaced by a concept of leadership which no longer trusts hierarchical instruction, but open negotiation processes. The commitment of members of self-responsible and self-organized units can only be gained through self-commitment which evolves in the process of open negotiation of different positions (Wimmer, 1996). We find a different approach to steering and control. To propose appropriate communication modes and structures has moved into the center of leadership. In contrast to hierarchy, leadership is no longer a means of complexity reduction, but a conscious attempt to allow for more variety. Leadership in this sense implies the constant production and reproduction of general conditions which support different units to use their autonomy in line with the overall organization.

3. *Teams*: Comprehensive organizational change projects increase the variety of the organization by establishing a new difference within the organization: the difference between the hierarchical organization and the project organization. Project teams are usually regarded as a counterpart to the hierarchy (Heintel & Kraintz, 1988). The extent, however, to which teams depend upon the hierarchy, is often ignored. If they do not receive their mission and their resources from the hierarchy, they at least have to negotiate with the hierarchy about these premises.

The project organization assumes an important function within the organization. The team requires horizontal communication and makes it impossible to escape it. Everything else in the team may be contingent: size, resources, technology, leadership; what is not contingent, but an absolute necessity, is communication within the team (Baecker, 1998). That is why everything in the team seems simpler and more personal. Teams allow for more trust and more information. In spite of the central role of horizontal communication, however, teams remain ultimately dependent upon the hierarchy. Especially when they want to implement their results into the overall organization, teams need to observe the hierarchy and place and evaluate all their decisions in the context of the hierarchy.

But it is also vice versa: the dual structure of formal organization and project teams creates a new difference which allows for more variety. Its main function is not to control complexity, but to make it observable for the hierarchy. Project teams in this sense are temporary institutions which enable the organization to observe, increase and manage its complexity. This, however, is a conception of management by complexity, not management of complexity.

4. *Networks*: The dynamics of the economic system in general, and deregulation and globalization in particular, have contributed to a development in which the organizations observe basic changes in their environment. Takers have become customers; formerly state-owned organizations have become enterprises. This has far-reaching consequences for decision premises which concern the identity of the organization and its observation patterns towards the relevant environment. The enterprises create more and more specialized markets for each other. The single organization finds itself within a dense network of customer and supplier relations, which in their dynamics can no longer be grasped with the notions of classical economy. In many industries, like the airlines, we find a simultaneity of cooperation and competition within worldwide networks and the competition between these networks.

Networks, too, are a form of increasing variety. They require communication between organizations, and they require communicating about contacts. Business relations between partners or between customers and suppliers have always existed. What is new is an intensified communication about contingency.

Every contact between two organizations can principally be substituted by a contact to another organization. In networks, one does not wait for the substitution to happen, but one attempts to head it off. Reasons for questioning the alliance and changing the partner are identified and eliminated at an early stage.

In networks, we find manifest and virtual cooperation. They comprise not only the cultivation of contacts with present cooperation partners, but also with potential future partners. This reintroduces a whole range of new uncertainties and contingencies into the organization. With networks, organizations install a surprise factor into the way they deal with complexity. They have to reckon that the other network organizations will change, be it in technology, product policy, culture, or just persons in top positions. Networks thus immensely increase the amount of intraorganizational contingency. On the other hand, it has also been observed that networks also increase the pressure on organizations to clarify their identity and to reemphasize the distinctive function of their borders (Wimmer, 1995).

LESS MAY BE MORE: SOME PRACTICAL CONSEQUENCES

Whereas it can be shown that organizations have successfully found different ways of increasing their variety and of dealing with change and innovation, this is not necessarily the case if we look at the organization members. For many of them, the problem is not deadlock and "more of the same," but rather contrarily a large number of rash and simultaneous change projects. Again and again, they find themselves in situations which force them to give up structural security before they have even gotten fully accustomed to it. In their view, an almost hysterical change of patterns and structures demands an almost daily "more of the new." Many organization members—management and employees alike—feel overrun by rash and radical changes. They feel they cannot cope and they feel rendered superfluous. They are vulnerable and distraught; many have lost their orientation.

Within organizations, the continuous emphasis on change and variety has produced a new difference of inclusion and exclusion: between those whose commit themselves to change and innovation and actively drive it forward, as member of management or of innovative project teams on the one hand, and those who suffer from these changes passively, who feel uninformed, shifted around, and forced into change. This difference between those who push forward and those who endure is reflected by a second distinction which gains prominence within the internal observation of organizations: the distinction between winners and losers. The former experience an increase in opportunities for influence, learning, and career; the latter experience the present primarily as a loss: loss of the past, of identity and elementary securities, expectation securities above all.

In an organizational world, which makes loss an everyday experience, we observe a widespread longing for permanence and security. It emerges less from organizational mechanisms, but rather from the people working in organizations. In many organizations, we find a strong undercurrent indicating a furor of conservation, a revolt of standstill. It is articulated by employees and part of the management alike and directed against more and more of the new. It opposes an incessant wave of more change, more variety, more innovation.

What makes so many members cling so desparately to the status quo is *Angst*, an anxiety nourished by the perception of being neglected and not being able to cope. People want to go into the future by themselves; they do not want to be pushed, driven, or forced into it. In their view, the contingency in the organization has become so extensive that they themselves as members are no longer necessary, but have become contingent.

No manager will get these members out of their anxiety by just explaining the necessity of change while continuing to move forward. What is needed is an interruption of the rigid loop between more of the new on the one hand and more of the same on the other hand. To interrupt this loop, an intervention is needed which neutralizes former problem solutions and converts them into the opposite. Watzlawick has called this the functional use of a deviation for its own correction (Watzlawick, 1985).

Not that management should or could promise a return to the securities of the past. The creation of nonthreatening communication contexts between management and employees, beween innovators and preservers, however, constitutes such an intervention. It allows making past traumata a topic and gives a signal for a process of mutual understanding. What organization members need is the credible assurance that while almost everything may have become contingent for the organization, its members remain absolutely necessary for its future operations. Without the restriction of membership, after all, organized social systems are incapable of operating.

Top management needs to reassure its members more by actual decisions than by words that the ongoing selections of the organization are not just adjuncts to the anonymous functional logic of the global economic system. Whatever the contingencies of the future may be, the organization members with their unique capabilities and resources will retain a privileged position, which is not just another choice. Only if members realize that they matter for the organization, will the organization and its goals matter for them. Only then will they contribute their indispensable share in overcoming blockades to modernization and get in line to help with long overdue change.

Organizations have become both compulsive corsets of necessities and confusing fireworks of contingencies. With the strong dynamics of present social change we find that the classical solution of the organization, the reproduction of more of the same, ends up in the paradox that the same is simultaneously not the same. The organization's redundancy consists of its increase of variety. Different as the two are, in one aspect they are very comparable. Opposite to their own intentions, they produce more of the same problem they had set out to solve.

I could perhaps not formulate the possibility of interrupting such rigid loops, had I not accompanied numerous organizations in their change processes as a consultant. In my experience, a cybernetically informed intervention repertoire makes an enormous difference for complex change processes (Ahlemeyer, 1996). Both for the sociological observer and the intervening consultant, it remains a challenge to successfully relate the distinctions of one's own observation to those used in the self-observation of the social systems concerned.

REFERENCES

Ahlemeyer, H.W. (1994). Administrativer Wandel. In K. Damman, D. Grunow & K.P. Japp (Eds.), *Die Verwaltung des politischen Systems. Festgabe zum 65. Geburtstag von Niklas Luhmann* (pp. 183-197). Opladen: Westdeutscher Verlag.

Ahlemeyer, H.W. (1996). Systemische Organisationsberatung und Soziologie. In H. von Alemann & B. Vogel (Eds.), *Soziologische Beratung. Praxisfelder und Perspektiven* (IX. Tagung für angewandte Soziologie), (pp. 77-88). Opladen: Leske + Budrich.

Ahlemeyer, H.W. & Königswieser, R. (Eds). (1998). *Komplexität managen. Strategien, Konzepte und Fallbeispiele*. Wiesbaden: Gabler.

Ashby, W.R. (1956). *An Introduction to Cybernetics*. London: Chapman & Hall.

Baecker, D. (1998). Einfache Komplexität. In H.W. Ahlemeyer & R. Königswieser (Eds.), *Komplexität managen. Strategien, Konzepte und Fallbeispiele* (pp. 21-50). Wiesbaden: Gabler.

Bateson, G. (1972). *Steps to an Ecology of Mind. Collected Essays in Anthropology, Psychiatry, Evolution and Epistemology*. New York: Chandler.

Heintel, P. & Krainz, E. (1988). *Projektmanagement. Eine Antwort auf die Hierarchiekrise*. Wiesbaden: Gabler.

Löfgren, L. (1977). Complexity of Descriptions of Systems: A Foundational Study. *International Journal of General Systems 3*, 197-214.

Luhmann, N. (1971). Reform und Information. Theoretische Überlegungen zu einer Reform der Verwaltung. In N. Luhmann, *Politische Planung. Aufsätze zur Soziologie von Politik und Verwaltung* (pp. 181-202). Opladen: Westdeutscher Verlag.

Luhmann, N. (1988a). *Die Wirtschaft der Gesellschaft*. Frankfurt/Main: Suhrkamp.

Luhmann, N. (1988b). Organisation. In W. Küpper & G. Ortmann (Eds.), *Mikropolitik. Rationalität, Macht und Spiele in Organisationen* (pp. 165-186). Opladen: Westdeutscher Verlag.

Luhmann, N. (1990). Haltlose Komplexität. In *Soziologische Aufklärung 5* (pp. 59-76). Opladen: Westdeutscher Verlag.

Luhmann. N. (1997). *Die Gesellschaft der Gesellschaft, 2 vols*. Frankfurt/Main: Suhrkamp.

Watzlawick, P. (1985). Management oder - Konstruktion von Wirklichkeiten. In G.J.B. Probst & H. Siegwart (Eds.), *Integriertes Management. Bausteine des systemorientierten Managements* (pp. 365-376). Bern: Paul Haupt.

Wimmer, R. (1995). Die permanente Revolution. Aktuelle Trends in der Gestaltung von Organisationen. In R. Grossmann, E. Krainz, & M. Oswald (Eds.), *Veränderung in Organisationen* (pp. 21-41). Wiesbaden: Gabler.

Wimmer, R. (1996). Die Zukunft der Führung. Brauchen wir noch Vorgesetzte im herkömmlichen Sinn? *Organisationsentwicklung 4*, 46-57.

Chapter 4

THE EMERGENCE OF SOCIETAL INFORMATION

Robert Artigiani

SCIENCE AND VALUE

For three centuries "Modern" science either ignored the "Big Questions" or trivialized them. Big Questions concern qualitative changes. Modern science, the science of Galileo and Newton, relegated qualities to the subjective realm of mental phenomena, where they could safely be ignored. Alternatively, Modern science insisted that all explanations be about the mechanical forces controlling the behaviors of material particles, which were describable in terms of Newton's laws. Thus, when a Big Question was asked, the answer was that an apparent qualitative change was "really" an epiphenomenon, whose behavior could be completely explained in terms of small material objects dashing about in ultimately familiar, wholly mechanical, if otherwise invisible, ways. However, recent scientific developments may make it possible to once again ask Big Questions and answer them interestingly.

One Big Question, of course, concerns the origin of life—accounting for the emergence of a level of reality qualitatively different from its historical predecessors. Modern science, initially, had no explanation for life, save that its spokesmen were certain no "ghost (lurked) in the machine." Living beings were only particularly complicated steam engines, to Modern science, and once all the atomic particles constituting life were observed, there would be nothing left to explain. The same was true of "mind," which T.H. Huxley promised to explain by computing its mechanical equivalent. But explaining life and mind proved impossible for Modern science. The most it has demonstrated is no mechanical determinism necessitates life and no particle constitutes mind.

To make progress towards answering Big Questions interesting, a new paradigm respecting the integrity of qualitatively different levels of being is needed. Then phenomena like "life" can be treated according to rules appropriate to their level of reality, rather than analyzed in terms of material atoms. Such a science would be more concerned to capture phenomena "whole" than to break them down into constituent parts. The key issue for the new science, therefore, is to describe the patterned processes by which wholes come into being. This suggests the attributes of particles are not rigidly fixed and may vary with relationships. Relations between material bits could then produce mutual transformations in how all the components are defined.

A science substituting relationships for things is radically different from its Modern ancestor, and for that very reason its explanations are suspect. To preserve the integrity of different levels of reality, it replaces smooth mechanical transmissions with symmetry-breaking discontinuities. The qualitatively new levels of reality that appear at symmetry-breaks are said to "emerge." Emergence seems to defy scientific explanation and must be accounted for systematically. The problem is made more acute by theorists who introduce randomness into the events triggering symmetry-breaks, for randomness by definition eludes explanation.

The new paradigm remains "scientific," however, because it finds patterned processes in the emergence of new phenomena throughout time and space. The new paradigm respects the differences between living systems and dead particles, and recognizes that some of the behaviors and capacities of living systems cannot be subsumed by force laws. Its legitimation rests on demonstrating that the same patterned processes tracking the emergence of life can be found in the emergence of the universe, subatomic and atomic particles, chemical molecules, hurricanes, and so on. Locating emergent qualities within natural processes, the new scientific paradigm introduces no plan or final purpose to the universe as a whole, but respects the importance of realities like life and mind.

Remaining as austere as possible, the new paradigm rests essentially on the Second Law of Thermodynamics. This seems contradictory, for the Second Law says the universe always tends to disorganize. But Ilya Prigogine showed there need be no contradiction between evolution and entropy (Prigogine, 1980). The Second Law, he argued, describes universal cosmic truths but says nothing about local conditions. Thus, order can emerge from disorder, provided there is a gradient down which energy can flow. The work done by energy flowing down gradients creates local systems of order, the sustaining of which requires work. Therefore, the rate of universal entropy production increases as more complex systems evolve. Since increased local order carries a cosmic entropy cost, evolution conforms to the Second Law.

Local order depends on the self-organization of systems, formed by correlating the behaviors of whatever previously independent smaller parts happened to be bouncing about. Simple logic tells us that what self-organizes is systems as wholes, not the previously independent components, which are what get caught up in the self-organizing event. If what self-organizes is a system, then the components which went into the system will be transformed by their membership in it. Their attributes are not universals frozen in time, but variables dependent on sequences of partly contingent interactions embedded in energy flows. Attributes do not exist in a wonderland of potentialities blissfully awaiting discovery. They come into being and pass away when interactions mutually transform previously independent elements and capture them as members of systems. Thus, the attributes present in self-organized systems depend on the systems—they cannot be explained as the additive products of previous material objects. Being a whole greater than the sum of its parts, a system is, quite contrary to Modern linear logic, the effect of its own causation. Since no logic and no matter crosses this line of self-organization unaffected, there is something present in system wholes that is irreducible to their parts.

Emergence can have the relatively modest meaning of something preformed and already existing rising up from a concealed state, as a leaping porpoise "emerges" from the sea. But if science is to answer the Big Questions—that is, to track the origins of newness—emergence must be accorded a bolder meaning. It must encompass the appearance of surprises, qualitative changes that cannot be deduced from first principles or even "explained" by their histories. This is a logically ticklish issue, since the conventional way to avoid determinism is to emphasize the contingencies of experiences in time. This solution is Pyrrhic, however, for it throws out the baby of comprehension with the bath water of determinism.

Nevertheless, because self-organization occurs at symmetry-breaking discontinuities, where accidents acquire meanings, emergent systems will be conditioned by their pasts if not determined by their histories. Irreducible wholes, systems cannot be entirely comprehended either by deduction from necessary causal laws or by narrating the sequence of events preceding their emergence. There is always an outcome, when phase changes occur, that could have been otherwise—and nothing determined the phase change itself. But a kind of intellectual order can be found in this chaos of events by focusing on pattern-making processes giving sequences coherence without making outcomes necessary. By finding orderly processes among the chaos of events, the new science understands the world without sterilizing it or freezing it in some deterministic configuration. Seen as an emergent phenomenon, life, far from being Monod's (1971) statistical miracle, becomes, for Prigogine, "as natural as a falling stone" (Prigogine & Stengers, 1984).

SOCIAL INFORMATION

The human sciences face comparably Big Questions in explaining the origin of culture—and have been equally prone to offer uninteresting answers to the question of where culture came from. Perhaps the two most boring explanations of culture are the biological determinist one, which reduces culture ultimately to genes (Wilson, 1978), and the conspiracy theory, which reduces culture to an unfair trick played by the privileged on the exploited (Schmookler, 1984). The biological answer derives cultures from the programed behaviors of the individual organisms making them up, thereby making cultural artifacts like Values, Ethics, and Morals (VEMs) simply our epiphenomenal way of representing electrochemical brain flows. Alternatively, the evil elites' interpretation of cultures as mechanisms for coercing the weak and poor to work for the rich and powerful, while drug-like rituals delude the victims into thanking their molesters for the privilege, is equally simplistic. Where the biological determinists explain human behavior by its genetic legacy, the conspiracy theorists attribute to the generations which founded societies the same powers of foresight, planning, and awareness found in our contemporaries. Both ignore the possibility that new human attributes emerge with cultures.

The new paradigm suggests using natural processes to track the emergence of social information. It recognizes the qualitative difference between genes and VEMs, yet respects the emergent quality of social systems. Moreover, with the new paradigm, the real existence of VEMs and their effect on all members of societies can be accepted. Thus, the emergence of cultures need be neither miraculous nor manipulative, for the new science models how thermodynamically triggered interactions changed people qualitatively when VEMs emerged and social systems self-organized. Human spirituality—VEMs, mind, consciousness, selfhood—then represents an emergent level of reality, storing information outside the bodies and brains of individual human beings. This new level of reality exists for perfectly good scientific reasons, for it preserves local order by correlating human behaviors and thereby it dissipates energy at higher rates. This result regrounds humankind in nature and finds meaning in existence without supernatural appeals.

It is neither possible nor necessary to reject all of Modern science to apply the new paradigm. Since, in particular, the goal is to understand the process of change, fundamental elements of evolution theory remain relevant. Thus, if a new, spiritual level of reality emerges, we can postulate that some selective advantage justifies it. Reconciling spirituality and selection was hard for Modern science. Its linear logic postulated that human behavior was driven by a desire to preserve the quantitative maximum of each individual's DNA. So science looked for some mathematical relation between altruism and genetics. This approach presumes selection works directly on the genes carried by individuals, ensuring the survival and reproduction of the offspring of those who help each other. In this vision, the environmental criteria for selection given in nature originally always apply, and all that "emerges" is what time unpacks.

However, if nature is a process, then the environment also evolves. Exchanges between open systems and their worlds, after all, release entropy and matter while dissipating energy. Thus, open systems, at least in part, create their selecting environments. Evolution takes place when systems acquire the ability to map more environmental states, some of which are new. If the scale and criteria on which selection occurs can change, then there is no need, for example, to reduce VEMs to altruistic genes. VEMs represent new kinds of information, which emerges when interacting people correlate their behaviors and create, in societies, systems whose environments act on social rather than biological realities.

If, moreover, the social systems in which VEMs emerge self-organize, they need not be the purposeful creations of intentionally acting individuals. To be sure, it seems reasonable to suppose that genetically programed survival behaviors guide aggressive individuals to impose social structures on weaker rivals. Moreover, some individuals win and some lose in the phase change from archaic to civilized societies, for the increased flow of resources released by altered environments is distributed no more equally than the workload. Yet although the relative positions people have can be permanently stabilized by environmental feedbacks, they may be accidental in origin. Momentary acts of cooperation solving the problem of survival for a population are simply preserved because self-organized systems remember their origins. So the descendants of founding generations will continue to experience the consequences of ancestral fortunes. A population dependent on agriculture, for example, survives by replicating the specialty skills and sustaining the behavioral roles that made generating sufficient resources possible.

The self-organization of an agricultural society exemplifies how natural processes could transform its human components. Agriculture, of course, does not invent the components creating new social systems, for there were people and plants before there was agriculture. But if people and plants mutually transform each other through interactions, then agriculture is part of the created information emerging in self-organized social systems. We do not know exactly how or why separately evolving plant and human populations interacted, but it is thought women invented agriculture looking for ways to increase the quantity or quality of food they gathered. Perhaps they were looking for ways to reduce the effort necessary to access resources. They could have done either while thinking only of themselves or, at most, their immediate associates. But the interaction between people and plants had consequences that cannot be explained by the genes of either and that were foreseen no more clearly by the former than the latter.

After the fact it is easy to see how the surprise occurred, but as the Adam and Eve story indicates, to the people alive at the time the change in human life was so dramatic it was attributed to divine intervention—and so unwanted it was considered a punishment. The point is simple: agriculture had increased resource availability. More food per unit of land, in turn, supported a larger human population. The first surprise was that, with agriculture, it was no longer necessary for expanded populations to fragment and migrate when naturally occurring local resources were stressed. Peoples who had invested energy in farming a locale altered their traditional nomadic behavior and became sedentary. At this point, an environment altered by human initiatives was selecting for altered human behaviors. And an autocatalytic loop was generated, for permanent settlement and prosperity attracted raiding nomads, encouraging the construction of defenses and making settlements even more prosperous, inviting, and difficult to leave (Carniero, 1970). Some bands of humans were thus carried through cascades of bifurcations to self-organize at a higher, social level of reality.

But the inventors of agriculture also constituted a selecting environment for the plants, which had, in their mutations, wandered through a genetic landscape even more unpredictable than the geographical space nomadic humans crisscrossed for millennia. By choosing particular wheats, corns, or rices for cultivation, the first farmers acted as a selecting environment, multiplying the population of one variation and condemning untold hosts of others to oblivion. In other words, the actions of people stopped the random mutation of the plants, while the reaction of the plants arrested the random wanderings of the people. Each was captured by the other it was capturing.

Sedentary human populations represent only a modest degree of emergent behavior. Feedbacks from the environment were triggering more important changes because the most productive grains selected by the first agriculturalists proved unusual in that, although naturally occurring hybrids, they did not reproduce naturally. The wheats and corns were encased in shells so tough the seeds rotted rather than germinated because they could not get through the shells to the soil fast enough. For the wheats and corn used in early agriculture to survive, people had to shuck the shells, store the seed, and later plant and irrigate the crops. Rice, of course, needs ponds of water to grow in. In either case, civilization was the plants' way of making more plants, and the human work required to create conditions in which selected plants would grow transformed the environment radically.

Here was the most unwanted surprise associated with emergence on the social scale. The transformed environment in which agriculture occurred proved much richer than anything naturally available, which is what caused the human population to explode. But, if the first agriculturalists were looking for an easier way to make a living, emergence surprised them! For the enlarged population to survive, the particular set of behaviors characteristic of agriculturalists had to be preserved, and it took more work to preserve the social relationships on which an expanded population depended for survival through agriculture than it had by scavenging and hunting. Adding the consequence of their linear development of gathering techniques to the construction of irrigation works, warehouses, and fortifications led to a phase change in which Max Weber's "iron cage" of seemingly endless labor literally enslaved many. Yet since working harder meant energy was dissipated at a greater rate, all these changes obeyed the Second Law, for the entropy of the universe increased as did the order of society.

Once population grew through human agency, the environment that people had collectively selected no longer acted directly on individual organisms. Had selection continued to be "natural," virtually all would perish, since not enough food grew naturally for people individually to survive. Once agriculture generated increased yields, individuals survived or perished as members of societies; they settled in one place, worked harder and more continuously, correlated their behaviors, built permanent structures, invented war, and became specialists. Selection now occurred within the society—not on the basis of what people were biologically, but on the basis of what they did behaviorally. Nonaverage behaviors—Social Roles—constrained individual options but made collective survival possible. As long as individuals chose and acted in ways that made continued farming of the settled spaces possible, the community solved problems individuals could no longer solve for themselves.

The emergence of society did not exempt humanity from nature's laws and the challenges of environmental selection. People were still affected by gravity, disease, climate, and so on. But the self-organization of social systems introduced a new level on which selection takes place. Preserving the system upon which the survival of all depended became essential. Society itself now became the object on which the environment acts, while within the society "artificial" criteria measured fitness in terms not of physical but behavioral attributes. Once a social system self-organized, individual physical attributes mattered less and behavioral tendencies counted for more.

But accident could not be relied upon to keep the system going. On the contrary, if the individuals forming a society continued to act in whimsical accordance with their biological drives, the interdependent system would fall apart. Individuals who slept, ate, mated, fought, or fled when they felt like it could not predict what the others would do next. Members of social systems have to work, share, bond, soldier, and die for the greater good. Societies extract sacrifices from individuals because, once interactions produce social relationships, societies operate top-down. Social rules capture biological propensities facilitating individual survival, contextualize them, and put them to work for the higher purpose of collective survival in a perfect example of the "bricolage" Jacob (1973) found typical of evolutionary nature. The results are then policed to preserve established orders.

THE SELF-ORGANIZATION OF MEANING

In societies, human behavioral choices depend on rules appropriate to their emergent level of reality, and these rules are moral rather than biological. Moral rules represent created information. They result from mutually captured and capturing human interactions. And the rules regularizing behavior in human social systems must be stored in the systems themselves—not in the individuals but in the relationships between them. But the new scientific paradigm should apply to the emergence of morals as well as to any other of the Big Questions—social rules simply map a structure spontaneously self-organized in a gradient.

Biological evolution had not made people in overcrowded spaces smart enough to survive on their own, so social rules make the difference. Information stored in social structures made people in groups smarter than they were in isolation. How this was done itself evolved. The first means of storing social information was probably discovered accidentally and then regularized by play, as Huizinga (1951) suggested. People having successfully performed some operation were likely to savor their success by repeating the action. Repeated actions become rituals, and rituals held people in particular positions relative to their colleagues and encouraged actions within a narrow range of behaviors. But rituals would not only preserve information about successful behavioral options, they would tend to excite people to recreate the very actions the rituals represent. Through rituals, therefore, societies became autocatalytic systems, storing in their structures the information necessary to recreate those structures.

Rituals were also, according to Alfred North Whitehead (1926), the first vehicles through which humankind became aware of the differences between nature and societies. The regularized behaviors and stable relations displayed in and created by rituals, said Whitehead, made nature stand out as apparently chaotic and disordered. Outside the rituals there were wild plants and unpredictable events; by performing rituals, however, a realm of ordered regularity was continuously recreated. As long as ritual practices organized people in networks of action generating surplus resources, the information stored in them would have selective advantage.

Moreover, since no two social groups would have bonded together into exactly the same pattern of behaviors, there was a population of social structures whose fitness varied. Thus, selection would continue to work on social systems, and, by favoring variations with even slightly more advantageous internal arrangements and behaviors, competition between systems composed of cooperating components would account for social evolution. Some societies would simply have organized their members in ways that permitted them—the societies—to survive longer. Those traits would then have the force of nature supporting them, for societies prevail because they increase the rate at which external entropy is produced by intensifying the work done within the system.

But each test successfully passed would leave an organization with the need to store more information, for success means the society has either found new environmental energy sources or more efficient ways to process energy. Success confronted social organizations with the problem of storing increasing amounts of information. Rituals worked initially, but success meant that rituals had to encode an ever-increasing number of organized behaviors. Moreover, societies soon found that they needed rituals to transition from one practiced set of behaviors to another. Ritual eventually proved too cumbersome and slow a medium for communicating information of different kinds at various rates. To continue surviving, societies with large populations eventually exceeded the informational carrying capacity of ritual.

Social evolution did not stop when ritual proved limited. Another vehicle for storing information was readily available and was soon being exploited. That instrument was language. Language was not invented to store social information, and it had, of course, evolved earlier as one of our biological properties. In this regard language initially probably contributed to individual survival by describing various activities, places, and people. But by allowing people to communicate, language facilitated the correlation of behaviors. It also bound together people whose communications increased available resources.

As speech led to cooperation in multiple circumstances demanding varied responses, the number of things people needed to say was increasing. To then use this originally primitive communication device selected for its individual benefits to map the ordered realm described by ritual was difficult. But there was no meta-medium available to describe the world language had helped create, so language itself had to be used. So language folded back upon itself and invented new words to name relationships created by communication and represent the power of social systems. VEMS emerged with the new words for deities and morally sanctioned actions.

As spoken words, VEMs were just sounds, physically no different from any other available words. But their task was not to represent what individuals were and did separately. VEMs had to represent what people had in common, what they knew as members of societies, and how they could solve problems collectively. To map an "us" rather than a world of "you's" and "me's," language transcended its origins and "myth" emerged. Like ritual, myth stores information outside human brains. Moreover, it stores information no individuals know from direct experience. Finally, as Frankfort (1973) showed, myth catalyzes the behavior it describes. Like DNA in organisms, myth stores the information on which the stuff of the systems it maps depends.

The conscious human being emerges in this mythically mapped domain, which Dilthey (1962) called "the mind-effected world." Symbolizing the information in myths that map the environments they have made—and using myth to guide actions—human beings encounter themselves and adjust their present actions in pursuit of a future resembling their remembered past (Artigiani, 1998). Shaped by mythical feedback, their perceptions and behaviors depend as much upon what they think as on the world in which they operate. For that reason, myth is lived, not contemplated. When peoples retell their myths—as when they perform their rituals—they act the myths out, thus exciting themselves to become what they describe. But actions could have any number of consequences, which vary depending on context. Consequences are what actions "mean," and, in particular environments, the social goal is to regularize them so that practiced behaviors trigger predictable consequences. It is these meanings that give people their social roles and their moral identities.

Using VEM symbols, myths describe the relationships defining the Social Roles and practiced behaviors constituting societies. But the emergence of myths suggests that people had become collectively aware of the order characteristic of their societies along with the confusion of nature. That awareness was captured in VEM symbols as the difference between the sacred and the profane. The difference between the sacred and the profane is the key binary distinction between in/out, us/them essential to a social system. The awareness captured in this distinction is the origin of religion, which suggests that while people were aware of their world they were not yet aware of their awareness.

THE EMERGENCE OF HUMAN CONSCIOUSNESS

Religion emerges with complex social systems. Functionally, religion represents the same sort of autocatalytic external information storage system discussed in terms of rituals and myths, perhaps at a higher level of abstraction. According to Clifford Geertz (1973), religion is "(1) a set of symbols which acts to (2) establish powerful, pervasive and long-lasting moods and motivations in men by (3) formulating conceptions of a general order of existence and (4) clothing these conceptions with such an aura of factuality that (5) the moods and motivations seem uniquely realistic" (p. 90). Religion, too, evolves, and its evolution tracks increasing social complexity. As social systems become more complex, the sense of awe shared by their members increases, for the power that societies exert increases and the perspective from which they must be viewed becomes more distant. Religion evolves as the image of God becomes more remote (Armstrong, 1994)—that is, as the society moves further from equilibrium. An original abstract monotheism, which deified the resource flows liberated from the Earth Goddess by female gatherers, first breaks into more detailed, differentiated gods symbolizing a more richly variegated environment. But then, says Armstrong, highly specialized individuals operating in a market economy feel increasingly self-conscious, since their Social Roles call attention to how they are different from others. Not only does society then specialize religious roles, from shaman through priest to ecclesiastical bureaucrat, it returns to a monotheism as a device for binding separate, conscious individuals together.

Thus, religion is a symbolic map of society, as Durkheim (1912/1954) said. Eliade (1959) adds that the ceremonial centers associated with religions effected recalibrations, for bands revisiting them at crucial moments in the annual ritual calendar were reminded of proper social relationships and admonished to replicate normative roles by behaving acceptably. Ceremonial centers accomplished this task because they embodied a "sacred canon" that was an architectural model of the world. Similarly, by capturing the meaning of behaviors, VEMs catalyzed behaviors replicating defining roles and relationships in successive generations. Sometimes, of course, peoples stray from divinely ordained—that is, environmentally represented—selecting flows, but institutionalized religions correct deviants, reminding them of proper social relationships, approved behaviors, and normative roles.

Although religions and VEMs are present in every society, not even biological determinists claim there is a religious gene. Religion is emergent information, a socially constructed reality that appears at symmetry-breaking discontinuities. But if every civilized society used religion to map itself in symbols powerful enough to constrain behavior and valuable enough to excite self-sacrifice, the particular religion characteristic of any society will vary contingently with the personalities of its founders, their relative positions, the exact nature of their relationships, and their contextualizing environments.

Variations between religions provide a population of society-shaping information carriers that can be more or less advantaged, like organisms, for, while religion may be a form of reality the materialism of Modern science could not accommodate, it is not wholly otherworldly. It cannot exist without biological human brains, for instance. But once biological human brains are entangled in a religious system, they, the brains, will behave differently. Like other symbologies, religion serves as an operating system for biologically evolved "wetware"; such operating systems were written when complex human societies self-organized. VEMs did not, of course, change the physical characteristics of the human brains with which they coevolved. But new operating systems did change the attributes of those human brains. Those whose VEMs encouraged social learning were the most privileged.

Although the availability of organized symbol systems, like mathematics, gave individuals the power to solve problems they individually might not have even been able to conceive, the greatest intellectual advances probably derived from the religious symbols themselves. Here the emergent attribute—consciousness—is so important we tend to think it our species-specific hallmark (Carrithers et al., 1985). While people probably became aware of mind around Plato's time (Snell, 1953), consciousness is not defined until well into the European Middle Ages. Then it meant thinking with others and thinking about the self (Fischer, 1989). The first part of the Scholastic definition of consciousness is easiest to understand, for if how and what we think is influenced by a shared symbolic operating system we are, literally, thinking with others. Thinking about the self is much harder to understand. But it is well-established that thinking about the self is not something people have always done or do as an inevitable part of their biological natures. It seems reasonable, then, to hypothesize that self-consciousness is an emergent attribute and that it emerges with the self-organization of complex societies (Artigiani, 1996).

There is negative evidence to support this hypothesis in the myths characteristic of ancient societies. Using Homer's epics as examples, neither Achilles nor Odysseus was self-conscious. Achilles simply acted, for the most part, and what he did was the result of Gods acting through him. Odysseus thought, but he was able to be very clever about the world because he never wasted any mental energy thinking about himself (Rubino, 1991). Odysseus looked outward, not inward. According to Karl Jaspers (1953), Homer's figures are quite typical of humankind generally, until the "Axial Age," 1500-500 BCE. In the Axial Age human nature changed, from China through India to the Middle East.

In this vast swath of space there were, of course, many different societies. But those that were undergoing the final stages of economic development as integrated territorial empires supported by irrigated agriculture, specialized labor, developing markets, and writing were all being stressed in similar ways. Long-term changes had been developing, but the final resolution of how societies should organize to process flows was not established. The human components of these societies, having biologically similar brains, reacted to the same sorts of stresses in similar ways. They were, to begin with, traumatized by the prospect of destabilized cooperative systems on which everyone depended disintegrating. Some, like Confucius, reacted to this possibility by postulating a previous stable state, sanctioned by the Mandate of Heaven, to which society should return. Others, like Buddha, advocated a sort of spiritual decoupling from the troublingly unpredictable material world. Finally, thinkers like Socrates advocated reflection on the self as a way to restructure behavior and stabilize society.

Heroes of the Axial Age were able to articulate their experience of a personal inner life in ways unlike heroes of old. They were aware of their existence with a new intensity, leaving them aware of being aware of themselves. Most, like St. Augustine later, seemed less than pleased by that experience, but others, like Socrates, at least, could proclaim it self-consciously as the only way to live. These differences may be slight, but iterated over generations they could evolve societies that were strikingly varied.

Regardless of the particular form of their reaction, all these representatives of the Axial Age were self-conscious because their societies had developed symbols representing their collective identity. These symbols told individuals which actions were socially sanctioned and which were taboo. It then became possible for people to choose between behavioral options by anticipating how their societies would react if they behaved one way rather than another. Since the societies' reactions had the moral authority of collective consequences rather than merely private pleasures and pains, the new symbols were mapping the "meaning" of actions.

It was not long before people realized that many of the things which made them personally happy—like resting a lot—destabilized societies. Since societies only endured when their individual components performed as trained and expected—and since the individuals only survived when their societies continued to solve problems the individuals could not solve for themselves—it was obviously to the individual's long-term advantage to do what society wanted. The difference, sometimes painfully perceived, between private, personal desires and VEM-defined public obligations is the origins of the Self. People became aware of their existence in the strain between biological urges and social responsibilities. It is likely that the sense of "sin" emerges in this context, too, as the symbol representing the experience of following natural urges at the risk of social stability.

To avoid sin, individuals could use shared symbols, mapping societies to project the consequences of their actions and predict how others would define them. People could then see the likely consequences of their choices and understand how the different choices would impact others. It was then possible for individuals to make meaningful choices, which not only further intensified the sense of Self but made freedom a moral category for the first time. People were no longer simply following whatever biological urges motivated them. Nor were they operating in a social vacuum, where the consequence of an action was experienced only by the initiator or receiver. In these earlier cases, many actions were possible but the difference between one choice and another was almost indistinguishable from any higher level perspective. People could do whatever they felt like doing, but there was no way to choose between actions.

Becoming moral agents with the emergence of complex social systems, people came closer to contemporary identities. The other side of this same coin, however, was that deception now entered into the repertoire of human attributes, as well. People who knew that socially disapproved but privately beneficial actions could cause them pain might, if they were clever enough, disguise personal profit as public gain. Now these are clearly people with the mental attributes necessary to trick others into subservient and exploited positions in societies.

But because people have attributes like consciousness and foresight after complex societies self-organize does not mean they used the attributes to create the societies. The new scientific paradigm, in fact, would suggest that at least some presently perceived attributes emerge with the social systems of which we are currently parts (Artigiani, 1995). We cannot produce a compelling mechanically or logically necessary account of how those attributes emerged. But on the other hand, ambiguity permits the evolution of nature to be modeled. It is also possible that, in the competition between civilizations, environmental selection favors societies which select for conscious, autonomous, even potentially dishonest individuals and VEMs that are characteristically ambiguous. Conscious, autonomous, active citizens can, through invention and behavioral variations, increase resource flows and privilege their societies. This, no doubt, confuses people and threatens the powerful. But the progressive nature of social evolution suggests human systems display nature's propensity to select for the possibility of further evolution, which occurs at the system state Langton (1990) calls "the edge of chaos."

EVOLUTIONARY VEMS

Once societies and their mythically communicated VEMs emerge, it is no longer changes in the physiology of individual human organisms that is interesting. Rather, the Big Question becomes "does the tale of exploitation, war, suffering, and woe that is the story of humankind's history mean anything?" Answering it requires that we stay within the scientific parameters laid out, but they provide at least the possibility of an encouraging answer. Perhaps history has a meaning, and its meaning is the individuation, moralization, and reflective self-awareness of human beings over time. Then the natural tendency to increase complexity as a way of maximizing entropy turns out to be a base for the evolution of social systems which it is fair to call "progressive."

Although somewhat startling in today's culture, this is actually not a very demanding argument. We have already conceded that every society maps itself distinctly, and we must further recognize that myths and religions are parochial devices separating people from one another. Of course, distinct social systems are likely to compete, sometimes through destructively intrusive behaviors like wars. There is no reason to justify such conduct morally, although it is clear that competing social systems do generate entropy. Measuring entropy rates by counting wasted human lives is cruelly quantitative. But it may have qualitative implications, for any society enjoying a marginal advantage can benefit in nonlinear ways from its distinction. If competition leads to more humane societies, then progress and increasing complexity emerge together.

Societies whose VEMs enable them to anticipate problems, access or process resources more efficiently, and recover from shocks more robustly tend to prevail. Cultural evolution is rapid because the information involved—VEMs— is cheaper than the information involved in, say, biology—genes. Societies can experiment more easily than species, for there is no way to correct bad genes except by destroying organisms. Mistaken ideas can be changed without destroying whole societies, however, and societies composed of self-conscious moral agents can change most quickly. Yet the process of cultural evolution, while accelerated, need not be peaceful and happy, for it follows the same patterned process of self-organization and selection characteristic of nature generally.

While there are good scientific reasons for progressive societies, we cannot blithely conclude that every society will evolve into relatively more humanistic patterns: Cosmic entropy can be increased through a virtually infinite number of ways. Moreover, there is no reason to assume that the self-consciously individual moral agents that have historically evolved in cultural contexts can bear the strain on their biologically given sensibilities associated with the ambiguity of life at the edge of chaos. And we certainly do not know whether these historical products of self-organized systems will, in turn, make a world meaningfully valuable to the future.

But a science that gives rational foundations to new, Post-Modern VEMs secularizing morals and emphasizing cooperation as well as competition, synergies as well as selfishness, creativity as well as responsibility may provide the psychological strength people need to negotiate virtually continuous change. The emergence of humanistic societies seems to imply there is a basis in natural processes for hope. Replacing sectarian myths turning members of self-organized societies against each other with a science searching for commonalities across nature should also help. The appearance of such VEMs may seem unlikely, but then the essence of emergence is its wonderful unpredictability.

REFERENCES

Armstrong, K. (1994). *The History of God.* New York: Knopf.
Artigiani, R. (1995). Self, System and Emergent Complexity. *Evolution and Cognition, 1,* 139-147.
Artigiani, R. (1996). Societal Computation and the Emergence of Mind. *Evolution and Cognition, 2,* 2-15.

Artigiani, R. (1998). Social Information: The Person Is the Message. *BioSystems, 46,* 137-144.
Carniero, R.L. (1970). A Theory of the State. *Science, 169,* 733-738.
Carrithers, M., Collins, S. & Lues, S. (1985). *The Category of the Person.* Cambridge, MA: Harvard University Press.
Dilthey, W. (1962). Pattern and Meaning. In H.P. Rickman (Ed.), *History.* New York: Harper Torchbooks.
Durkheim, E. (1912/1954). *The Elementary Forms Of The Religious Life.* New York: Macmillan.
Eliade, M. (1959). *The Sacred and the Profane.* New York: Harcourt Brace.
Fischer, R. (1989). Why the Mind is Not in the Head. *Diogenes, 151,* 1-28.
Frankfort, H. (1973). *Before Philosophy.* Baltimore: Penguin.
Geertz, C. (1973). *The Interpretation of Cultures.* New York: Basic Books.
Huizinga, J. (1951). *Homo Ludens.* Boston: Beacon Press.
Jacob, F. (1973). *The Logic of Life.* New York: Pantheon.
Jaspers, K. (1953). *The Origin and Goal Of History.* New Haven, CT: Yale University Press.
Langton, C. (1990). Computation at the Edge of Chaos. *Physica D, 42,* 12-37.
Monod, J. (1971). *Chance and Necessity.* New York: Knopf.
Prigogine, I. (1980). *From Being to Becoming.* San Francisco: Freeman.
Prigogine, I., & Stengers, I. (1984). *Order Out of Chaos.* New York: Bantam.
Rubino, C. (1991, 1992). The Least Deceptive Mirror of the Mind. *The St. John's Review, 41,* 61-73.
Schmookler, A. (1984). *The Parable of the Tribes.* Boston: Houghton Mifflin.
Snell, B. (1953). *The Discovery of Mind.* Oxford: Blackwell.
Whitehead, A.N. (1926). *Religion in the Making.* New York: Macmillan.
Wilson, E.O. (1978). *On Human Nature.* Cambridge, MA: Harvard University Press.

Chapter 5

ON THE INTERPENETRATION OF SOCIAL SUBSYSTEMS: A CONTEMPORARY RECONSTRUCTION OF PARSONS AND LUHMANN

Michael Rempel

INTRODUCTION

This chapter reconstructs two major theories of social differentiation: the systems theories of Talcott Parsons and Niklas Luhmann. Despite their persistent influence, these theories fail to explain a number of important and intensifying social trends facing contemporary advanced industrial societies. Such trends involve growing patterns of intersection, or interpenetration, among social influences rooted historically in distinct institutions. To wit, contemporary political deliberations increasingly respond not only to the influence of distinctly "political" ideologies (e.g., left and right) but also to forms of technical expertise rooted in economic or scientific institutions. Legal deliberations increasingly respond not only to existing laws and legal precedents but also to the "extra-legal" guidance of social scientists and therapeutically trained social workers. Also, scientific deliberations regularly respond not only to quasi-objective "scientific" influences but to economic considerations of which research projects can garner outside funding and to political considerations of which agenda funders would like to promote. In general, deliberations in one institution seem increasingly to incorporate social and technical influences rooted historically in others. This tendency is hardly unique to contemporary societies, but I argue that it is currently growing more prevalent. This leads me to develop a concept of subsystem interpenetration as the centerpiece of a more adequate theoretical approach to social differentiation. This concept can frame the accelerating tendency for influences rooted in otherwise differentiated institutions to conjoin in empirical practice. Instead of abandoning past systems theories altogether, I use the concept of interpenetration to reconstruct the approaches of Parsons and Luhmann.

I proceed in three sections. The first section pulls together a few key points from the theories of Parsons and Luhmann, the second section reconstructs their theories using the concept of interpenetration, and the third section reviews what this chapter's reconstruction accomplishes.

PARSONS AND LUHMANN ON SOCIAL DIFFERENTIATION

The social systems theories of Parsons and Luhmann provide two of the more influential accounts available of social differentiation in modern societies. Both theories divide societies into a few major subsystems, each responsible for executing a different function for the whole society. Otherwise, however, Parsons and Luhmann move in radically dissimilar directions. The next two subsections elaborate.

Parsons' Social Action System

Parsons offers two approaches for understanding social differentiation, functional and structural. Many theorists discuss only one or the other approach, or conflate them, but I find it important to draw an explicit distinction.

The functional approach divides social systems into four subsystems, with each responsible for addressing one of four "functional imperatives" of the larger society (Parsons & Smelser, 1956; Parsons, 1961). The economy specializes in adaptation (A), the polity specializes in goal-attainment (G), the integrative subsystem (I) specializes in integrating or generating social cohesiveness among society's members, and the pattern-maintenance subsystem specializes in maintaining "latent" (L) cultural "patterns." This last function involves imparting the core values of the larger society, such as democracy, individual rights, or other values.

The structural approach divides societies into an unspecified number of concrete subsystems, or "collectivities" (Parsons, 1961). Each consists of a "membership" of interacting persons, as in the concrete membership of a business firm, scientific institute, or church.

In comparing these approaches, the functional retains an axiomatic position that there are four abstract types of actions which all social systems organize: adaptive, goal-attaining, integrative, and pattern-maintaining. The structural approach demands the actual empirical study of what are a particular society's most influential action-organizing collectivities (e.g., its most influential formal organizations). Rather than divide actions a priori among just four subsystems, the structural approach provides a set of concepts—social system, collectivity, and action—for empirically studying the actual social divisions that exist in a given society. The resting of Parsons' functional approach on a strictly theoretical rather than an empirical foundation hinders its ability to correspond plausibly with a changing social universe. For instance, Parsons' theoretically based scheme seems ill-equipped to illuminate anything about the growing significance of science and technology, and of the operations performed by universities and research institutes. Onto which of the four functionally defined subsystems should one map scientific work? For that matter, onto which functionally defined subsystem should one map work performed in hospitals, or in social service organizations? Whereas Parsons' functional approach yields an inflexible list of four subsystems, the structural approach suffers from a failure to propose any parts of society as particularly important. To this extent, the structural approach abdicates any responsibility for suggesting guidance as to the major sectors into which contemporary societies appear to be organizing themselves.

Luhmann's Social Communication System

Luhmann theorizes the differentiation of social subsystems in a radically different way than Parsons. Whereas Parsons defines a social system to consist of socially structured actions, Luhmann defines it to consist of conceptually structured meanings. Luhmann explains that these meanings organize themselves communicatively, or into linguistic elements that one can communicatively express to others. Each of Luhmann's social subsystems is a particular form of communication. Each stands for a particular cognitive perspective for viewing the world and a particular language for communicating that perspective (e.g., see Luhmann, 1982, 1989, 1995). For instance, Luhmann's economic subsystem is a form of communication regarding the calculation and communication of economic costs and benefits. This subsystem is therefore not a set of concrete actions and organizational structures, such as business firms, but a kind of conceptual language and logic that, in empirical practice, business firms will probably tend to employ.

Parsons does not altogether ignore the import of meaning and language, but the meanings discussed are primarily normative. They concern what persons should do and what general considerations of value persons should bring to bear. Luhmann emphasizes the cognitive dimension of meaning. He presumes that contemporary social life proceeds primarily because persons do what they technically can, not because persons do what they normatively should. According to Luhmann, persons do what existing subsystems of meaning and communication make linguistically and cognitively possible, regardless of normative "should-oriented" recommendations. Luhmann sees contemporary, institutional conduct as critically constrained by issues of technical skill: by what is technically and logistically feasible in different situations.

Luhmann's approach seems more adequate to contemporary, expertise-based societies. His theory is consistent with Giddens' (1991) observation of contemporary societies as increasingly divided into "expert systems," each composed of highly specialized expert techniques and forms of knowledge. Unlike Giddens, Luhmann actually specifies six subsystems that he considers particularly consequential in contemporary societies: economic, political, legal, scientific, educational, and religious. Note that his naming of these subsystems

Table 5.1
Major Communication Subsystems in Contemporary, Advanced Industrial Societies

Subsystem[1]	Binary Code	Language of Social Communication	Basis of Competence and Authority	Medium of Communication
economic	payment vs. non-payment; or property-ownership vs. non-ownership	prices	ability to pay; or property ownership	money
political	holding vs. not holding political office; or government vs. opposition	adversarial struggle for political gain	holding political office	power
ideological[2]	left vs. right; or progressive vs. conservative	political culture values, or ideological preferences	holding &/or seeking to advance an ideological position	substantive political values or ideologies
legal	legal vs. illegal	the law, legal discourse, or legal precedents	legal training	law and credentials
scientific (basic)	truth vs. falsity	scientific truth discovery techniques	technical/ scientific credentials	truth
therapeutic[3] (clinical)	functional vs. dysfunctional (psychological)	communications on psychological functioning and quality of life	therapeutic credentials	psychological states
medical[3] (clinical)	functional vs. dysfunctional (physiological)	physical remedy discovery techniques	medical credentials	physiological states
educational	better vs. worse; pass vs. fail; or succeed vs. fail	comparisons & ratings; & languages of various educational subjects	right to evaluate, compare, and select; teachers or administrators	grades, or exam scores

[1] All subsystems synthesized from Luhmann, 1982, 1989; Rempel, 1996, 1998. The specification of four distinct elements for each subsystem draws directly on the ideas of Niklas Luhmann but is itself an original reformulation of those ideas, initially developed in Rempel (1996) but significantly modified since that paper's publication.

[2] Luhmann does not in any work explicitly differentiate an "ideological" from a "political" subsystem. Luhmann (1982) formulates a concept of a "political" subsystem that is roughly akin to this table's "ideological," while in a later work, Luhmann (1989) abandons any notion that ideologies matter in expert, differentiated societies. Hence Luhmann (1989) defines the "political" subsystem solely in terms of the adversarial struggle for office (see "political" as defined in this table).

[3] The idea of this subsystem is strictly unique to this scheme.

depends on his empirical observation of societies, not on an axiomatic position, as in Parsons' functional approach. Thus one can adhere to Luhmann's basic theory and still add or subtract subsystems for specific purposes or in accordance with perceived social changes.

Building further on Luhmann, Table 5.1 provides a slightly revised listing of the major subsystems in contemporary societies. I consider each subsystem to consist of a (1) binary code, (2) language of social communication, (3) basis of competence and authority, and (4) medium of communication. The particular role of binary codes in organizing how a given communication subsystem will process meaning is a role Luhmann strongly emphasizes throughout all of his works. The binary code is the initial cognitive tool, indicating which matters fall in and outside of a given subsystem's range of concerns and through what cognitive lenses the matter is to be assessed. (For a more extended discussion of the indicated subsystem elements, see Rempel, 1996, 1998; and also see Luhmann, 1982, 1989.)

A Preliminary Synthesis of Parsons and Luhmann

Neither Parsons' nor Luhmann's approaches adequately account for all the major types of influences over institutional deliberations in contemporary, advanced industrial societies. Parsons' focus on action, and on the normative dimension of meaning, does not apprehend the differentiation of societies into fundamentally dissimilar cognitive perspectives and expert languages. Those working in different organizational settings may not only have different action responsibilities but may employ fundamentally different paradigms for thinking and communicating about issues (e.g., see Kuhn, 1962). At the same time, Luhmann's cognitivistic focus ignores the impact on social deliberations of concrete social relations among different persons and organizations. In particular, the opportunity to raise given topics, express given interests, or use given languages, logics, or styles of communication depends on the system of socially structured action relations that one is located within. A communication subsystem has no import unless concrete organizations and acting persons have the organizational structures and linkages for using that communication subsystem.

The next section further indicates why to combine subsystem concepts drawn respectively from Parsons and Luhmann. For now, consider the following stipulation. It is that one may define each major institution in society to consist

Table 5.2
Major Social Institutions in Contemporary, Advanced Industrial Societies

Institution	Communication Subsystem	Action Subsystem Most Typical Collectivities	Action Subsystem Most Typical Membership	Primary Functional Imperative
economic	Economic Communication Subsystem	business firms	for-profit business owners, managers, and workers; economists.	A: Adaptation
political	Political + Ideological Communication Subsystems	government & political party organizations	politicians, political party workers, and government bureaucrats	G: Goal-attainment
legal	Legal Communication Subsystem	court systems; legal firms; and law schools	lawyers, judges, and legal scholars	I: Integration
scientific (basic)	Scientific Communication Subsystem	research institutes or labs; research universities	humanities, natural, & social science scholars; other technical experts	???
psychological (clinical)	Therapeutic Communication Subsystem	counseling organizations; and psychiatric hospitals	social workers, clinical psychologists, & some psychiatrists	I: Integration ??? L: Latent pattern-maintenance ???
medical (clinical)	Medical Communication Subsystem	hospitals; doctor's offices	medical doctors, and psychiatrists	???
educational	Educational Communication Subsystem	schools; educational bureaucracies; testing firms	school bureaucrats-administrators, teachers, parents, & students	L: Latent pattern-maintenance

of: (1) an action subsystem composed of the institution's regularly interacting members, and (2) a communication subsystem composed of the set of communicable meanings regularly used within the institution. An institution then consists of an action subsystem coupled with a historically related communication subsystem. Historically, social differentiation thus involves conceptual communication subsystems codeveloping alongside concrete action subsystems. For instance, a society's legal communication subsystem—the conceptual logic used to communicate in legal institutions—influences and takes shape in light of concrete decisions within the legal action subsystem, where the latter consists of actions by such actors as judges, lawyers, and legal scholars. In effect, each institution's communication subsystem provides the meaningful content that infuses the thought and communications of persons working in the corresponding action subsystem.

Pursuant to the foregoing stipulations, consider the eight institutions described via Table 5.2.

This table replicates the contents of Table 5.1 but with several additions. First, for each communication subsystem, Table 5.2 includes a historically related action subsystem composed of (1) a certain type of collectivity (formal organizations or other social grouping), and (2) a concrete membership of interacting persons. Second, to join this synthesis with Parsons' functional approach, where possible, I note which functionally defined subsystem each institution's operations are most likely to fall under. The many blank spaces in this part of the table reinforces the inadequacy of using Parsons' functional approach for a comprehensive differentiation theory.

TOWARD A THEORY OF INTERPENETRATION

Parsons and Luhmann both ground their theories on the presupposition that social differentiation takes the form of a radical segmentation of society's major institutions. The idea is that distinct organizations and forms of knowledge arise to handle distinct types of issues: economic, political, legal, scientific, therapeutic, religious, and so forth. For example, legal institutions supposedly develop their own, uniquely legal organizations (the action-based component) and their own technical language and logic (the communication-based component). This means that considerations of economic costs and benefits, partisan political advantages, social research findings, or advice from therapists are supposedly irrelevant to what occurs in legal deliberations. Yet all of the preceding "extralegal" considerations do in fact bear on legal deliberations, a reality to which most persons with a borderline awareness of current events can attest. Even though Parsons, Luhmann, and other differentiation theorists usually insert various caveats on how institutional operations are not as neatly segmented as their basic models suggest (with some caveats discussed below), these theories ultimately rest on a segmentationist foundation. The initial, overriding vision portrays modern society as segmented into highly distinct institutions, or subsystems, each concerned with a subsystem-specific function and set of operations. This chapter rejects the segmentationist view. It instead assumes the ubiquitousness and hence social centrality of subsystem interpenetration. Broadly described, interpenetration refers to a connection or conjoining among historically separate contents, such as historically differentiated organizations, social networks, or forms of communication.

The Ubiquitousness of Interpenetration

Why is this chapter's change of theoretical orientation needed at this time? Consider just a few recent trends that illustrate the ubiquitousness of interpenetration.

Interdisciplinary Forms of Knowledge: Researchers with a primary training in one scientific field, from biology to psychology to sociology, increasingly combine concepts, methods, and arguments rooted in others (e.g., Wallerstein, 1997). Also, numerous academic programs have arisen since the 1960s, focusing on some substantive questions by bringing to bear many disciplinary perspectives (e.g., Women's Studies, Gay and Lesbian Studies, or American Studies).

Interlocking Organizational Structures Joining Government, For-Profit, and Nonprofit Organizations: Indicating interpenetration among different formal organizations, interlocking organizational structures have grown substantially over recent decades (e.g., see Powell, 1990). These structures involve formal, contractual arrangements among different organizations, whereby some of their members join together in the pursuit of a common project. One particularly publicized trend is the expanded privatization of many government services. This involves private business firms in carrying out tasks formerly carried out by government agencies (e.g., education, mass transit, or social service delivery). However, the private agencies carry out these tasks under close, regulatory oversight from government, and in this sense, there arise tight, formally regulated network ties across the two types of organizations. As another example, many researchers now document the rise of contractual arrangements and joint ventures between profit and nonprofit charitable organizations (Powell, 1990). These examples illustrate a kind of "interpenetration" of organizational structures.

"Multifunctional" Workers: Multi-functional workers combine several different types of skills instead of possessing only a single, highly specialized form of training (Castells, 1996; Jacobson, 1996). The advantages of multifunctionality (see Jacobson, 1996), as well as the reality of its current diffusion, counter Luhmann's (1982) position that to simplify the vast complexity of the world, the prevalent solution has been to divide operations into increasingly specialized expert communication subsystems. The challenge which multifunctionality poses to earlier differentiation theories, for instance of Weber or Durkheim, goes without saying.

The Increasingly Global Penetration of Money, Markets, and Free Market Economic Thinking: Communications technologies since the early 1980s, including fax machines, e-mail, and the Internet, tremendously heighten the global circulation of information. Among other effects, this improves the ability of multinational business firms to engage in a global coordination of their operations. This may increase the global power of both business firms and the free market economic thinking (i.e., the "economic communication subsystem") upon which such firms characteristically base their decisions. One conceivable outcome is a global penetration by business firms and by economistic thinking throughout a wide array of social settings (e.g., see Galtung, 1984). Indeed, in our ordinary lives, we encounter evidence of this trend every day. From Hollywood decisions on what movies to produce, to prospective funding-based decisions of what scientific research to undertake, to insurance company/economic "bottom line"-influenced medical decisions of what procedures to sanction, economic calculations of costs and benefits figure prominently in an expanding number of contemporary institutions.

In each of these examples, one can identify two or more social influences and a growing intersection, or interpenetration, among them. The first example—interdisciplinary fields of knowledge—involves a growing interpenetration among conceptual perspectives. The second example—inter-organizational linkages—involves a growing interpenetration among concrete governmental, for-profit, and nonprofit types of organizational entities. The difference between these two examples illustrates the two fundamental forms that interpenetration can take. It also demonstrates why this chapter joins both action-based and communication-based subsystems concepts. The first example concerns an interpenetration of knowledges, or of cognitively based languages and logics—as indicated by Luhmann's concept of a communication subsystem. The second example concerns an interpenetration of concrete organizational entities—as indicated by Parsons' concept of an action subsystem. Rephrasing again, the first example concerns an interpenetration of disciplinary ways of thinking, whereas the second concerns an interpenetration of acting persons initially rooted in different organizations (e.g., governmental and for-profit).

The foregoing implies the relevance of two distinct types of interpenetration, corresponding to the two types of social subsystems stipulated above: (1) interpenetration among action subsystems, and (2) interpenetration among communication subsystems. I introduce each type in the following subsections.

The Interpenetration of Action Subsystems

Action subsystems interpenetrate when the members of formally distinguishable collectivities (e.g., business firms and government agencies) jointly take action on a substantive project, such as developing environmental regulations, building bridges, or managing public schools. A simple way to think about the interpenetration of action subsystems is in terms of network theory. The essential idea is that close network ties exist between persons formally connected to different organizations. So in practice, organizations that are formally differentiated appear to closely confer, cooperate, engage in mutual influence, or jointly decide plans of action. Laumann and Knoke (1987) in effect observe systematic patterns of interpenetration through their network analysis of decision-making in the United States energy and health care policy domains. They carefully map the network ties between different organizations—both governmental and nongovernmental—so as to reveal which organizations come into contact in the course of seeking to influence energy and health care policies. Concerning both of these policy domains, Laumann and Knoke find that governmental agencies are at the center of decision-making, but members from an array of nongovernmental organizations are closely implicated. The methods of Laumann and Knoke lead them toward an empirical analysis of political decision-making based, in effect, on a theoretical presupposition that processes of action subsystem interpenetration are rampant. A strictly network-based approach, however, grounded as it is on a kind of neo-Parsonian action framework, ignores the implications of growing interpenetration among communication subsystems (see below).

Notably, Parsons and Smelser (1956, p. 142) already observe that among action subsystems, there are regions of operational overlap, or "zones of interpenetration." Theirs is a kind of mathematical set theory metaphor, whereby one imagines two subsystems, each with boundaries defined by a circle, but whose boundaries overlap in some intermediate area. However, this view limits interpenetration to obvious, mundane instances. An example which Parsons and Smelser provide is the overlap between the economic and political subsystems when it comes to actions regarding government regulation of the economy, or the government's need to seek greater financial revenues. This example reveals a self-evident confluence of relevance among political and economic organizations; hence, they interpenetrate.

More to the point of this chapter's concerns, however, are instances of interpenetration among organizational entities that lack a self-evident common relevance on the substantive issues under deliberation. An example would be if tight, exclusive influence relations exist between business leaders and political officials with regard to public interest-related decisions, as on environmental protection or health care. Another important example is the actual, contemporary trend toward privatizing many government services, from child welfare to education to prison services. There is no absolutely compelling, self-evident relevance of for-profit organizations on these issues, as compared to their self-evident relevance on issues of business taxation or government regulation of the economy. An example like the privatization of government services goes more to the point of what this chapter seeks to highlight, as compared with the kinds of nonproblematic examples cited by Parsons and Smelser. For this chapter, the set theory metaphor does not work, in the sense that before the interpenetration develops, one would not necessarily position the interpenetrating organizations right next to one another, as though the interpenetration consequently involves a kind of natural and self-evident overlap of function. Rather, one's visual metaphor is more of highly mobile, in-motion circles (i.e., organizations) seeking to extend themselves to contact and influence other circles lying initially in all kinds of locations within social space.

Compare interpenetration with Parsons and Smelser's (1956) related concept of "boundary interchange." The latter involves one subsystem in sending money, raw materials, processed goods, or other exchangeable qualities to another subsystem. Like interpenetration, boundary interchange involves mutual contact between two or more action-based subsystems. However, there is a critical difference. In interpenetration, it is not just that one subsystem releases an output that becomes an input for another subsystem, but that two or more subsystems jointly participate, in the first place, in the creation of the output. Interpenetration does not signify an exchange but signifies integral, joint participation in social deliberations.

The Interpenetration of Communication Subsystems

Communication subsystems interpenetrate when more than one such subsystem enters into some set of social deliberations. As a simple example, President Clinton's deliberations in the "Monica Lewinsky scandal" jointly considered what would advance the president's legal position and his political popularity—with the latter thought about independent of the relevant technical legal issues. This constitutes an interpenetration of the legal and political communication subsystems. If certain legal deliberations incorporate economic models when considering what penalties to charge industrial polluters, there is an interpenetration of legal and economic communication subsystems. Or if medical deliberations consider the possible impact of both prescription drugs and therapeutic work in alleviating medical symptoms, there is an interpenetration of what I term the medical and therapeutic communication subsystems.

Since, by definition, communication subsystems are strictly conceptual in nature, to have social relevance, their interpenetration must always occur in a concrete action setting. Conceptual communication subsystems do not magically conjoin but do so in a specific social and geographical space where real persons communicate and act.

Implications for the Study of Institutions

Two questions arise in studying some sets of institutional deliberations. First, do the deliberations in that institution involve an interpenetration of distinct action subsystems—for example, distinct types of collectivities, of those listed under Table 5.2, column 2? Second, which of a society's communication subsystems interpenetrate in the relevant action space? Often, the answer to one of these questions helps to answer the other. For instance, if certain business firms—for example, historically rooted in an economic action subsystem—regularly penetrate certain deliberations, it is plausible to hypothesize that the economic communication subsystem regularly interpenetrates as well. This is insofar as business firms, and the persons representing such firms, are likely to communicate in terms of maximizing quantitative economic benefits and minimizing costs. Thus if business organizations have close network ties with government agencies, that may imply that decisions for which those government agencies are ostensibly responsible will be heavily influenced by an economistic logic—by the economic communication in addition to the economic action subsystem. Or to give another example, the introduction of acting social scientists and social workers into the formulation of criminal justice policies may correspond also with a greater interpenetration of scientific and therapeutic communication subsystems with the legal.

Importantly, it can be problematic to assume a priori that certain action subsystems always use one and not any other type of communication subsystem. Nonetheless, Luhmann implicitly makes this problematic assumption, even though he never develops an explicit action-based subsystem concept. This assumption also underlies network-based studies, such as Laumann and Knoke's (1987) study of the energy and health care policy domains in the United States. Network-based approaches focus on the concrete action-based influence relations among the members of concrete organizations (or individual persons) but tend not to study, as a potentially separate, independent variable, which communicative influences predominate within given action-based settings.

To illustrate what is here at stake, consider as a case-in-point Ferman's (1996) research of policy-making in the city of Pittsburgh. She finds that since 1969, Pittsburgh has incorporated an exceptionally wide array of community-based and other interest groups in its public policy deliberations. Hence a strictly action-based analysis would reveal extensive action subsystem interpenetration. In plain language, Pittsburgh appears to be run according to a highly inclusive and democratic form of decision-making. However, Ferman also finds that underlying Pittsburgh's policy-making deliberations since 1969 has been a dominant assumption that political decisions must maximize aggregate economic growth in the city and aggregate profits for the business community.

Read in this chapter's terms, Ferman in effect reports that policy deliberations in Pittsburgh have been dominated by an economic communication subsystem—even though the business community is not a dominating action-based presence in the policy-making process. So whereas a strictly action-based (e.g., network) study would reveal a wide array of organizational influences in Pittsburgh (i.e., inclusive democracy), a communication-based study would reveal the lack of a wide array of communicative influences (i.e., authoritarian domination by particular ways of thinking). This example illustrates the weaknesses of a network-based empirical study, as well as of a strictly Parsonian theoretical approach.

WHAT DOES INTERPENETRATION SYSTEMS THEORY ACCOMPLISH?

Refocusing social systems theory around a dynamic concept of interpenetration productively updates existing theories of social differentiation. For instance, it does not make sense merely to have a theory of "boundary interchange," as in Parsons and Smelser (1956), if subsystems on the receiving end of an exchange often participated in the development of the exchanged products in the first place. Increasingly, the most relevant question does not concern which subsystems participated in "boundary interchange." Rather, more relevant is which subsystems interpenetrated during the deliberations leading to the construction of the exchanged items. For instance, economic subsystems may not only receive outputs from the political subsystem but may also extensively influence the formation of those outputs—as in the case of Pittsburgh cited above.

As a qualifier, this chapter's theoretical reconstruction need not involve an insistence that interpenetration was an infrequent process only until recent decades. Nonetheless, empirical research of post-1960s organizational trends by Powell (1990), Castells (1996), Lash and Urry (1994), and Jacobson (1996), among others, does point to a qualitative increase in the inadequacy of segmentationist frameworks. This research indicates a marked rise in the interdisciplinarity of organizations and knowledge. Such research calls for a response from social theory. The concept of interpenetration is a broad conceptual intervention for unifying a variety of different but qualitatively related trends that different empirical researchers have respectively documented.

While redirecting differentiation theory to study the interpenetration of subsystems, I maintain that it can be analytically illuminating to identify the original subsystems whose influence is at work. By beginning with coherent distinctions among differentiated action and communication subsystems, it is only then possible to gain clear insight into what exactly is interpenetrating in a given instance. By understanding what broadly defines the legal communication subsystem, or the political, or any other noted in Table 5.2, one begins with a coherent guide for interpreting which subsystems may be interpenetrating in a given instance. Hence this chapter remains tied to systems theory, building on Parsons and Luhmann rather than abandoning their projects altogether. A grounding on some initial model of actual, major subsystems in society seems to provide a more productive guide to subsequent analysis than vague, undeveloped theses that many "expert systems" are out there.

Figures 5.1 and 5.2 summarize this chapter's position. Figure 5.1 models the assumptions of a classic, segmentationist differentiation theory, such as Luhmann's (see analyses in the previous sections). Such a theory presumes that deliberations in each particular type of institution respond to a particular action-based influence and a historically related communication-based influence. For example, the assumption is that deliberations in legal institutions primarily respond to the influence of (1) judges, lawyers, or others working in legal organizations, and (2) a legalistic language and logic of communication. By comparison, Figure 5.2 models the assumptions of interpenetration systems theory. It is that processes of interpenetration are becoming increasingly rampant and, consequently, the baseline concepts of a differentiation theory should be reoriented to study interpenetration. This means that, for a given domain of social deliberations (e.g., rendering political decisions, enforcing laws, educating citizens, or performing medical diagnoses), analysis stems from

Figure 5.1:
Implicit, Ideal Type Assumptions of a Segmentationist Theory of Social Differentiation (e.g., Parsons or Luhmann)

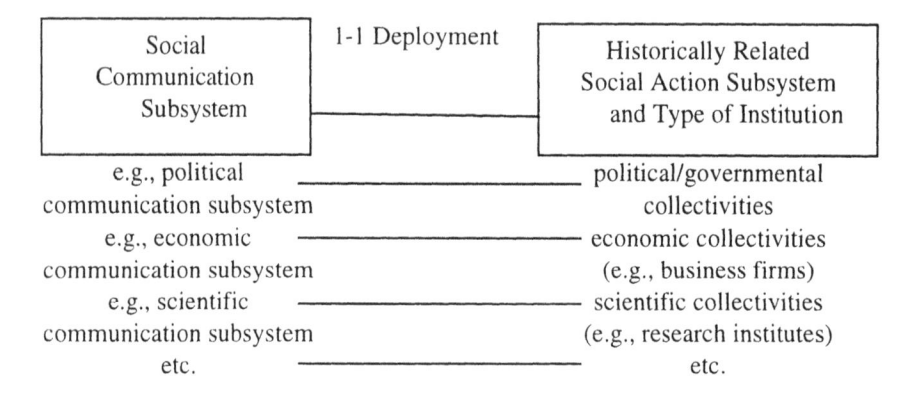

Social Communication Subsystem	1-1 Deployment	Historically Related Social Action Subsystem and Type of Institution
e.g., political communication subsystem	————————	political/governmental collectivities
e.g., economic communication subsystem	————————	economic collectivities (e.g., business firms)
e.g., scientific communication subsystem	————————	scientific collectivities (e.g., research institutes)
etc.	————————	etc.

Figure 5.2
Implicit, Ideal Type Assumptions of an Interpenetration Systems Theory

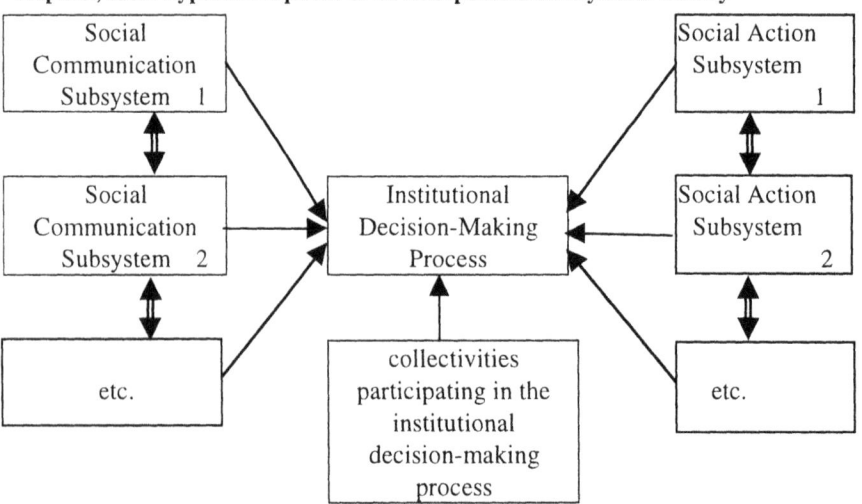

Social Communication Subsystem 1		Social Action Subsystem 1
Social Communication Subsystem 2	Institutional Decision-Making Process	Social Action Subsystem 2
etc.	collectivities participating in the institutional decision-making process	etc.

The uni-directional (single) arrows indicate processes of deployment.
The bi-directional (double) arrows indicate processes of interpenetration.

the initial assumption that empirical study will reveal interpenetrating influences of more than one action-based and more than one communication-based subsystem. Notice, however, that an effort to theorize what are the major subsystems in contemporary societies, and thus to offer a systems-theoretic framework, does not disappear with this reorientation of theory to the interpenetration phenomenon.

Interpenetration Systems Theory and Social Instability

Although the concept of interpenetration does not imply the obliteration of systems theory, the concept does lead systems theory closer to a "postmodernist" recognition of growing social fragmentation and instability. The notion that it makes sense to discuss total, unified "social systems" does not make sense if the distinct parts of such a system are interpreted to be highly mobile and thus not ordered in any stable interrelation. Systems theory therefore becomes subsystems theory. This move is, for one, starkly contrary to Parsons' long-standing insistence that it is possible to see societies as unified "systems." For Parsons, this higher level of unity appears in his alleged cultural system (e.g., Parsons & Shils, 1951). Also, Parsons perceives unity at a higher "system" level insofar as given subsystems allegedly emerge as efficient, specialist sectors designed to make a subsystem-specific contribution to the attainment of generalized, societal goals (e.g., Parsons, 1960b/1982). Luhmann already rejects this integrationist position of Parsons. Luhmann holds instead that communication subsystems establish radical closure from each other's influence and contents (e.g., Luhmann, 1982, 1989). Luhmann argues that by establishing closure from each other, subsystems can therefore focus attention and gain expertise in handling a narrow, subsystem-specific range of concerns. Yet, even as Luhmann rejects social system unity, he accepts social stability as the consequence of subsystem differentiation processes. Societies are supposedly stable and efficient overall, because self-enclosed, specialist subsystems emerge with improved expertise in key domains of social functioning (see especially Luhmann, 1982). By comparison, interpenetration systems theory implies less stability and more uncertainty in whether and how functioning really occurs in each social domain. Rather, under interpenetration systems theory, a host of problematic questions arise. Which action and communication subsystems actually interpenetrate in a given domain of operations? How stable is the current pattern of interpenetration? And are operations in fact conducted efficiently, or might interpenetrating subsystems precipitate inefficient conflicts over what perspective to apply to the issues at-hand, and what policies to implement? Such uncertainties extend beyond those anticipated in both Parsons' and Luhmann's accounts.

On Interpenetrating "Extrainstitutional" Communication Subsystems

Many communication subsystems possess initial, historical ties to one particular type of social institution. For example, the language of the legal communication subsystem ostensibly developed alongside formal legal institutions (e.g., courts, the legal profession, and those working within that profession). Or the language and logic of the medical communication subsystem ostensibly developed alongside formal medical institutions (e.g., the growth of hospitals, medical professionals, and various medical organizations). However, this chapter's approach assumes that although a given communication subsystem may have a formal and historical tie to a particular institution, and to a particular action subsystem, that communication subsystem may regularly penetrate social deliberations elsewhere. If communication subsystems are thus mobile, economic reasoning can influence political deliberations, therapeutic reasoning can influence medical deliberations, or political reasoning can influence legal deliberations. To review, the possession of a historical tie to a particular institution, or to a particular action subsystem, is therefore not a necessary condition for holding social influence. This, in turn, implies that some influential communication subsystems in contemporary societies may lack any such tie at all. Cornell (1992) articulates gender as just such an "extrainstitutional" communication subsystem. Cornell defines the gender subsystem as a set of meanings, respectively attached to men and women, that construct gender differences and privilege what is male. What is significant about Cornell's work is the relative ambiguity of the gender subsystem's precise historical origins in one particular social institution, coupled with the reality of its interpenetration in many institutions.

Other widely interpenetrating communication subsystems, besides gender, may lack a clear, integral tie to any one institution (or action subsystem). Think about the following added examples as representing highly influential types of mobile, extrainstitutional communication subsystems, each definable using the same concepts introduced in Table 5.1.

- a communication subsystem developed out of the logic of bureaucratic regularity, expediency, and efficiency (e.g., interpreted from drawing on Weber, 1947).
- a communication subsystem developed out of a logic of surveillance, regulation, and gaining maximal information about all individuals (e.g., interpreted from drawing on Foucault (1979) on "disciplinary practices").
- a communication subsystem developed out of a logic of calculating and allocating time to social activities, whereby given activities must occur in set, regular, and consciously calculated times (e.g., interpreted from drawing on Postone, 1993).

SUMMATION

This chapter endeavored to advance two aims. The first was to synthesize a few basic systems concepts from both Parsons' and Luhmann's theories, because a synthesis that productively builds on both of their approaches is not currently available. In particular, the concepts of action and communication subsystems have not before been integrated as two independently important dimensions of social differentiation. Rather, action-based approaches influenced by Parsons, or cognitivistic, communication-based approaches influenced by Luhmann, at present exist as largely nonsynthesized alternatives.

The second aim was to contribute beyond Parsons and Luhmann by placing a concept of interpenetration at the center of social systems theory. I argued that the need for the concept has intensified specifically in conjunction with several intensifying social trends of recent decades. Orienting differentiation theory to interpenetration implies that social boundaries and processes have become uniquely unstable and uncertain. Still, a focus on interpenetration need not obliterate the idea of social differentiation, nor should it argue for the abandonment of social systems theory. Rather, I argue that it can be analytically illuminating to model what are the most broadly influential subsystems in contemporary societies that may therefore become systematically involved in particular instances of interpenetration. In Tables 5.1 and 5.2, I in fact present a typology of eight subsystems that appear now to be especially important. Although such a typology is subject to continual, empirically based revision, it nonetheless seems preferable to rigid, theoretically generated typologies like Parsons' four-subsystem functional approach. In the contemporary world, social theory can provide frameworks for interpreting major social processes, but those frameworks must be flexible in the face of continuing, dynamic change.

REFERENCES

Buckley, W. (1967). *Sociology and Modern Systems Theory*. Englewood Cliffs, NJ: Prentice-Hall.
Castells, M. (1996). *The Rise of the Network Society*. Malden, MA: Blackwell.
Cornell, D. (1992). The Philosophy of the Limit: Systems Theory and Feminist Legal Reform. In D. Cornell, M. Rosenfeld & D. Gray Carlson (Eds.), *Deconstruction and the Possibility of Justice*. New York: Routledge.
Ferman, B. (1996). *Challenging the Growth Machine*. Lawrence: University Press of Kansas.
Foucault, M. (1979). *Discipline and Punish*. New York: Vintage Books.
Galtung, J. (1984). The Dialectic Between Crisis and Crisis Perception. *International Journal of Comparative Sociology 25*, 1-2.
Giddens, A. (1991). *Modernity and Self-Identity: Self and Society in the Late Modern Age*. Stanford, CA: Stanford University Press.
Gouldner, A. (1970). *The Coming Crisis of Western Sociology*. New York: Basic Books.
Jacobson, D. (1996). Structural Integration and Contemporary Organizational Movements. Draft M.S.
Kuhn, T. (1962). *The Structure of Scientific Revolutions*. Chicago: University of Chicago Press.
Lash, S., & Urry, J. (1994). *Economies of Signs and Space*. London: Sage.

Laumann, E.O., & Knoke, D (1987). *The Organizational State*. Madison: University of Wisconsin Press.
Luhmann, N. (1982). *The Differentiation of Society*. New York: Columbia University Press.
Luhmann, N. (1989). *Ecological Communication*. Chicago: University of Chicago Press.
Luhmann, N. (1990). *Political Theory in the Welfare State*. New York: Walter de Gruyter.
Luhmann, N. (1995). *Social Systems*, trans. John Bednarz, Jr., with Dirk Baecker. Stanford, CA: Stanford University Press.
Lyotard, J-F. (1984). *The Postmodern Condition: A Report on Knowledge*. Minneapolis: University of Minnesota Press.
Parsons, T. (1960a/1982). Durkheim on Organic Solidarity. In L.H. Mayhew (Ed.), *On Institutions and Social Evolution*. Chicago: University of Chicago Press.
Parsons, T. (1960b/1982). Some Considerations on the Theory of Social Change. In L.H. Mayhew (Ed.), *On Institutions and Social Evolution*. Chicago: University of Chicago Press.
Parsons, T. (1961). An Outline of the Social System. In T. Parsons, E. Shills, K.D. Naegele & J.R. Pitts (Eds.), *Theories of Society: Foundations of Modern Sociological Theory*. New York: Free Press.
Parsons, T. (1972). Response to Clark on "Structural-Functionalism, Exchange Theory, and the New Political Economy." *Sociological Inquiry, 42*, 275-298.
Parsons, T. & Shils, E.A. (Eds.) (1951). *Toward a General Theory of Action*. New York: Harper Torchbooks.
Parsons, T. & Smelser, N.J. (1956). *Economy and Society: A Study in the Integration of Economic and Social Theory*. Glencoe, IL: Free Press.
Postone, M. (1993). *Time, Labor, and Social Domination: A Reinterpretation of Marx's Critical Theory*. New York: Cambridge University Press.
Powell, W.W. (1990). Neither Market Nor Hierarchy: Network Forms of Organization. In B.M. Straw & L.L. Cummings (Eds.), *Research in Organizational Behavior*. Greenwich, CT: JAI Press.
Rempel, M. (1996). Systems Theory and Power/Knowledge: A Foucauldian Reconstruction of Niklas Luhmann's Systems Theory. *International Journal of Sociology and Social Policy, 16*, 58-90.
Rempel, M. (1998). *Interpenetration Systems Theory: A Systems Approach to Social Differentiation and Power in Contemporary Societies*. Ph.D. Dissertation. University of Chicago.
Wallerstein, I. (1997). *Differentiation and Reconstruction in the Social Sciences*. Paper presented at the ISA Research Council Meetings, Montreal, August 6.
Weber, M. (1947). *The Theory of Social and Economic Organization*, trans. A. M. Henderson & T. Parsons. New York: Oxford University Press.

PART II

AUTOPOIESIS

Chapter 6

INFORMATION, MEANING, AND COMMUNICATION: AN AUTOPOIETIC APPROACH

John Mingers

INTRODUCTION

In their early papers on autopoiesis, Maturana and Varela (Varela, Maturana & Uribe, 1974; Maturana, 1974, 1975, 1978; Varela, 1977) were very skeptical of concepts such as "information" and "communication." They argued that since organisms were structurally determined systems and since the nervous system was organizationally closed, it was not possible for there to be "instructive interactions"—that is, interactions (including linguistic ones) that themselves determine the effect they will have on the receiver. This means that traditional ideas such as objective information, and communication as the transmission of information from one person to another, are not tenable. More recently, Luhmann has developed an autopoietically based social theory in which society consists of a network of communications that trigger further communications. In this theory, information becomes relative to the observer, and is related to meaning.

This chapter aims to develop the connection between, on the one hand, a conceptualization of information and meaning at the level of interactions between individuals, and, on the other, communication at a societal level. This development is based on a range of earlier work by the author. First, a review of existing theories of information especially with regard to semantics and meaning (Mingers, 1996c). This led to a reconceptualization of the relation between information and meaning (Mingers, 1995a) that tried to synthesize concepts from autopoiesis, Habermas' (1984, 1987) theory of communicative action, Dretske's (1981) theory of information and knowledge, and semiotics (Morris, 1938). It argued for two separate domains, that of information— existing objectively, and carried and transmitted by events and signs, but not directly accessible to humans; and that of meaning as the interpretation and significance of information for individual subjects, generated through a process of embodied cognition (Mingers, 1996b).

Second is consideration of the possibility of autopoiesis at the social or organizational level. The first analysis mainly concerns the individual subject generating meaning from the information carried by a sign or utterance. If we move up to the social level then it is possible to relate this analysis to Luhmann's (1995) theory of an autopoietic society based on communication. The question of whether or not a society can be taken ontologically to be autopoietic is highly controversial (Mingers, 1992, 1995b; Bailey, 1997), but I have argued that the communicative theory can be utilized without committing oneself to social autopoiesis. Instead, we can use the less restrictive notion of organizational closure, of which autopoiesis is one particular type.

This leads to the third area of background—a typology of types of organizationally closed (or, as I argue, self-referring) systems (Mingers, 1997). The typology as so far conceived stops short of social systems, and that is the particular contribution of this chapter—an enhancement that links the individual, through social networks, to organizations and society. The resultant synthesis provides a framework at a variety of levels, from that of information as a conceptual category in its own right, through the processing of information into meaning and action at the level of the individual (a process of "embodied cognition" [Mingers, 1996b]), up to the communicative networks of societies and organizations.

LEVELS OF ORGANIZATIONAL CLOSURE

The idea that societies, institutions, or organizations[1] could be taken ontologically (rather than metaphorically) to be autopoietic systems is very difficult to sustain (Mingers, 1992). Two essential components of the definition of autopoietic, self-producing, systems are: that of a self-generated and self-maintained boundary thus forming a unity or whole; and that of a process of production of components which themselves participate in further production processes. In the case of social systems it is difficult to see how such notions could be instantiated. What are the self-producing products of a social system and what might its boundary components be? In Luhmann's formulation the answer is communications that trigger further communications, and distinguish themselves from other communications that belong to a different part of the social system. This approach, however, raises serious questions of its own: it excludes people from the social system per se, relegating them to being in the environment of society; and it appears to require that communications, in themselves, have the capacity for action or at least generating further communications (Mingers, 1995b).

There is, however, a more general notion propounded by Maturana and Varela, that of organizational closure, of which autopoiesis is a special case

Figure 6.1
Typology of Organizationally Closed (Self-Referential) Systems

Level in Boulding's Hierarchy	Type	Characteristic	Example
1	Self-referring systems	Structural reference to self by position or symbolism (pictorial or linguistic)	"This is a sentence," Escher's *Drawing Hands*, Magritte's *The Treason of Images*
2	Self-influencing systems	Dynamic systems that involve circular causality and causal loops	Size and birth rate of population, inflation, the nuclear arms race
3	Self-regulating systems	Maintenance of a particular variable at a particular level	Thermostat, body temperature
3	Self-sustaining systems	All parts of the system are necessary and sufficient for operation of the whole, but do not produce each other	Gas pilot light in heating boiler, autocatalysis
4	Self-producing systems (autopoietic)	Autonomy, the system both produces and is produced by itself	Cell, computer model of Autopoiesis
5	Self-recognizing systems	Systems that are able to recognize their own parts and reject others	Immune system within an organism
5	Self-replicating systems	Systems that can build replicas of themselves	Organisms that reproduce, computer viruses
6	Self-cognizing systems	Systems that generate cognitive identity through recursive neuronal activity	Animals with nervous systems interacting symbolically
7	Self-conscious systems	Able to interact with descriptions of them self. The observer observing the observer	A person saying "I acted selfishly today"

(Varela, 1977, 1979; Maturana & Varela, 1980). Mingers (1997) argued that organizational closure simply requires some form of self-reference, whether material, linguistic, logical, or social, rather than the more specific process of self-production. A typology of self-referential systems is reproduced in Figure 6.1.

In this typology, the numerical "level" refers to Boulding's (1956) Hierarchy of Systems as modified by Mingers (1997). The primary feature that distinguishes the different levels is the type of relation that emerges at each level. Systems at a particular level involve the relations of that level plus those from preceeding levels. Level 1 systems are characterized by static relations of topology, level 2 by dynamic relations of order, level 3 by feedback relations, level 4 by relations of self-production, level 5 by relations of structural coupling between components, level 6 by symbolic relations, and level 7 by relations of self-awareness (for more detail see Mingers, 1997).

The first type of organizationally closed system is thus characterized only in terms of spatial or topographic closure since it is not dynamic or processual. I have called these self-referring systems. They are usually symbolic or representational in a general sense, and refer to themselves either by some form of pointing (e.g., a signpost pointing to itself); by containing an image of themselves within themselves; or by referring to themselves linguistically. They include all of the many paradoxes and tautologies (Hughes & Brecht, 1978), for example, "This sentence is in French"; or "This assertion is not true." Pictorial examples are Escher's drawing (*Drawing Hands*) of two hands drawing each other, and Magritte's pictures, one (*The Treason of Images*) of a smoking pipe with the words (in French) "this is not a pipe," and another (*The Human Condition*) in which the picture contains a picture of part of the scene.

It might be objected that as many of these are symbolic and linguistic examples they should be at a much higher level in the typology. This however is to confuse the output from a system with the system itself. While they may be the results of complex linguistic processes, in themselves they only embody level 1 relations. By analogy, a table may be the result of a complex sociotechnical production process, but it, itself, is a simple level 1 system.

At level 2 are systems I identify as self-influencing systems. These are examples of what are often called causal loops or circular causality. That is, patterns of causation or influence which become circular: for instance, the larger a population, the greater the number of births, and thus the larger the population in the next time period. This is a positive loop leading to exponential increase or decrease and, more commonly, there are negative loops which lead to, at least temporary, stability—for example, the price/demand relations for a normal good. The economic and ecological domains are full of complex patterns of just such mutual causality.

At level 3, I distinguish two types of systems: self-regulating and self-sustaining. Self-regulating systems are organized so as to keep some essential variable(s) within particular limits. They rely on negative feedback and specified limits. Obvious examples are a thermostat and the blood temperature control system. They are distinct from the self-influencing systems in that they maintain a prespecified level determined by the wider system of which they are a part. Self-influencing systems may stabilize through negative feedback but do so at essentially arbitrary levels.

The next type I call self-sustaining systems. In Maturana and Varela's terms these systems are organizationally closed but not self-producing. Their components and processes close in upon themselves so that their own elements are both necessary and sufficient for their own continuance. Such systems do not however produce their own components. A good example is the gas heater pilot light found on many central heating systems. In such a system, the gas pilot light heats a thermocouple which controls the flow of gas to the pilot light which allows the pilot light to function in the first place. Once it is in operation, it sustains itself. However, once it stops it cannot restart itself—it needs some form of outside intervention to begin the cycle again. Other examples are systems of autocatalysis where a chemical reaction produces at least some of the chemicals that are necessary for the reaction to occur; and the nervous system where every state of nervous activity is triggered by a previous state and triggers, in turn, the next state.

At level 4 we have autopoietic systems which are self-producing in both their components and their own boundary. They are more than self-sustaining in that they actually produce the components necessary for their own continuation. Such systems have properties such as autonomy, since they depend mainly on their own self-production, and identity, since they maintain their own individual autopoietic organization despite changes in their structure. The main examples are living systems—molecular embodiments of autopoiesis—but it is also possible to conceive of abstract self-producing systems such as Nomic, a game that produces its own rules (Suber, 1990; Mingers, 1996a), and the computer model of autopoiesis produced by Varela (Varela et al., 1974; McMullin & Varela, 1997).

At level 5 in the hierarchy (multicellular systems), I again distinguish two types: self-recognizing systems and self-replicating systems. The prime example of a self-recognizing system is the body's immune system (Varela & Coutinho, 1991). This is a network of glands and chemicals throughout the body, one function of which is to fight off cells and organisms that do not belong to the body. In order to do this, it must be able to recognize its self—that is, its own cells as opposed to another organism's. Self-replicating systems are those that are capable of producing a copy or replica of themselves. This includes all living systems as well as, for example, a computer virus. Note that the ability to reproduce is not definitory of living systems: some individuals, or even species such as the mule, are sterile yet living, while most people would say a computer virus is not living.

At Level 6 are self-cognizing systems that are integrated by a brain and nervous system The nervous system is an organizationally closed network of interacting neurons in which all states of relative activity lead to, and are preceded by, other states of activity thus leading to recursive closure. Certain parts of the nervous system (the effector and sensory surfaces) do interface to the bodily or external environment, and can thus be triggered by outside events, but the vast majority of the nervous system is composed of interneurons that only interact with each other. The coupling of the circular processes of the nervous system and the linear interactions of the organism as a whole over time give rise to new domains of behavior based on abstract and symbolic representations of the organism's interactions. This allows for the development of increasingly varied and ontogenetic modes of behavior in the more developed species. It also necessitates, for the individual organism, the construction of their own cognitive self. The nervous system integrates the perceptions and actions of the organism as it operates as a whole within an environment. Through its circular, recursive operation it continually establishes and maintains the distinct, coherent self of the individual at the same time as projecting onto the environment a structure of signification that is relevant to its own self-continuance.

The symbolic interactions enabled by the nervous system lead to the emergence of many new domains of interactions—for instance, consensually coordinated behaviors, the distinctions of objects and the relations between them (observing), and finally self-consciousness. That is, systems that can, through language, create descriptions of themselves and then interact with these descriptions as if they were independent entities, thus recursively generating the conscious self. Human beings are the main example of such languaging systems at this point in time. Such interactions are mainly linguistic utterances, either latent or manifest, such as, "I am lying" or "I hereby promise to ...," but can also be embodied in gestures or facial expressions.

ORGANIZATIONAL CLOSURE IN THE SOCIAL DOMAIN

The typology in Figure 6.1 stops short of the higher levels of social organization, and it is these that the chapter will now explore. I shall consider the nature of organizational closure in the social domain at four levels: the embodied individual, the social individual, the social group, and the organisation or societal subsystem. In Figure 6.2 these are characterized in terms of their components, their structural[2] relations, their mode of organizational closure, and their emergent properties.

The Embodied Individual

At this level, which is level 7 in Figure 6.1, we are dealing with cognitive systems whose manner of being essentially involves languaging—for example, human beings. The components of such systems are the physical bodily structure, integrated by a complex nervous system, the processes that occur between components, and the actions performed by the system as a whole. The structural relations involved are those within the body and the nervous system, and importantly, those between the two as described in the previous section.

One of the important properties to emerge at this level is the ability to draw a distinction between information and meaning (Mingers, 1995a). Signs, and the information they carry, cannot be transferred wholesale into peoples' consciousness. Rather, the complex analog stimulus that is received by the nervous system is progressively transformed through a process of digitalization that results finally in the meaning of the sign for a particular person. This fits in well with Maturana's argument that information cannot determine its effects on a

Figure 6.2
Levels of Social Organizational Closure

Level	Type of components	Structural Relations	Mode of Organizational Closure	Emergent Property
The Embodied Individual	Body and nervous system; Action	Relative neuronal and bodily relations	Enactive/ Embodied cognition	Distinction between information and meaning
The Social Individual	Direct interaction between people	Expectations of other's behavior (structural coupling between individuals) in terms of meaning, emotion and behavior	Double contingency	Distinction between action and communication
Social Networks	Recurrent interaction within groups	Structural coupling to a behavioral domain in terms of meaning, legitimation, power	Conversations	Enduring social cultures / practices
Society/ Organization	Communications	Interaction generates society, society structures interaction	Establishment of closed communicational domains	Closed networks of communications

receiver, it can only ever trigger structure-dependent change. At every stage the receiver's knowledge, intentions, and context determine what counts as information, and which aspects of the analogue information available are actually digitalized into meaning. Information and meaning are clearly distinct and nonoverlapping domains; information is ever-present, yet human consciousness only ever exists within the domain of meaning.

Of great importance is the recognition that this process of digitalization is carried out largely subconsciously by the body and nervous system. Cognition is not a Cartesian or Husserlian processing of pure thoughts, but is essentially embodied and enactive (Mingers, 1996b), better exemplified by the phenomenology of Merleau-Ponty (1962, 1963, 1969). For Husserl cognition was essentially pure thought, freed from the daily world; in contrast, Heidegger made our everyday activities the starting-point, at least for his analysis of being. Merleau-Ponty (1962) takes a more radical step by revealing the extent to which human subjectivity is essentially an embodied phenomenon:

when I reflect on the essence of subjectivity, I find it bound up with that of the body and that of the world, this is because my existence as subjectivity is merely one with my existence as a body and with the existence of the world, and because the subject that I am, when taken concretely, is inseparable from this body and this world. (p. 408)

The basis of Merleau-Ponty's concerns was laid out in *The Structure of Behavior* (1963) where he argued that human behavior could neither be explained in a behaviorist way in terms of external causes, nor internally in terms of conscious intentionality. Rather, it had to be explained structurally in terms of the physical structures of the body and nervous system as they develop in a circular interplay within the world. The world does not determine our perception, nor does our perception constitute the world, rather both arise within structurally-coupled interactions.[3] One of the significant emergent properties of cognitive systems is the ability to draw a distinction between information and meaning.

Action and Communication

Having looked at the level of the individual we now move up to consider the emergence of communication—a reciprocal interaction between two individuals. Luhmann (1986, 1995), in fact, argues that communication (between at least two people[4]) is the most fundamental social category, more so than an individual action. This is because first, actions need not be inherently social whereas communications are, although this does verge on the tautological since for Luhmann the social is defined as a system of communications. Second, social actions already presuppose communications in the sense that they rely on or raise the expectation of recognition, understanding, and acceptance by others. In other words, a social action is inevitably already a communication. Yet, third, a communication is more than simply an action. It involves and therefore includes the understanding of another party and so goes beyond the individual action to form the link necessary for social operations. A communicative act in itself leads to nothing, it is only when it generates some understanding in another that it can trigger a further communication.

It is important to understand what Luhmann means by communication since he uses the term in a very specific sense. He stresses that it is not what we might normally mean by a communicative act, such as a statement or utterance by a particular person. Indeed, it is at a different level to people and their thoughts and actions. For Luhmann, these are not part of the social system at all, but are part of its environment. He characterizes a communication as an event consisting of three indissoluble elements—*information, utterance* (communication or action), and *understanding* (comprehension)[5]—which can enable further communications to occur. Each of these elements is said to be a selection. That is, one possibility chosen (but not necessarily by a person) from many.

Broadly speaking, information is what the message is about—its propositional content to use the terminology from Mingers (1995a); utterance is the form in which it is produced (its illocutionary content): how? by whom? when? And understanding is the sense or meaning that it generates (which can include misunderstanding) in the receiver. There must be at least two parties involved, the communicator and the communicatee (my terminology), but these may well not be individual people. All these elements are generated or coproduced together as a unity, and this event allows the possibility of further communications. It is important to stress that all three aspects are distinctions made by the system: the system determines what is information for it, how it may be embodied, and how it may be interpreted. This is the closure of social systems. Note that Luhmann is critical of the traditional transmission model of communications with self-conscious senders and receivers.

Of the three, understanding stands in a particular relation to the other two. Understanding draws the distinction between information and utterance (Luhmann, 1982, p. 183) and recognizes that they are selections in different dimensions. Even more important, it is the understanding of the receiver that ultimately determines the nature of the communication. Only when a further communication is generated (or perhaps not generated) "in reply" does the nature of the initial communication become established. The question may have been interpreted as a command; the joke as a rebuffal. Information is the "what" of the communication—it is produced by the system out of the perturbations the system undergoes, and the system determines whether it originates or refers outside the system to the environment. The utterance is the "why now," the "how," and the "who" of the communication and so is inevitably autoreferential. Again, these distinctions are made by the communication itself, which is attributed to an agent rather than being the conscious production of an agent. It is this distinction between information and utterance, which allows for an arbitrariness between the two, that provides the possibility of further autopoietic production for without it understanding would simply be perception rather than communication. This provides a model of the dynamism of communication both at the level of the individual interaction and moving up to the level of the social system.

The closure of this systemic interaction can be seen in terms of what Luhmann (1995, ch. 4) calls the problem of "double contingency." In initiating an interaction, A needs to consider what B's expectations are, but equally B needs to consider what A's expectations are. "I will do what (I think) you expect of me if you do what (you think) I expect of you." Given that each individual is opaque to the other, the interaction is underdetermined, how is it that communication occurs at all? For Luhmann, it is the resolution of this problem in practice that generates social structure itself. Presupposing at least a minimal interest in the relevance of the other's communication for the selves, the two self-referential systems will interact based only on what they can observe of the other, and the influence that their actions have. "In this way an emergent order can arise that is conditioned by the complexity of the systems that make it possible but that does not depend on this complexity's being calculated or controlled. We call this emergent order a social system" (Luhmann, 1995, p. 110). The inherent uncertainty (contingency) in this system becomes stabilized through the generation of shared expectations that in turn constrain or limit future interactions. For Luhmann, social structure is precisely the structure of expectations that develop in response to the double contingency of interaction.

Social Networks: The Emergence of Cultures and Practices

At the next level we can consider patterns of repeated social communication between groups or networks of individuals such that particular cultures or practices emerge that transcend the individuals. Particular members of such groups may join or leave but the social organization (Maturana, 1980) carries on. Examples are families, clubs, organisations (and subcultures within them) and (other) informal but enduring networks.

For Maturana, such systems are not themselves autopoietic, but constitute the medium in which other autopoietic systems exist and interact in such a way that the interactions become bound up with the continued autopoiesis of the components. In other words, a group of living systems (not necessarily human) takes part in an on-going series of interactions with each other. These coordinations of action will contribute to the continued survival of the individual autopoietic systems. This will generate networks of particular interactions and relations through the structural coupling of the organisms, and these networks will become involved in the continued autopoiesis of the organisms. The resulting system (or unity distinguished by an observer), consisting of the living components, their interactions, and the recurrent relations thus generated is characterized by a particular organization—the social organization.

The relationship between people and their social networks is a circular one. The participants, as structure-determined entities, will have properties and behavior determined by their structure. These properties and behaviors realize the particular social systems to which they belong. But this, in turn, selects particular structural states within the participants as in all structural coupling. In other words, a social system inevitably selects or reinforces behaviors which confirm it and deselects those which deny it. People are members of many different social networks. They may enact them successively, or at the same time. These domains all ultimately intersect in the body and nervous system of the individual and may well involve different and possibly contradictory modes of behavior. Membership is very important in human social systems. To become a member means taking on the behaviors appropriate to the domain (consensual coordinations of action), becoming structurally coupled, and then being accepted as such by other members. Decisions about acceptance and rejection are emotional rather than rational and form an implicit boundary for the system.

The mutually reinforcing nature of social networks means that they are inevitably conservative in the sense that they operate so as to maintain their present organizational relations. Change can only come about through a change in the behavior of the participants—it cannot be imposed in some sense by the system. Such change can happen, despite the homeostasis of the social system. An individual may enter a social network and not become structurally coupled to it initially, instead altering the behaviors of the other members by becoming structurally coupled to them later, in the course of coordinations of action that do not confirm the social system. Or, already existing members can reflect upon their experiences in other domains and choose to modify their own behaviors, thus realizing an altered social network.

For humans, interaction is essentially communicational and social systems can therefore be seen as networks of recurring conversations (series of interlocked communications). Conversations are a braiding of language, emotion, and bodyhood, and social interactions involve all three. This is in fact the mechanism whereby the structural coupling of the social system takes place since linguistic interactions are inevitably physical, involving the body and the nervous system.

Society and Organizations

At the final level we move from social interaction to social systems. From the Lebenswelt to the encompassing domain of society and its subsystems, or on a smaller scale, from particular subcultures to the organization within which they occur. Following (for the moment) Luhmann, we can visualize the whole system as an ongoing network of interacting and self-referring communications of different types, and see how they can be separated from the particular people involved. The people will come and go, and their individual subjective motivations will disappear, but the communicative dynamic will remain.

Luhmann conceptualizes society as consisting of a network of communications that continually regenerates itself. Communications trigger new communications in a continuous self-defining process. A communication is not a communicative act nor a particular message but the connection of an utterance conveying information with the understanding it generates. Society consists only of communications and of all communications. Communications are not entities but events produced at a point in time—they have a duration but only that of their actual occurrence. They do not exist after their occurrence. When completed their very absence calls for another event or else the system will no longer exist. Moreover, the next event cannot be a repetition of the first, but must be a different event occurring in time.

Modern societies are not homogeneous, but have become internally differentiated. Particular types of communications (e.g., legal and economic ones) have separated themselves out from the rest to form their own self-defined subsystems. These are not outside of or different to society, they are merely particular communicational domains which have achieved a certain autonomy from the others. Each subsystem becomes self-defined, operating around a particular distinction—in the case of the law, that of legal/illegal. They too form closed networks of communications—each one only being able to process or deal with communications of its own type.

For subsystems, the other functional subsystems exist as part of their environment and there are much greater interactions and dependencies between subsystems than between society and its environment. The subsystems have become autonomous and independent, but at the same time more interdependent since they rely on the existence of the other subsystems to carry out particular functions. Interactions between subsystems are reasonably well defined—legal communication can give rise to economic ones which in turn trigger political ones. When a subsystem is triggered by its environment and generates a communication about a particular matter, this is called resonance. Luhmann (1989) extends the metaphor to describe the resonance of society as a whole—that is, the subsystems with each other.

However, I would not wish to go along wholly with Luhmann's analysis. In particular, I would not accept that the network of communications produces an autopoietic system, rather just an organizationally closed one. This is for the reasons outlined at the beginning—that societal communication does not qualify as production, nor is it possible to specify bounded wholes in the way that autopoiesis requires. I also would not wish to make the strong distinction that Luhmann does between society and people—for Luhmann society consists only of communication and excludes people. Rather I would propose that the relation be viewed more in the light of structuration theory (Giddens, 1984; Mingers, 1996a).

Giddens distinguishes between social system (patterns of observable social activity) and social structure (virtual rules and resources that enable social systems) and argues for two different perspectives or forms of analysis. In analysing strategic conduct we focus our attention on the way actors draw on the social structure. In institutional analysis we look at the way structural rules are reproduced through social interaction. In an analogous manner, we can either consider the way social interaction gives rise to networks of communication that form patterns at the societal level, or we can focus on the way communications limit and constrain the forms of social interaction at the interpersonal level.

In fact, we need to consider the relationship between this duality of interaction and society, and the social structure that underpins it. I would argue that it is possible to synthesize Luhmann's view of structure as consisting of expectations, instantiated at both individual and societal levels, with Giddens' view of structure as virtual rules that both enable and constrain interaction. We would thus end up with a twofold relation: that between observable system and underlying structure on the one hand, and within the system, that between individual interaction and societal communication.

CONCLUSIONS

This chapter has aimed to make a connection between a range of levels of sociological analysis using concepts from the theory of autopoiesis. The four levels are: first, that of the individual subject, embodied and enactive within the world—here it is argued that embodied cognition is in part a process of generating subjective and intersubjective meaning from objective information; second, that of the social individual engaged in a communicative interchange with another—here, the distinction is drawn between individual action and social communication; third, that of the social network from which emerge enduring patterns of activity, or practices that transcend the individual members; finally, that of the society or organization wherein networks of communications emerge that form self-defining, closed subsystems or cultures.

The main characteristics that emerge from this analysis of social systems are:
- Interactions in society or organisations are based around the conversation: a braiding of language, body, and emotion. These need not be face-to-face but could be virtual.
- Emergent from these are many different domains of social practices and cultures.
- These can be analyzed from either the interaction or the communication perspective. The link between the two is social structure: a patterning of expectations in terms of signification, legitimation and domination.

Social systems differentiate themselves into closed communicational domains, although
- Individuals move between them
- Interactions between social systems is in terms of perturbation/compensation rather than cause and effect
- The effect of a communication on a system (if any) is determined by the structure of the system; the same communication may trigger different responses in different subsystems

Further research is needed into the complex relations between social interaction, societal communication, and the underlying social structure of meaning and rules that both enables and constrains communication and interaction.

ACKNOWLEDGMENT

This chapter is a slightly revised version of an article with the same title which originally appeared in *Cybernetics and Human Knowing* Vol. 6, issue 4 (1999), pp. 25-41. The editors wish to thank the copyrightholder for the permission to use the original text.

NOTES

1. From now on I shall use "organization" in the autopoietic sense, and "organisation" to refer to particular institutions such as universities.
2. "Structure" is used here in its autopoietic sense as a contrast to "organization."
3. For a discussion of the importance of embodied cognition for information systems, and a review of the increasing importance of the body within social theory, see Mingers (1996b, p. 238).
4. By "person" Luhmann intends something wider that an actual, individual, human being. The addressors and addressees of communication may themselves be social systems (see Luhmann, 1995, pp. 107-111).
5. The terms in parentheses have also been used by Luhmann.

REFERENCES

Bailey, K. (1997). The Autopoiesis of Social Systems: Assessing Luhmann's Theory of Self-reference. *Systems Research and Behavioral Science 14*, 83-100.

Boulding, K. (1956). General Systems Theory—The Skeleton of Science. *Management Science 2*, 197-208.

Dretske, F. (1981). *Knowledge and the Flow of Information.* Oxford: Blackwell.

Giddens, A. (1984). *The Constitution of Society.* Cambridge: Polity Press.

Habermas, J. (1984). *The Theory of Communicative Action, Vol. 1: Reason and the Rationalization of Society.* London: Heinemann.

Habermas, J. (1987). *The Theory of Communicative Action, Vol. 2: Lifeworld and System: A Critique of Functionalist Reason.* Oxford: Polity Press.

Hughes, P. & Brecht, G. (1978). *Vicious Circles and Infinity.* Harmondsworth: Penguin.

Luhmann, N. (1982). *The Differentiation of Society.* New York: Columbia University Press.

Luhmann, N. (1986). The Autopoiesis of Social Systems. In F. Geyer & J. van der Zouwen (Eds.), *Sociocybernetic Paradoxes* (pp. 172-192). London: Sage.

Luhmann, N. (1989). *Ecological Communication.* Cambridge: Polity Press.

Luhmann, N. (1995). *Social Systems.* Stanford, CA: Stanford University Press.

Maturana, H. (1974). Cognitive strategies. In H. von Foerster (Ed.), *Cybernetics of Cybernetics* (pp. 457-469). Biological Computer Laboratory, University of Illinois.

Maturana, H. (1975). Communication and Representation Functions. In J. Piaget (Ed.), *Encyclopédie de la Pleiade.* Paris: Gallimard

Maturana, H. (1978). Biology of Language: The Epistemology of Reality. In M.G. Lenneberg & E. Lenneberg (Eds.), *Psychology and Biology of Language and Thought: Essays in Honour of Eric Lenneberg* (pp. 27-63). New York: Academic Press.

Maturana, H. (1980). Man and Society. In F. Benseler, P. Hejl & W. Kock (Eds.), *Autopoietic Systems* (pp. 11-31). Frankfurt: Campus Verlag.

Maturana, H. & Varela, F. (1980). *Autopoiesis and Cognition: The Realization of the Living.* Dordrecht: Reidel.

McMullin, B. & Varela, F. (1997). *Rediscovering Computational Autopoiesis*. Sante Fe: Santa Fe Institute.
Merleau-Ponty, M. (1962). *Phenomenology of Perception*. London: Routledge.
Merleau-Ponty, M. (1963). *The Structure of Behavior*. Boston: Beacon Press.
Merleau-Ponty, M. (1969). *The Visible and the Invisible*. Evanston, IL: Northwestern University Press.
Mingers, J. (1992). The Problems of Social Autopoiesis. *International Journal of General Systems, 21*, 229-236.
Mingers, J. (1995a). Information and Meaning: Foundations for an Intersubjective Account. *Information Systems Journal, 5*, 285-306.
Mingers, J. (1995b). *Self-Producing Systems: Implications and Applications of Autopoiesis*. New York: Plenum Press.
Mingers, J. (1996a). A Comparison of Maturana's Autopoietic Social Theory and Giddens' Theory of Structuration. *Systems Research 13*, 469-482.
Mingers, J. (1996b). Embodying Information Systems. In M. Jones, W. Orlikowski, G. Walsham & J. DeGross (Eds.), *Information Technology and Changes in Organizational Work* (pp. 272-292). London: Chapman & Hall.
Mingers, J. (1996c). An Evaluation of Theories of Information with Regard to the Semantic and Pragmatic Aspects of Information Systems. *Systems Practice 9*, 187-209.
Mingers, J. (1997). Systems Typologies in the Light of Autopoiesis: A Reconceptualization of Boulding's Hierarchy, and a Typology of Self-referential Systems. *Systems Research and Behavioral Science 14*, 303-313.
Morris, C. (1938). Foundations of the Theory of Signs. In O. Neurath (Ed.), *International Encyclopedia of Unified Science*. Chicago: University of Chicago Press.
Suber, P. (1990). *Paradox of Self-Amendment*. New York: P. Lang Publishers.
Varela, F., Maturana, H. & Uribe, R. (1974). Autopoiesis: the Organization of Living Systems, Its Characterization and a Model. *Biosystems 5*, 187-196.
Varela, F. (1977). The Nervous System as a Closed Network. *Brain Theory Newsletter 2*, 66-68.
Varela, F. (1979). *Principles of Biological Autonomy*. New York: Elsevier-North Holland.
Varela, F. & Coutinho, A. (1991). Second Generation Immune Networks. *Immunology Today 12*, 159-167.

Chapter 7

ARE FIRMS AUTOPOIETIC SYSTEMS?

Lucio Biggiero

INTRODUCTION

More than 25 years since its introduction (Stengers, 1985; Varela, 1996), the paradigm of autopoiesis has been extensively disseminated in various scientific communities, with alternate fortunes and enthusiasm. Although many theorists treat it as a new paradigm shift in science, owing to its philosophical novelty, it is curious that the disciplines that were most reluctant to embrace such a new "Kuhnean revolution" were indeed biology, on which autopoiesis is founded, and philosophy, about which autopoiesis is supposed to have something radically new to say. The most promising developments in fact were attained in sociology (Luhmann, 1990; Ulrich & Probst, 1984), political science (Jessop, 1990, 1992), law (Teubner, 1988, 1993; Teubner & Febbrajo, 1992), ecology (Zeleny, 1995, 1996), and management (Kickert, 1993; von Krogh & Roos, 1996; von Krogh & Vicari, 1993; Morgan, 1986; Zeleny & Hufford, 1992; Vicari, 1991). This chapter focuses on the latter field. It is wondered whether firms are autopoietic systems—that is, whether the paradigm of autopoiesis is applicable to for-profit organizations. Although only applications to other sciences will be touched upon, it will be clear that results can be extended to all kinds of social systems. This argument can be summarized as follows:

> **Thesis I**: Autopoiesis is not applicable to profit organizations or, in other words, firms are not autopoietic systems.

However, many of the constitutive concepts of the autopoiesis paradigm, taken in a weak sense, may be useful to explain firms and social systems. These concepts are self-organization, self-reference, self-maintenance, autonomy, identity, and recursive communication networks, for these are cybernetic concepts, which lie at the core of the autopoiesis paradigm. If appropriately reformulated they can be saved. Therefore, second-order cybernetics, by clarifying its basic concepts and epistemology, has much to gain from abandoning rather than espousing autopoiesis. This argument leads to the following:

> **Thesis II**: Autopoiesis does not coincide with second-order cybernetics, whose basic concepts, if not taken as on/off conditions, can be applied to social systems.

Rescuing cybernetics from autopoiesis makes it possible to renew the application of second-order cybernetics to the social sciences. Through this "surgery" many philosophically naive concepts and some unacceptable managerial implications deriving from the autopoiesis paradigm can be avoided, thus overcoming resistances of philosophers and management scholars.

The next section will outline the basic concepts and main developments of autopoiesis, while the third section applies them to firms, developing fundamental aspects: invariance and change; closure and boundaries; system and environment; identity and membership; communication networks. Differences between autopoiesis and second-order cybernetics are highlighted, and a "degree approach" is developed as an alternative to the on/off approach. The fourth section outlines the demarcations between autopoiesis and second-order cybernetics, and calculates the gains of their separation. As the scope of the discussion is limited to operational concepts, methodological and epistemological questions are not dealt with.

BASIC CONCEPTS AND DEVELOPMENTS

Definitions

The concept of autopoiesis reached the international scientific community through an article published by Varela, Maturana, and Uribe in 1974 (Varela et al., 1974), sponsored by von Foerster (Varela, 1996). Its roots lie in cybernetics and in the neurophysiology of cognition, as developed at MIT by McCulloch and at the Biological Computer Laboratory (BCL) by von Foerster (Stengers, 1985). The autopoietic approach was subsequently refined and developed over a period of five years (Maturana, 1975, 1978; Maturana & Varela, 1980; Varela, 1979). Two readings edited by Zeleny (1980, 1981) established in quite a definite manner the essence of the autopoiesis paradigm, as well as differences between Maturana and Varela as to the possibility of its applications to the social sciences. Their last book (1987) marks the end of their collaboration and agreement.

The main purpose of developing autopoiesis was to answer a classical question: what is life? In characterizing a living system, Maturana and Varela moved away from what was the emerging trend in molecular biology, which sought a solution in DNA and its programming code, as well as from population geneticists, who looked at evolution, with its properties of reproduction, adaptation, and selection. Yet, the stand taken by Maturana and Varela was far removed from the weak answers which were suggested by many biologists, in terms of a list of many features possessed to a varying extent by a system. Maturana and Varela were looking for a precise and definite answer, a property or a set of properties—all necessary and sufficient—which the system was supposed to have, and which were to define an on-off condition: living or nonliving system. On the first page of their seminal article (Varela et al., 1974) we find at once the global outline:

We assert that reproduction and evolution are not constitutive features of the living organization and that the properties of a unity cannot be accounted for only through accounting for the properties of its components. In contrast, we claim that the living organization can only be characterized unambiguously by specifying the network of interaction of components which constitute a living system as a whole, that is, as a "unity." We also claim that all biological phenomenology, including reproduction and evolution, is secondary to the establishment of this unitary organization. (p. 187)

Hence *the essence of autopoiesis is neither reproduction nor evolution nor adaptation, but rather self-production of the invariant organization of a closed network.* That invariant organization represents and guarantees the identity of the system as a whole, as a unity.

The autopoietic organization is defined as a unity by a network of productions of components which (i) participate recursively in the same network of productions of components which produced these components, and (ii) realize the network of productions as a unity in the space in which the components exist. (Varela et al., 1974, p. 188)

Invariance and Perturbations

The property of organizational invariance is essential as it addresses that of autonomy: being invariant, an autopoietic system does not adapt to the environment, at least unless nonadaptation to environmental features or changes menace its organizational invariance. Indeed, an autopoietic system filters, enacts, and reacts to the environment in order to maintain its autopoiesis (i.e., its self-production). That property is what was initially called organizational closure and subsequently operational closure (Varela, 1979). A system exchanges—is open to exchange—matter, energy, and information with the environment, but it neither receives inputs nor gives outputs. It only receives and gives perturbations, (i.e., a sort of "neutral inputs and outputs") which do not affect system unity and organization. While traditional cybernetic meanings of inputs and outputs refer to some sort of possible orientation or control or governance of the system, an autopoietic system is autonomous and maintains its own identity. Autopoietic systems do suffer only from environmental perturbations, which are defined as incapable of modifying the system's organization. They are supposed to leave unchanged the relational network between system elements. It is implicitly assumed that perturbations can affect the system's organization only if the system is not autopoietic, or in case it dies and transforms into another auto- or allopoietic system.

Operational closure

Operational closure is a fundamental concept, which should be analyzed using the notions of operations and closure. The former refers to component actions, which are determined by component role and nature, and by their reciprocal interconnections. Operations are all self-contained, which explains autonomy and self-reference. What can be exchanged with the environment is only energy, matter, and information, provided that the latter is not in the form of components. Closure refers to the relationship between system and environment. Any environmental change is selected (perceived, enacted) by the system, in order to maintain its organization (i.e., its autonomy [identity]). A system can give rise to structural changes as needed to adapt to environmental changes, always maintaining (preserving) the existing organization (identity). If it fails to do so, then that systemic identity perishes and the autopoietic system may transform itself (1) into another autopoietic system, with a new organization; (2) into an allopoietic system, owing to the loss of its autonomy; or else (3) it can disintegrate and disappear. Of course, if systems are closed and autonomous, they cannot be controlled or managed from outside. Among supporters of autopoiesis it is debated whether autopoietic systems could be, at least partially, steered or "governed." Radical constructivists reject such a possibility. On the contrary, Varela (1979) does not deny the existence of a control dimension of autopoietic systems, usually carried out by engineers. He reconciles autonomy (deriving from organizational closure) and control, arguing that they are complementary. However, this is not true because autonomy and control are not two different dimensions, but rather the same dimension in different degrees: maximum autonomy = minimum control.

Types of Autopoietic Systems

Autopoietic systems are a large set, comprising the subset of living systems. First-order autopoiesis is at cell level, the second-order is at a multicellular (organism) level, and third-order autopoiesis is at a multicellular set level, as social systems are. First- and second-order autopoiesis occur in the same kind of organizational space, that of the physical space of biology, while third-order autopoiesis occurs in the social space, which is usually defined as a communication, or linguistic, or cognitive space, even if these three labels do not indicate exactly the same things. However, what is most interesting for our purpose now is that if autopoiesis can occur in different organizational spaces, then we can also find autopoietic systems in nonphysical and nonbiological space. This would confirm that the class of living systems belongs to, but does not identify with, the class of autopoietic systems. This is the path followed by Maturana (1978, 1980, 1981) and, with significant differences, by Luhmann (1990), who distinguishes psychic, biological, and autopoietic systems. On the opposite Zeleny (1996) equates social and biological systems under their autopoietic character, and, reversing the causal relation, argues that, because of its autopoietic nature, also biological systems are social systems. On the other hand, Fleischaker (1988) and Varela (1979, 1981) argue that autopoiesis should be limited to biological space, beyond which only a metaphorical usage is acceptable.

Boundaries

Autopoietic systems must have a clearly identifiable boundary, like a cell membrane, independent of both the internal production network and the environment. This property, like some others, has been neglected or weakened in subsequent developments of the autopoiesis paradigm. However it maintains a relevant role, because without precise boundaries, system identity, invariance, and closure become vague and uncertain, and the threshold between living and nonliving systems is no more an on/off state. By the theory of nearly decomposable systems (Simon, 1962), it may be said that under some sort of sensitivity, threshold linkages between the system and its environment are not significant and do not influence system operations and identity. The system simply remains invariant. Therefore, boundaries are identifiable and precise only over certain sensitivity thresholds. Beyond the difficulty of establishing the threshold values, autopoiesis literature lacks any proposal in this direction.

System, Organization, and Structure

During the 1980s, Maturana and Varela (1980) and Varela (1979) delved into the question of the difference between system, organization, and structure. In short, the organization is a network of relations between system components, and its invariance gives an identity to the system—that is, the class it belongs to. The structure is the concrete and observable manifestation of the organization: it is the system's existence in a given space. Lastly, the system is the concrete existence of an organization through a specified structure. Moreover, Maturana and Varela suggested this kind of conceptual differentiation for all systems theory and all types of system. Here is an example: suppose we can define a chair as a network of relations between components (i.e., a horizontal plane supported by at least one strut). That is the organization of the seat class. Since both plane and strut can be made of various materials (i.e., wood, iron, plastic, etc.), each member of the seat class may have a different structure. A specific member of the seat class, together with its defined structure, is a system.

APPLICATIONS TO FIRMS

Invariance and Change

Of course invariance cannot pertain to employees, because they change very often, because they are not operations and because they are not produced by the system itself. An organizational network could be invariant with respect to roles, rather than to people. If people change but roles remain, then we can speak of an autopoietic system. There are, however, quite a few problems in that approach. First, within the context of an organization, roles are very ambiguous, equivocal, and ill-structured, and therefore defy any attempt at identifying a network of roles. It would be like speaking about a network of vagueness, because since Simon's early works (March & Simon, 1958) it has been clear that the definition and design of even very simple tasks constitute a difficult challenge to human rationality. Any version of the "Tayloristic dream" encounters the problem of bounded rationality (Simon, 1978). Second, recent organization theories no longer speak of roles, but rather of competencies: what is organized are competencies and not roles. And competencies are even more difficult to define than roles. At least they are much more generic and vague. That is all the more true for knowledge-based organizations, which are the trend in the industrial world. Moreover, neither routines (Nelson & Winter, 1982) nor decision-making (Janis & Mann, 1977) could be taken as invariant operations, because recent studies on cognitive maps (Weick, 1979; Weick & Bougon, 1986), ambiguity (March & Olsen, 1976), and equivocality (Sims & Gioia, 1986) argue that the heaviest and most dominant work in organizations is sense-making (Weick, 1995) rather than decision-making. Whenever possible, before taking a decision one needs to give sense to and make sense of the world. As a matter of fact, the situations where problems and actions are well structured and defined, regardless of their solvability, are the exception and not the rule. Rather paradoxically, emphasis on sense-making is sustained even by supporters of autopoiesis (von Krogh & Roos, 1996; Luhmann, 1990; Maturana, 1978; Winograd & Flores, 1986), but it is inexplicable how it corresponds with invariance.

Roles and competencies are all but invariant: they are continuously changing and hence no invariance is recognizable. In fact organizations are always in motion through departments, divisions, strategic business units, and the like, and they keep on redefining individual roles and competencies. Even if we were to accept searching for roles or competencies rather than for people, it would be impossible to recognize any invariance, except in very generic and meaningless terms. On the contrary, a large and growing part of organization and management science is stressing the relevance of change and development, and many scholars point out that all organizations are always changing, more or less broadly. The scientific problem is to succeed in classifying and studying how incremental rather than radical changes, which often alternate with one other, do emerge and develop. There is only one answer to such criticism: if organizations maintain their unity and identity, then their change is only apparent, because they do so only to the extent that it does not entail a modification of their identity—that is, maintaining their invariance. However, we believe that the first part of that answer fails to deal with and conceals the crucial point: a prior definition and identification of invariance, or invariant relations. The second part instead is pure tautology: *organizations do only what they can do*.

Closure

Even if roles and behaviors were organized, it would be impossible to make a clear-cut division, separating people from roles and behaviors. It appears to be a rehashing of the old classical approach, which also separated people from formal roles. All nonengineering approaches to organizations, since that of human relations, emphasize that people enter organizations in their entirety and not only in a manner limited to the formal or predefined part of their being. Studies conducted in the 1960s and 1970s pointed to the role played by personality as a whole in organizational behavior and, consequently, in human resource management. Recent studies (Kets de Vries & Miller, 1984; Park, Sims & Motowildo, 1986; Weick, 1979, 1995) further underlined the impact of emotions and nonintentional cognitive processes. One could argue that all these factors are involved in internal recursive cognitive processes, and therefore the pure self-referential approach is not disturbed. This is not the case, because multiple membership is a characteristic of social systems: people belong to many different organizations at the same time, carrying their personality, emotions, and cognition everywhere. They are vectors in polluting self-organization and self-reference, which would leave each organization with a closed "self." *Simultaneous memberships break closures and pollute self-organization and self-reference.*

Boundaries

Identifying organizational boundaries is an old and recurring theme in organization theory, to which the dominant answer of late is that they are very unstable, vague, and arbitrary. Physical boundaries, the external walls of organizations, clearly do not matter. Juridical definitions leave the solutions fully open and vague. Accounting approaches are very partial ones, because they would include only people paid by the organization, but many people can extend the influence of an organization without receiving any payment. Yet from both a juridical and an accounting point of view, it is not clear what can be considered internal or external. Transaction cost economics (Williamson, 1975, 1985) shows that boundaries change frequently, depending on production and transaction costs. Resource dependence theory (Pfeffer & Salancik, 1978), highlighting the role of both the power and requirements of effectiveness, argues that boundaries are highly disputable and changing. Recently, pointing to the growing trend of firms to construct interorganizational networks, scholars spoke of "boundaryless" (Ashkenas et al., 1995) or "borderless" (Jarrillo, 1993) organizations. Organizations have all but stable, precise, or objective boundaries. Last, it appears quite strange to view firms as operationally closed systems when all organizational science surmises, and is also suggesting, the opposite, as the only way to face and cope with the growing environmental uncertainty of our times. Authoritative reviews, journals, and magazines keep recommending that firms be opened up, as the sole way to survive in complex environments. Firms are all but closed systems, at least because they must search for effective and efficient resources and clients, as well as for technologies and current and potential competitors. Inputs and outputs still remain very important concepts for firms, because an error in their identification could cause their death. One might answer either that any change in inputs and outputs is to leave the system invariant, or that inputs and outputs change to the extent that they maintain the same autopoiesis. The first answer is erroneous, because nearly any change in strategy and in type of inputs and outputs almost invariably affects the organizational structure and design as well. The second one leads back to the same tautology: organizations do only what they can do.

Perturbations

The distinction between inputs-outputs and perturbations is one of the most problematic questions. First, some supporters of autopoiesis refer to the concepts of structural coupling between system and environment, which happens through perturbations. However, structural coupling is still a basic concept of first-order cybernetics (Ashby, 1956), and expresses the same meanings using inputs and not perturbations. What does it change, then? If it is not just a linguistic preference, then what difference is there between the structural coupling of first-order cybernetics and the structural coupling of autopoiesis? The second problem is that there is no ex-ante criterion of distinction between perturbations and input. In other words, a way to distinguish perturbations from inputs must be found independently and before the system's reactions, which could leave the system's organization untouched. It is necessary to be able to escape from such tautological definitions as "the system is autopoietic because it interacts with environments only through perturbations and not inputs."

In fact, since one may say also that "interactions are perturbations and not inputs because the system is autopoietic," given our lack of a way to distinguish perturbations from inputs or, independently, to distinguish auto- and allopoietic systems, we would fall into a tautology. The latter involves perfectly identifying the system's organization and then checking that it does not change after interactions with environments. Then we have to test all the other criteria that define a system as autopoietic. If the result is positive, we may say that the interactions occurring between system and environment are perturbations and not inputs. Adopting this method, the criterion of distinction between perturbations and inputs is in terms of residual. In the alternative case, an independent criterion of distinction between perturbations and inputs would be simpler and would involve distinguishing auto- and allopoietic systems as well. However, the literature on autopoiesis does not offer any test or operationalization of either of the two alternatives, remaining encapsulated in tautology. Although recent literature on enactment, interactionism, and population ecology of organizations points to limits of adaptation feasibility, due to organizational inertia (Hannan & Freeman, 1989), recognition and activation selections (Weick, 1979), and problems of observation (Biggiero, 2001) and interaction (Zan, 1995), no one really rules out an environmental influence on a system, nor its partial ability to adapt.

Identity and Belonging

In Maturana's (1978) and Luhmann's (1990) perspective of autopoietic social systems, the question of identity is central, because it coincides with a system identification. The means to achieve such an identity is recurring self-reference: identity is the "fixed point," the "attractor" of its self-referring process. The problem, however, is that in order to converge to a fixed point the self-referring system must always contain the same elements. Now, if those elements are people, there is a multiple membership problem because each of us belongs to many different systems at the same time: families, lobbies, parties, and so on. All the organization sciences have traditionally argued that people enter organizations with their own unity, with their whole personality, and that they do not do so only to the extent required by their own role or competence. In any event, since both competence and personality are strictly related to what occurs in all the other systems to which anyone belongs, then the self-referential process can be only partial, and nobody knows whether it converges.

Membership is the most important property of social systems: people belong to many different systems. As a consequence, every time one identifies a social system, this is connected to someone else through "communication embodiments" (people). Therefore, however good one's capacities to make subtle and precise distinctions, these would "break" people. In mathematical terms, this means that all society is an enormous, single network, and that all systems we could define are subnetworks (subsystems). Multiple membership is just a cross-boundary property, because people are at the same time elements of different communication networks. Where is closure? In our minds? Are we schizophrenic and partitioned beings, so that we activate separate parts of our neuronal networks depending on the system we are immanently faced with? And are these parts speaking different languages and creating different meanings reacting to the same things? This is not my opinion, and I point to two issues. First, Wittgenstein considers language a public affair, and hence emerging from interactions, which reciprocally influence nonclosed systems. Second, translation is a sign of openness.

Two More Questions

The theoretical perspectives of management sciences differ from the autopoiesis paradigm under two subtle but relevant aspects. The first refers to the difference between formal and empirical sciences. When we say that we define a system by applying a certain criterion, the system of course gains an identity and becomes "closed" to that criterion, because a criterion of distinction is per se an inclusion-exclusion criterion as well. It is merely saying that A=A. However, such a staticity, precision, and clarity concerns formal sciences but not empirical sciences, where identity and closure cannot be presupposed. They are just the object of inquiry; and a special object: an evolutionary one, whose future behaviors are quite complex (unpredictable). Hence, in empirical sciences, as management sciences are, no one knows ex-ante what the multidimensional definition (criteria of distinction) is that makes it possible to precisely identify (the borders of) social systems. It is merely conjectural knowledge, concerning how complex systems evolve and what their temporary identities and operations may be. As such, operational closure cannot be presupposed, but rather it is a hypothesis to be empirically tested. "Communication network" is definitely generic and does not permit any meaningful distinction. Whenever we attempt to operationalize definitions, we find that people belonging to the identified system communicate with people outside the system. Hence, no closure. The only solution is to refer to isolated communities somewhere in the world, which are actually like individual examples of mankind.

The second subtle difference between management sciences and the autopoiesis paradigm concerns the radicalism of the latter, which claims precise distinctions and on/off conditions. Living systems are supposed to be precisely distinguishable from nonliving systems, system identities are supposed to be precisely distinguishable from one another, boundaries are supposed to be clearly defined, and so on. Moreover, organizational closure is supposed to be as such 100%, as well as self-organization. After many decades of debate on organizational boundaries and a few years on organizational identity (Biggiero, 1998b), management sciences are assuming nonradical orientations. In other words, closure-openness, identity, self-organization, and boundaries are matters of degree and not of on/off states. Up to now we conclude that, under the characteristics we discussed, firms are not autopoietic systems, which was our first thesis.

SECOND-ORDER CYBERNETICS AND AUTOPOIESIS

Now we may ask ourselves whether second-order cybernetics needs autopoiesis, as this would seem to be the case considering the growing use of this term among systems theorists. I believe that there is no need for it, because the characteristics that define autopoiesis are much more restrictive than those of second-order cybernetics. While autopoiesis is not applicable to firms and to social systems at all, second-order cybernetics can help towards understanding social systems, if concepts like self-organization, self-reference, and autonomy are interpreted as a question of degree and not as on/off conditions. Second-order cybernetics stressed some concepts already introduced by first-order cybernetics, like feedback functions and recursivity (Ashby, 1956), self-organization (Ashby, 1962), subjectivity of observations (Ashby, 1956), and such. Engineering culture and applications highlighted openness and control, underestimating sources of complexity (Biggiero, 2000). Second-order cybernetics has the benefit of reducing illusions of controlling living and social systems and of stressing self-organizing processes.

As frequently occurs in the history of ideas, a school of thought emphasizes and radicalizes what its predecessors ignored or denied. At the very core of second-order cybernetics there are: (1) self-organization, based on feedback properties; (2) system identity, based on a certain degree of organizational closure; (3) organizational closure, based on a certain degree of organizational boundaries; (4) nonrealistic or antirepresentationalist epistemology, based on the perspective of observer subjectivity; (5) and a new theory of knowledge, based on self-reference and relational complexity (Biggiero, 2001). Often these issues are collected and addressed as a new perspective in epistemology, called constructivism. Now, the point is that all these issues can hold true without claiming an extreme position. In no way does second-order cybernetics imply joining radical constructivism (or autopoiesis). A moderate constructivism is compatible with second-order cybernetics and with a "degree approach." Even postpositivist and antirealist epistemology are compatible with second-order cybernetics and moderate constructivism, while they are not compatible with relativism, idealism, skepticism, and radical constructivism (or autopoiesis) (Biggiero, 1998a). Ashby, Bateson, Klir, Wiener, and even Von Foerster can be usefully distinguished from Von Glasersfeld, Luhmann, Maturana, and Varela.

In management literature, explicit treatments of the applicability of the autopoiesis paradigm to organizations can be divided into groups. Kickert (1993) and Morgan (1986) argue for a limited metaphorical use, helpful mainly in highlighting the relevance of self-organizing processes and in explaining the formation of organizational identity and inertia. These are merely concepts that autopoiesis borrowed from second-order cybernetics. On the contrary, Kickert (1993) points out that "a serious limitation of the original formal model of autopoiesis is its notion of closedness, albeit closure on a higher meta-level of organization.... Yet the model of autopoiesis unfortunately suggested that organizational stability had something to do with closure" (p. 271). He concludes that "the possibilities of a strict conversion of the autopoiesis model into a valid model that can be used in the administrative sciences are limited. The usefulness of the model does not seem to lie in strict adherence to the original and literal translation, but rather in its power as a source of a creative lateral thinking. It can inspire highly interesting and relevant ideas" (p. 276).

However, we know that once amended from operational closure, invariance and self-production, autopoiesis "retrenches" to second-order cybernetics. On the contrary, Zeleny (1996), von Krogh (von Krogh & Roos, 1996; von Krogh & Vicari, 1993), and Vicari (1991) explicitly do take sides on the autopoiesis paradigm. While Zeleny and Vicari point out operational closure and its consequences for management and organizations, von Krogh focuses mainly on corporate epistemology—that is, on consequences for strategy and decision making deriving from a paradigm change in the theory of knowledge and of information. The traditional perspective encounters a new one, which is characterized by three basic aspects: (1) the world is not pre-given; (2) knowledge is connected to observation; and (3) information is not an object but an observer's state. Many interesting findings are discussed by von Krogh in the field of strategic management and corporate epistemology. Although this chapter is not intended to investigate epistemological aspects, we wish to stress that we agree with nearly all the ideas argued by von Krogh & Roos (1996), but they imply neither an antirepresentationalist epistemology, nor the autopoiesis paradigm. They are compatible with postpositivist orientations, and particularly with moderate constructivism and second-order cybernetics. Moderate constructivism has been applied to organizations, strategic alliances, and industrial districts (Biggiero, 1998b, 1999). Relative closure, multiple fuzzy boundaries, identity, and recursivity assume a sound meaning and match the literature in management and social psychology with no reference to autopoiesis.

CONCLUSIONS

Management literature regards organizations as systems which, through inputs and outputs, are open to changing environmental conditions. To ensure system survival, a fit must be found between system structure and environmental conditions. The autopoiesis paradigm, developing second-order cybernetics, goes to the opposite extreme: cognitive, living, and social systems are totally autonomous and operationally invariant. They "select" the environment, and not vice versa. Environmental perturbations allow for changes of system structure as long as these do not affect its operations, which guarantee system identity and closure. Such a perspective is not applicable to firms, nor to social systems. Although they have a significant and variable degree of autonomy, closure, and identity, in no way is it possible to radicalize these aspects as on/off and ex-ante conditions. Inputs cannot be distinguished from perturbations, and organizational boundaries are all but stable, precise, and independent. However, the recognition and study of those aspects of firms and social systems, if considered as matters of degree, can open up interesting research programs and easily join and integrate second-order cybernetics in the field of management. The former does not imply the autopoiesis paradigm or radical constructivism, and has everything to gain from separating their destiny, which would prevent a further move of management sciences away from cybernetics, as we already have witnessed over the past three decades.

ACKNOWLEDGMENT

I wish to thank my colleagues on the Sociocybernetic Research Committee and in the SOEIS Project for the exciting and challenging discussions we had on this topic over two years.

REFERENCES

Ashby, R.W. (1956). *An Introduction to Cybernetics*, London: Chapman & Hall.
Ashby, R.W. (1962). Principles of the Self-Organizing System. In F. von Heinz & G.W. Zopf (Eds.), *Principles of Self-Organization: The Illinois Symposium on Theory and Technology of Self-Organizing Systems,* London: Pergamon; reprinted in Walter Buckley (Ed.) (1968) *Modern Systems Research for the Behavioral Scientist.* Chicago: Aldine.
Ashkenas, R., Ulrich, D., Jick, T. & Kerr, S. (1995). *The Boundaryless Organization.* San Francisco: Jossey-Bass.
Biggiero, L. (1998a). *Faces of Constructivism: Steps Toward an Epistemology of Management,* Paper presented at SOEIS meeting, Bielefeld, <www.luiss.it/facolta/economia/biggiero>.
Biggiero, L. (1998b). *The Creation and Evolution of District Identity: Theoretical and Empirical Observations*, Paper presented at LIUC Conference on "SMEs and Districts: Hybrid Governance Forms, Knowledge Creation & Technology Transfer," Castellanza (Italy) 1998.
Biggiero, L. (1999). Markets, Hierarchies, Networks, Districts: A Cybernetic Approach, *Human Systems Management, 18,* 1-16.
Biggiero, L. (2000). Sources of Complexity in Human Systems, *Nonlinear Dynamics and Chaos in Life Sciences, 5,* 3-19.
Biggiero, L. (2001). Managerial Action and Observation: A View of Relational Complexity, *Systemica,* forthcoming.
Fleischaker, G.R. (1988). Autopoiesis: The Status of its System Logic, *BioSystems, 22,* 37-49.
Hannan, M. & Freeman, J. (1989). *Organizational Ecology,* Cambridge, MA: Harvard University Press.
Janis, I.L. & Mann, L. (1977). *Decision Making.* New York: The Free Press.
Jarrillo, C.J. (1993). *Strategic Networks: Creating the Borderless Organization*, Butterworth: Heinemann.
Jessop, B. (1990). *State Theory*, Cambridge: Polity Press.
Jessop, B. (1992). The Economy, the State and the Law: Theories of Relative Autonomy and Autopoietic Closure. In G. Teubner & A. Febbrajo (Eds.), *State, Law and Economy as Autopoietic Systems: Regulation and Autonomy in a New Perspective* (pp. 187-265). Milano: Giuffrè.

Kets de Vries, M.F.R. & Miller, D. (1984). *The Neurotic Organization.* San Francisco: Jossey-Bass.
Kickert, W.J.M. (1993.) Autopoiesis and the Science of (Public) Administration: Essence, Sense and Nonsense, *Organization Studies, 14,* 261-278.
von Krogh, G. & Roos, J. (Ed.) (1996). *Managing Knowledge.* London: Sage.
von Krogh, G. & Vicari, S. (1993). An Autopoiesis Approach to Experimental Strategic Learning. In P. Lorange, B. Chakravarthy, J. Roos & A. Van de Ven (Eds.), *Implementing Strategic Processes: Change, Learning and Cooperation* (pp. 394-410). London: Blackwell.
Luhmann, N. (1990). *Essays on Self-reference.* New York: Columbia Uuniversity Press.
March, J.G. & Olsen, P. (1976). *Ambiguity and Choice in Organizations.* Bergen, Norway: Universitetsforlaget.
March, J.G. & Simon, H.A. (1958). *Organizations.* New York: John Wiley & Sons.
Maturana, H.R. (1975). The Organization of the Living: A Theory of the Living Organization, *International Journal of Man-Machine Studies, 7,* 313-332.
Maturana, H.R. (1978). Biology of Language: The Epistemology of Reality. In G.A. Miller & E. Lenneberg, (Eds.), *Psychology and Biology of Language and Thought* (pp. 27-63). New York: Academic Press.
Maturana, H.R. (1980.) Autopoiesis: Reproduction, Heredity and Evolution, In M. Zeleny (Ed.), *Autopoiesis, Dissipative Structures, and Spontaneous Social Orders.* Boulder, CO: Westview Press.
Maturana, H.R. (1981). Autopoiesis. In M. Zeleny (Ed.), *Autopoiesis: A Theory of Living Organization.* New York: North Holand.
Maturana, H.R. & Varela, F.J. (1980). *Autopoiesis and Cognition: The Realization of the Living.* Dordrecht: Reidel.
Maturana, H.R. & Varela, F.J. (1987). *El arbol del conocimiento,* translated in English as The Tree of Knowledge, (1992) Horticultural Hall, MA: Shambhala Pub.
Morgan, G. (1986). *Images of Organization.* London: Sage.
Nelson, R. & Winter, S. (1982). *An Evolutionary Theory of Economic Change.* Cambridge, MA: Belknap.
Park, O.S. Sims Jr., H.P. & Motowildo, S.J. (1986). Affect in Organizations: How Feelings and Emotions Influence Managerial Judgment. In H.P. Sims & D.A. Gioia (Eds.), *The Thinking Organization* (pp. 215-237). San Francisco: Jossey-Bass.
Pfeffer, J. & Salancik, G.R. (1978). *The External Control of Organizations.* New York: Harper & Row.
Simon, H.A. (1962). *The Architecture of Complexity.* Proceedings of the American Philosophical Society, December; reprinted in H.A. Simon (Ed.) 1969, *The Sciences of the Artificial* (pp. 193-229). Cambridge, MA: MIT Press.
Simon, H.A. (1978). Rationality as Process and as Product of Thought. *American Economic Review, 67,* 76-90.
Sims, Jr., H.P. & Gioia, D.A. (Eds.) (1986). *The Thinking Organization.* San Francisco: Jossey-Bass.
Stengers, I. (1985). Les généalogies de l'auto-organisation. *Cahiers du CREA, 8,* 7-104.
Teubner, G. (Ed.) (1988). *Autopoietic Law: A New Approach to Law and Society.* Berlin: de Gruyter.

Teubner, G. (1993). *Law as an Autopoietic System.* Oxford: Blackwell

Teubner, G. & Febbrajo, A. (Eds.) (1992). *State, Law, and Economy as Autopoietic Systems.* Milan: Giuffrè

Ulrich, H. & Probst, G.J.B. (Eds.) (1984). *Self-organization and Management of Social Systems.* Berlin: Springer.

Varela, F.J. (1979). *Principles of Biological Autonomy.* New York: North Holland.

Varela, F.J. (1981). Describing the Logic of the Living: The Adequacy and Limitations of the Idea of Autopoiesis. In M. Zeleny (Ed.), *Autopoiesis: A Theory of Living Organization.* New York: North Holland.

Varela, F.J. (1996). The Early Days of Autopoiesis: Heinz and Chile. *Systems Research, 13,* 407-416.

Varela, F.J., Maturana, H.R. & Uribe, R. (1974). Autopoiesis: The Organization of Living Systems, its Characterization and a Model, *BioSystems, 5,* 187-196.

Vicari, S. (1991). *L'impresa vivente.* Milan: Etaslibri.

Weick, K.E. (1979). *The Social Psychology of Organizing.* Reading, MA: Addison-Wesley.

Weick, K.E. (1995). *Sensemaking in Organizations.* Beverly Hills, CA: Sage.

Weick, K.E. & Bougon, M.G. (1986). Organizations as Cognitive Maps: Charting Ways to Success and Failure. In H.P. Sims Jr. & D.A. Gioia (Eds.), *The Thinking Organization.* San Francisco: Jossey-Bass.

Williamson, O.E. (1975). *Markets and Hierarchies.* New York: The Free Press.

Williamson, O.E. (1985). *The Economic Institutions of Capitalism.* New York: The Free Press.

Winograd, T. & Flores, F. (1986). *Understanding Computers and Cognition.* Reading MA: Addison Wesley.

Zan, L. (1995). Interactionism and Systemic View in the Strategic Approach. *Advances in Strategic Management, 12,* 261-283.

Zeleny, M. (Ed.) (1980). *Autopoiesis, Dissipative Structures, and Spontaneous Social Orders.* Boulder, CO: Westview Press.

Zeleny, M. (Ed.) (1981). *Autopoiesis: A Theory of Living Organization.* New York: North Holland.

Zeleny, M. (1995). Ecosocieties: Societal Aspects of Biological Self-Production. *Soziale Systeme, 2,* 179-202.

Zeleny, M. (1996). On the Social Nature of Autopoietic Systems. In E.L. Khalil & K.E. Boulding (Eds.), *Evolution, Order and Complexity.* London: Routledge.

Zeleny, M. & Hufford, K.D. (1992). The Application of Autopoiesis in System Analysis: Are Autopoietic Systems Also Social Systems? *International Journal of General Systems. 21,* 145-160.

Chapter 8

THE AUTOPOIESIS OF SOCIAL SYSTEMS: AN ARISTOTELIAN INTERPRETATION

Colin Dougall

INTRODUCTION

This chapter addresses a problem which has dogged researchers off and on for more than a quarter of a century and which goes under the rubric of "social autopoiesis." Simply put, the problem is how to apply, or "port," or otherwise make use of Maturana's theory of autopoiesis in the context of social systems other than merely metaphorically and in a way that does not visit damage on the original theory. This is the problem of social autopoiesis as articulated by Mingers (1992, p. 231), a problem which has been debated extensively in recent years. Recently a special issue of the *International Journal of General Systems* (Vol. 21, 1992) lent its pages to just such a debate. The debate took the form of a focal paper by Zeleny and Hufford arguing that social systems are also autopoietic systems, a claim which was then debated and challenged by the other participants (Fleischaker, Mingers, Robb, Swenson, Kenny, Geyer, de Zeeuw) who unanimously concluded that Zeleny and Hufford had failed to demonstrate the truth of their claim. This is not to suggest that all of the participants ranged against Zeleny and Hufford were unanimous in the view that social systems are categorically not autopoietic systems or that there is anything wrong with the notion of "social" autopoiesis per se—only that Zeleny and Hufford have gone about proving their case in the wrong way. Robb and Geyer, in their different ways, are clearly sympathetic to the idea of social autopoiesis whereas Fleischaker, Swenson, and Kenny are opposed to it. Mingers' position is that while he does not completely rule out the idea, he has yet to come across convincing arguments for it.

This question (are social systems autopoietic?) was again debated by a special interest group, the Research Committee on Sociocybernetics of the

International Sociological Association, at the 14th World Congress of Sociology in Montreal, July 1998. Predictably, opinion was divided but what was perhaps most notable was the tacit assumption that social theory is the most appropriate vehicle for tackling this particular problem. Somewhere between Maturana and Varela's original elaboration of autopoiesis theory in the early 1970s and the 1998 World Congress, "nonphysical" autopoiesis had somehow been hijacked—it seemed that if we were to speak at all of autopoiesis outside of biology, then sociology and social theory were the appropriate narratives. To date, however, sociological models or approaches have signally failed to make any inroads towards a solution to this problem. In the sections below I present what I have called the M-A model as just such a solution. Luhmann has argued that since autopoiesis theory as we understand it is "tied to life," it cannot aspire to the status of a general theory. The M-A model is presented as a conceptual edifice and explanatory ground of both physical and nonphysical autopoiesis alike at the level of generality Luhmann aimed at but never achieved. To put this into perspective, the Organic model of Maturana and what I call the Enterprise model, are posited as special (Lat. *specialis*: as species) cases of the more general M-A model and are assumed to share its distinctive generic features (see Figure 8.4 below).

SOME PRELIMINARIES

The term "autopoiesis" is a neologism coined by Maturana and Varela (Varela et al., 1974) from two Greek words—*auto* meaning self, and *poiesis* meaning to produce. The appropriate Greek phrase is ην αυτοι ποιεσις *(en-heautoi-poiesis)* which can be glossed as "bringing forth from within itself," thus we get autopoiesis: to self-produce. The notion of self-production is not a new idea, and neither is it original to Maturana and Varela, although it is with Maturana that it is currently most often associated. Mingers (1995, p. 132), for instance, notes that the work of Bourdieu, Touraine, and Giddens implicitly or explicitly relates to autopoiesis inasmuch as these authors can be thought of as having some conception of self-production or self-organization at the societal level developed independently of Maturana (the title of Touraine's 1977 work is *The Self-Production of Society*). To this list we can add Aristotle who, as we shall see, has a conception of autopoiesis closer to Maturana and Varela than any of the above. Of the above, only Aristotle and Maturana develop their ideas on self-production specifically in a biological context—Touraine, Giddens, and Bourdieu do so in a specifically social context. This is an important distinction since it has a direct bearing on what it is that each of the two camps is attempting to explain. Aristotle and Maturana attempt to explain not only change but also constancy. Moreover, it is the constancy of a subject taken as a unified whole. Touraine, Bourdieu, and Giddens, in their different ways, attempt to explain not a unified subject but a society. Touraine in particular is at pains to make this explicit in his work (Touraine, 1977, p. 22). Autopoiesis theory properly understood has as its central concern, I will argue, a unified substantive subject. Social theorizing on the self-production of society, on the other hand, does not.

The *leitmotif* of autopoiesis theory is persistence (of the subject) in the face of constant change—a persistence which can be expressed by the perturbation/compensation formula. According to Maturana and Varela, an autopoietic unity is capable of bearing and surviving change (structural perturbations) and hence of persisting as the same subject (maintaining identity) by virtue of the plasticity of its *structure*. What persists throughout the change process is its *organization* and hence its identity, and this persistence is explainable in terms of "structural compensations." We find a similar *leitmotif* in Aristotle whose two key figures, form and matter, are by analogy the same thing as Maturana and Varela's organization and structure. It might be argued that a similar *leitmotif* runs through the work of Touraine, Bourdieu, and Giddens insofar as they attempt to explain the persistence of societies in terms of their self-production. While this may be true insofar as it goes, they neither have nor employ direct analogues of Maturanian organization and structure.

In comparing the work of Giddens (structuration theory) with that of Maturana, Mingers finds a number of prima facie points of contact or resonances (Mingers, 1995, p. 136). These points of contact notwithstanding, Mingers nevertheless concludes that a straightforward assimilation of autopoiesis to structuration theory is not possible. The relevant comparison, he argues, is not between autopoiesis and structuration theory but between Giddens' and Maturana's social theory—structuration theory is a social theory, autopoiesis theory is not. Although Giddens may seem to employ similar concepts to Maturanian organization and structure, Mingers argues that they are incompatible. Giddens' "system" is not the same thing as Maturana and Varela's "structure." It may be observable and exist in space-time but it does not meet the formal requirements autopoiesis theory demands of structure. The same is true of Giddens' "structure" and Maturana and Varela's "organization." Maturanian organization, Mingers argues, has no causal or enabling powers. Neither does it generate the particular behavior or properties of the unity's components. Giddens' structure, on the other hand, does (Mingers, 1995, p. 137).

It is worth noting that this last point regarding the causal nature of Maturanian organization is true if it is taken as a simple universal. It is not so clear that it is true if we treat organization as something other than this, a point Maturana (1993, p. 40) seems to recognize. If, as I have argued elsewhere (Dougall, 1999a), we rethink Maturanian organization as Aristotelian form, it can to a certain extent be seen to determine the properties and behaviors of the particular unity it is the organization of. The overall conclusion of the above discussion is that autopoiesis cannot be assimilated to any social theory of self-production because the objects of such theorizing (i.e., social systems) do not meet the formal requirements of autopoiesis theory. Whatever else such theories may be, they do not describe autopoiesis as we understand that term from Maturana and Varela.

AUTOPOIESIS AND CAUSALITY

Although the ancient Greeks had a general notion or conception of "auto poiesis" it is Aristotle who takes it up and reworks it into a technical explanatory notion which he incorporates into his explanation of nature and natural things and into his metaphysics in general. Heidegger, whose philosophical orientation is generally taken to be consonant with Maturana's (Mingers, 1995, p. 109; Winograd & Flores, 1987), finds "auto poiesis" (as we would understand that term post-Maturana) in Aristotle—in particular in Aristotle's analysis of nature (*phusus*) and in the doctrine of the causes as set out by Aristotle in the Physics[1]. In his interpretation of the Aristotelian doctrine Heidegger (1978) reads cause (L. *causa*) not as a way of effecting or bringing about, but as a translation of the Greek *aition*, that to which something else is indebted. That out of which something is made is the *causa materialis*. That into which something enters is the *causa formalis* (*eidos*, form). They belong together and in their own way are coresponsible for something's coming into being. A third cause is the *causa finalis*—telic finality. Heidegger does not translate *telos* as "aim" or "purpose." Rather it is that which in advance gives bounds to a thing. We have to consider carefully here what Heidegger means by this. By "in advance" he is suggesting that the silver chalice is confined to being what it is before it is what it is—that is, it is confined to "chaliceness" by virtue of its aspect (*eidos*, form) before it is produced, and by virtue of its form and matter after it is produced. It is precisely this circumscribing that gives bounds, since if it didn't we would not be able to identify a chalice as a chalice or produce it in the first place (if its boundary was not given over in advance we would not be able to tell when we had produced one). It is from out of these bounds that it begins to be what it is and can be.

There is a fourth cause which, according to Heidegger, has been misinterpreted as a *causa efficiens*. It would be, he argues, a mistake to view the silversmith of his example simply as a *causa efficiens*. As a fourth cause the silversmith is coresponsible for the finished chalice. In making sense of this it helps if we remember that in the context of the production of the chalice we are looking at what Maturana calls allopoiesis. The "bringing-forth" of the chalice is in the silversmith (*en alloi*, in another). His responsibility is that of the origin of this bringing forth. The four ways of being responsible bring something into appearance, from not yet present into presence. In his typically opaque language Heidegger calls this an "occasioning" and an "inducing to go forward." It is precisely this occasioning that Heidegger sees as the essence of causality as thought by the Greeks. Occasioning is to be found in bringing. Such a bringing is *poiesis*, a bringing-forth. *Poiesis* however is not only the arts and crafts of men and women. In its purest form it is *physis*, the arising of something from out of itself (*en heautoi*), a bringing-forth. This he contrasts with the bringing-forth of artifacts which has its origin in another (*en alloi*).

What we have then are two modes of *poiesis*, namely *en-heautoi-poiesis* (autopoiesis) and *en-alloi-poiesis* (allopoiesis). Heidegger addresses the question of how bringing-forth happens and what such a bringing-forth is. His answer is that it happens in revealing and what it is is truth. *En-heautoi-poiesis*, as bringing-forth, is a revealing. More precisely it is a revealing from out of itself into itself, self-revealing if you like. Whether or not Heidegger is correct in this last point (alethia = revealing = truth) is the subject of much debate and controversy among Heideggerian scholars. What is less controversial is that ην αυτοι ποιεσις as Aristotle reworks it and the neologism of Maturana and Varela as applied to the biological subject, even although separated by nearly 2,500 years, are indistinguishable. This is not as remarkable as it may at first seem. Aristotle and Maturana are first and foremost biologists and as such their starting point in their analysis of natural things is not definition but observation.

It is on the back of such observations that both are led to construe nature in such a way as to make explicit the differences as well as the similarities between the products of nature (biological subjects) and the products of art (artifacts). If we disregard their method of production then both can indifferently be called products (Woodbridge, 1965, p. 146), a point Aristotle makes at Physics 199a12. Once we consider the method, however, we can see that they are radically different—the growth and development of, for example, a plant is directed from within. In the case of artifacts such direction is from without. This of course is the difference between autopoiesis and allopoiesis. Maturana and Aristotle offer an account of change in biological (natural) subjects that places due emphasis on the persistence of the changing subject—a radical point of departure from most modern "change" theories. To be sure, their language is different. Where Maturana, with the benefits of modern technology, can describe autopoietic processes at the cellular level, Aristotle speaks of an "internal principle of change and stasis." Where Maturana speaks of organization and structure, Aristotle speaks of form and matter. As I shall attempt to demonstrate, however, the language may be different but both are describing the same phenomena.

To know or to explain something then is to know its causes. The objects of explanation, however, are not to be thought of as what we might loosely call events such as, for instance, the state opening of Parliament or meeting a friend on the way to the market. Rather they are the myriad objects and artifacts that constitute the furniture of the world, the *ta onta* of everyday life such as tables and chairs, birds and bees, cabbages and kings. Causes enter into the explanation of such things as explanatory factors and the explanations are couched in realist terms—hence anyone explaining things in this way might be termed an "explanatory realist." The causes account for how it is that something comes into being.

Moravcsik (1975) suggests that the causes are best viewed as generative factors and the doctrine of the "causes" is Aristotle's attempt at a metaphysical theory of understanding. By this he means that Aristotle held that there is a lasting and stable relation between the structure of human understanding and certain configurations in reality that make understanding possible and that the theory of the causes is Aristotle's attempt to uncover and spell out these relations. The *aitia*-relations themselves are taken to be ontological relations

Figure 8.1a
Meeting the Bootstrap Requirement

formal (organization)

X

efficient (relations of production)

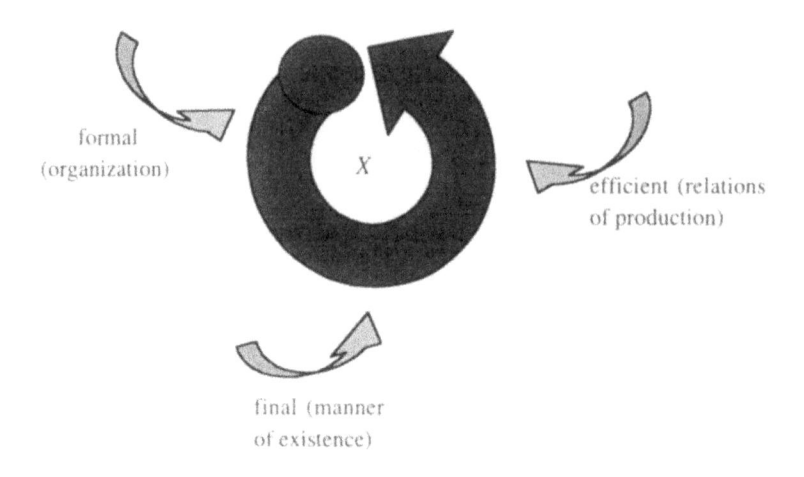

final (manner of existence)

Figure 8.1b
Failing the Bootstrap Requirement

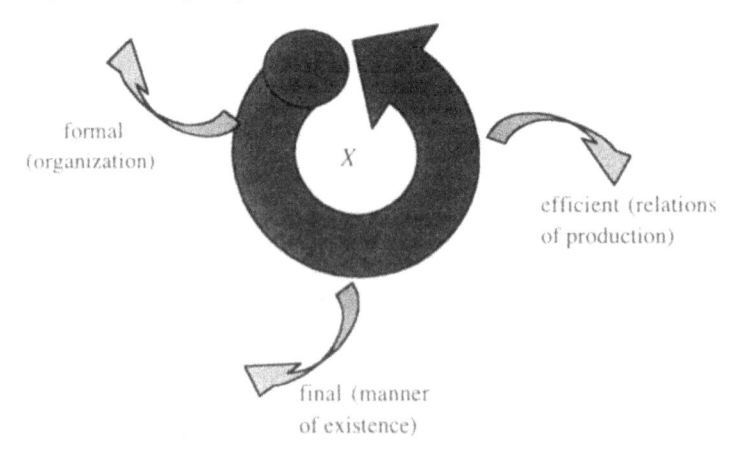

formal (organization)

X

efficient (relations of production)

final (manner of existence)

between things, the grasping of which allows the investigator to understand some important aspect of whatever it is that is under investigation. Since they yield explanatory power the *aitiai* are, according to Moravcsik, more than simply causes, however broadly we interpret this term. Neither are they simply explanatory factors or fashions. Rather, they are generative factors and what they generate is not only the conditions of the possibility for the understanding of a thing, but more importantly the thing itself. The sense of this is captured in Moravcsik's labels for the *aitiai* as the constitutive factor (material), the distinguishing factor (formal), the agentive factor (efficient), and the telic factor (final). Cause then (or *aitia*), is another of those things "said in many ways" (*pollachos legetai*). Since it is said in many ways, its underlying meaning must be ambiguous and best understood by the context of its use. Aristotle believed that in the case of things said to exist "by nature" the formal, final, and efficient *aitiai* coincide and for lack of a better expression I have called this, for reasons which hopefully will become clear later, the "bootstrap requirement" (see Figure 8.1).

THE CAUSES IN AUTOPOIESIS THEORY

We can straightaway identify the distinguishing and constitutive *aitiai* to be found in autopoiesis theory as organization and structure which correspond more or less exactly with Aristotle's form and matter. It might be thought that the perturbations to a structurally coupled system that cause it to move or act can be taken as being the agentive *aitia*. Aristotle would presumably adopt such a view: the physician who heals the patient is the efficient cause of health in the patient. In autopoiesis theory the physician administering his potions would be seen as a perturbation to the autopoietic system that is the patient. As such he neither causes nor determines the direction of change in the perturbed system: he can only act as a trigger and possibly select from among those states that are possible to the patient given his or her current structure. The direct cause of change then is the system itself, or more precisely the relations or processes of production that are its agentive cause. This is a slight reinterpretation of the moving cause although it is consistent with Aristotle's belief that in the case of natural things, the moving cause is internal. More controversially, we can identify the telic *aitia* in autopoietic systems in much the same way Aristotle identifies it in natural systems. Recall that for Aristotle the final cause in living things is the mature species form towards which the growing embryo moves. Maturana has consistently eschewed all notions of teleonomic reasoning; however, I take his position to be based on a modern misconception of telos as goal or purpose. In fact Maturana seems to have backtracked somewhat and in a 1993 paper seems to offer a distinctly Aristotelian account of final causality: "Living systems are characterized and realized as the kind of systems that they are by a particular organization that defines their class identity as well as their manner of existing in a domain of interactions and relations" (Maturana, 1993, p. 40).

I take "manner of existing" to be Maturana's version of the "telic factor" referred to above. To give an example, that a fish has a "particular organization" determines that it will grow from immaturity towards the mature species form and be an actual fish, behaving and acting in fish-like ways. Having identified the four causes or *aitiai* of autopoiesis theory we can contrast them with the Aristotelian originals using Moravcsik's labels as shown in Table 8.1.

We noted above that Aristotle believed that in natural things the formal, final, and efficient *aitiai* coincide (meet the bootstrap requirement) and are internal to such things. The same can be said of an autopoietic unity whose

Table 8.1
Aitiai in Aristotle and Maturana

Aristotle:	constitutive (material	distinguishing formal	agentive efficient	telic final)
Maturana:	structure	organization	relations of production	manner of existence

organization, manner of existence, and relations of production distinguished as *aitiai* are internal to it in exactly the same way and so meets the bootstrap requirement. We can represent this notion schematically as follows and contrast it with an allopoietic unity whose *aitiai* are external to it and which hence fails to meet the bootstrap requirement. The question "are social systems autopoietic?" can then be rephrased as "does a particular class of social systems meet the bootstrap requirement?"

As the father of modern biology Aristotle left it with his complementary concepts of telos and form (or *eidos*) very much at its explanatory center: the endpoint or telos of a developing specimen, its *terminus ad quem*, is the mature species form (this is not uncontroversial, cf. the papers by Balme in Gotthelf & Lennox, 1987). This idea however has been steadily expunged from modern biological thinking from at least the seventeenth century onwards (Grene 1976, p. 5). Evolutionary biology, with its view of the organism as an aggregate of adaptive mechanisms, has suffered as a consequence: without some modern analogue of Aristotelian form we have no unambiguous concept of adaption, of the adjustment of these means to that end (Grene, 1976, p. 16).

It is in the elaboration of autopoiesis theory that we find the "modern analogue" that Grene finds so lacking in contemporary biological theories of adaption—the "modern analogue" in question is of course Maturana and Varela's autopoietic organization. The irony is that its application has been most keenly pursued not in the biological sciences but in the management and social sciences, particularly in the context of business organizations as complex evolving and adaptive systems (see, for instance, the Proceedings of the Conference on Organizations as Complex Evolving Systems, University of Warwick, December 1998).

Maturana and Varela use autopoiesis as a technical term with a clearly defined and precise meaning. Since it was first formulated in the late 1960s it has grown in ways that could hardly have been imagined. It is considerations such as these that no doubt led King (1993) to describe it as more a theoretical paradigm that comes in several forms than as a unified theory. In a similar vein Von Glasersfeld (1997) notes that Maturana is one of the few authors who nowadays engage the construction of a wide, complete, explicatory system, comparable to those of Plato or Leibniz. Maturana certainly engages a wide, complete, explicatory system although, as I have been arguing, it is more comparable to Aristotle than to either Plato or Leibniz. In the construction of such a system he has to a great extent "invented" many of his own metaphysical terms—for instance "organization" and "the observer," to give just two examples—and attaches to them meanings quite different from the ordinary language usage of such terms. Researchers from many disciplines have assimilated autopoiesis into their theoretical toolkits. The debates and questions it has triggered on the nature of family reality, the ontology of law, the self-constitution of social systems, and the grounding of cognitive science and artificial intelligence seem, on the face of it, to be far removed from considerations of the autopoiesis of simple physical cells. Neither is it at all clear how the two are related. In order to understand or see the connection we must pay some regard to the particular metaphysics Maturana has felt the need to elaborate since, and as a direct consequence of, his "discovery" of autopoiesis.

By metaphysics we simply mean considerations with regard to the broad structures of reality. Although it is sometimes taken to be mumbo-jumbo it is, at heart, a rational project:

What is distinctive of metaphysics is that it is, like science, a rational project. What this means is that the metaphysician purports to give grounds for his large conclusions that are not founded either on the appeal to divine authority or on a claim to experience of a privileged kind. The metaphysician aspires, and pretends, to reach his conclusions by logical arguments commencing from assumptions which would be readily accepted by any reasonable person. From the pig's ear of our experience he fashions the silk purse of his vision of the cosmos. (Lawson-Tancred, 1998, p. xiii).

Maturana's vision and conclusions are large indeed. The world we experience is radically and literally one of our own making, one where nothing has any independent existence and where hallucination is indistinguishable from the "really real." This, Maturana argues, is a consequence of our biology. Mingers for one has voiced his reservations over this. Specifically, he argues that the claims Maturana makes from his theories are self-contradictory and are in fact inconsistent on two different levels. First, Maturana advances the claim that all knowledge is relative to the knower (or community of knowers), hence no theory can claim objective truth. Given the self-referential nature of this claim it must equally apply to the claim itself. If we accept this we are not compelled to agree with the theory; if we reject it then the theory is inconsistent (Mingers, 1995, p. 112). Second, Maturana's own theories specifically require that there be an independently existing world. Mingers finds this requirement peppered throughout Maturana's work in various different guises in the distinctions he makes.

Such inconsistencies in Maturana's philosophical position are indicative of problems with his metaphysics in general. Maturana's metaphysical position can be likened to those Loux (1998, p. 9) has called "conceptual schemers" and among whom he numbers Collingwood, Korner, Rescher, Putnam, and Rorty. Notwithstanding their philosophical diversity, what such metaphysicians have in common is a shared metaphysical agenda inherited from Kant, namely that the metaphysical enterprise is an inquiry into the structure of human thought. This is something quite different from the more traditional Aristotelian view, which sees the metaphysical enterprise as an inquiry into the structure of the world. If one takes the view, as Aristotle seems to have (Grene, 1976), that one mirrors the other then the outcome will be the same—typically, however, "conceptual schemers" don't believe this. To be sure, Maturana does not directly speak of conceptual schemes in the sense referred to above and neither does he explicitly articulate a metaphysical agenda in terms of such. His conclusions, however, are the same and they are drawn for the same reasons, although he arrives at them from biology rather than philosophy. This places Maturana squarely within the idealist tradition of metaphysics normally associated with Kant (Mingers, 1995, p. 93), although Maturana's position is more consonant with the more radical species of idealism Loux identifies with, among others, Rorty. On this account the conceptual framework or frameworks is all that there is—the very idea of an object separate from, and independent of, the conceptual scheme by which we form our representations is incoherent (Loux, 1998, p. 9). Loux finds the same sort of inconsistency in this neo-Kantian account of the project or agenda of metaphysics as Mingers finds in Maturana's radical constructivism, namely its destructive self-referential nature. A way out of this metaphysical bind is to concede the point to traditional (Aristotelian) metaphysics and accept that there is such a thing as a subject-independent reality. In this view, our conceptual frameworks, far from screening us from things as they really are, are on the contrary our routes to such things and our way of gaining access to them (Loux, p. 11). As I argue, reconstructing Maturana's metaphysics in this light saves it from its worst excesses and renders his project more coherent.

THE SUBSTANTIVE SUBJECT OF AUTOPOIESIS THEORY

I have argued elsewhere (Dougall, 1999a, 1999b) that autopoiesis theory, properly understood, has as its central concern a unified substantive subject. This substantive subject, which I take to be a synthesis of Maturanian and Aristotelian metaphysics, I have presented as the M-A model (reproduced in Figure 8.2). The M-A model brings together Maturana's notion of organization with Aristotle's notions of form-actual. In doing so it purges organization of its relational character and brings to form-actual Maturana's important notion of organizational closure. It also brings together Maturanian structure with Aristotelian matter-potential. Following Aristotle and Maturana it asserts both the priority of act over potency and the ontological dependency of accidents of substance on substance. Last, with the clear separation of organization and structure I argue that a more coherent picture of Maturanian unity emerges.

In terms of the above model the substantive subject is to be found on the persistence side—that is, it is organization-form-actual. One of the difficulties with the above model from the social autopoiesis perspective lies in the matter-structure-potential side. A formal requirement of autopoiesis theory is that all

Figure 8.2
The M-A Model as Substantive Subject

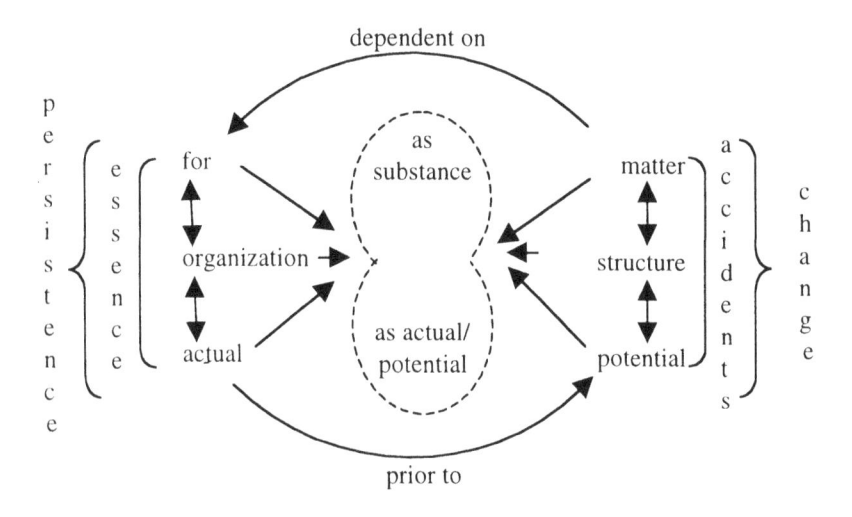

material system components be produced by the system itself. This does not seem to be the case with the social model. The solution to this is to broaden our conception of structure so as to include Aristotle's perceptible/intelligible distinction regarding matter which he makes at Metaphysics 1036a10.[1] Bogen (1996, p. 184) identifies four "levels" of Aristotle's hylomorphic analysis of matter and form and presents these as a hierarchy with the most primitive at the base and the most intelligible at the apex. In ascending order of intelligibility these are (1) the primary elements of Earth, Air, Fire, and Water (level 4), (2) the uniform parts (level 3), (3) the nonuniform parts (level 2), and (4) an organized body (level 1). We can modify this slightly in order to make more explicit the complexity of organic structures and introduce a new level between 1 and 2 (level 1a) which we shall call nonuniform composites. Such nonuniform composites are composites of the nonuniform parts. For example the nervous system, as a nonuniform composite, is a composite of brain, spinal cord, nerve tissue, and so on. Other examples of nonuniform composites would be the immune system, the cardiovascular system, the gastrointestinal system, and so on (see Figure 8.3).

As we move up the hierarchy the matter becomes more intelligible and less perceptible—that is, closer to form, and as we move down the reverse is the case. Thelonius' highest level of matter is his actual living body and his highest level of form is his Soul.[2] Thelonius' body can be analyzed into its lower level matter (the nonuniform parts of level 2) along with their appropriate lower level form. The nonuniform parts can themselves be analyzed into their lower level matter (the uniform parts of level 3) and their appropriate lower level form.

Figure 8.3
Thelonius' Matter/Form Hierarchy. Adapted from Bogen (1996, p. 184).

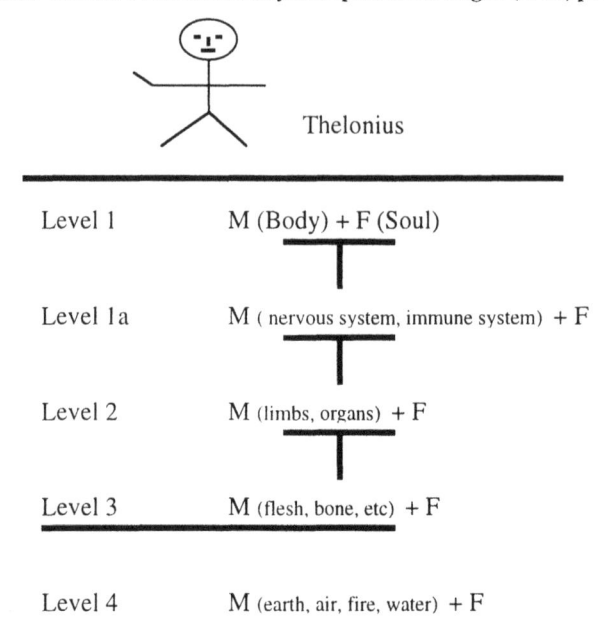

Level 1	M (Body) + F (Soul)
Level 1a	M (nervous system, immune system) + F
Level 2	M (limbs, organs) + F
Level 3	M (flesh, bone, etc) + F
Level 4	M (earth, air, fire, water) + F

Finally, the uniform parts can themselves be analyzed into their lower level matter (the primitive elements of level 4) and their appropriate lower level form. The matter at each of the first three levels is what Bogen (1996, p. 184) calls a concurrent constituent of Thelonius by which he means that the matters are actually present in Thelonius while he is alive and that the duration of their existence is the same as the duration of Thelonius' actual existence. The task of unifying the various perceptible and intelligible parts floating around is given to form: as the perceptible matter is differentiated into a perceptible unity (e.g., Socrates, Polly the parrot) by the form, the intelligible matter is organized into an intelligible unity in the form (Furth, 1988, p. 245). To give an example, as well as the individual perceptible parts such as heart, lungs, brain, and so on, Thelonius also has the following intelligible parts: (1) the nervous system, (2) the gastrointestinal system, (3) the cardiovascular system, and (4) the skeletal-muscular system and so on. According to our analysis so far these parts, as intelligible matter, belong to and are "parts" of form (soul). They are organized into an intelligible unity in the form. Form however is not simply these intelligible parts, it is also the relations between them. This of course has a distinctly Maturanian flavor to it. Since Maturana doesn't distinguish between perceptible/intelligible, however, Maturanian organization is left as simply "relations."

At De Partibus Animalium (PA) 642a9-13 Aristotle argues that a particular form can and will entail restrictions on the sort of matter that will be appropriate

THE AUTOPOIESIS OF SOCIAL SYSTEMS

to that form. At the crudest level of description where "matter = stuff and form = shape" (Furth, 1988, p. 86) a statue of Socrates can be made out of soap, marble, or clay and so on but it cannot be made out of wine, custard, or mercury and such things. This same argument holds as we proceed up the hierarchy. Aristotle doesn't give a particularly helpful example of what he means by "intelligible matter," although it seems clear that what he is getting at or trying to pick out is the generic conformation that underlies "divergent final differentiations" of whatever it is that is under consideration. Furth (1988) gives an example of bovine head-forms. The head-forms of the American Bison and Tibetan Yak are "divergent final differentiations" of the more generic underlying bovine head-conformation (dubbed bucocephalic by Furth). Here the generic underlies the more specific as "intelligible matter." Furth has argued that in the case of social systems the perceptible matter consists of the people who periodically fill the roles, while the intelligible matter consists of the roles or offices specified in the constitution of the system. Such roles or offices are no different in principle from the roles that the organs of, say, a human body fill (or en-matter).

Aristotelian matter then cannot be thought of simply as lumps of rock or wood or any other such basic materials. Depending on the context, the relevant "matter" may be, or include, anything from the basic elements through highly organized complete organic systems (cardiovascular, gastrointestinal, respiratory, skeletal-muscular, etc.) right up to and including "an organized body, potentially having life in it."

Much of this has a familiar Maturanian ring to it in spirit if not in exact detail. The structure of a unity (level 4) can be decomposed into its nonuniform parts (level 3), which can be further decomposed into their uniform parts (level 2), which can ultimately be decomposed into the basic elements (level 1). Each of these has its own appropriate organization which at the lower levels determines their function and which at the top level determines the manner of existence of the unity. Similarly, a unity can be realized by many different structures but not by just any structure. Arguably Maturana also makes the perceptible/intelligible distinction referred to above. To say that structure consists of the actual relations and the actual components just is to say that matter has a perceptible and intelligible dimension. A cardiovascular system is intelligible matter, its organic bits and pieces are its perceptible structure.

THE PROBLEM OF SOCIAL AUTOPOIESIS

In the opening paragraph of this chapter we articulated the problem of social autopoiesis as how to apply, or "port," or otherwise make use of Maturana's theory of autopoiesis in the context of social systems other than merely metaphorically and in a way that does not visit damage on the original theory. Luhmann, whose work is undoubtedly the most extensive, coherent, and rigorously worked out in this area in recent years, chooses to ignore it. For Luhmann (1986) the autopoiesis of society and its subsystems turns on the production of communications. Such communications are not to be confused with conscious thoughts (and hence language), behaviors, or actions. Rather they are communicative events (Mingers, 1995, p. 141). A communication is an event consisting of three elements: information, utterance (communication or action), and understanding (comprehension). Information is what the message is about, utterance is the form in which it is produced—how?, by whom?, why?,— and understanding is the sense or meaning that it generates. Autopoietic closure is to be found in the fact that it is the system itself that determines what falls under each category. Crucial to communicative autopoiesis is the next communicative event, since without it autopoiesis stops. Society itself, taken as the sum total of all its autopoietic subsystems, is also autopoietic.

In assessing Luhmann's work on social autopoiesis, Mingers, although noting the boldness of his approach and his consistency in avoiding domain confusion, nevertheless argues that where Luhmann is less successful is (1) in resolving the problem of boundaries—there is no boundary consisting of particular boundary components; (2) he does not use the distinction between organization and structure in spite of its potential usefulness and importance to autopoiesis theory; (3) it does not seem possible to conceive of new autopoietic systems emerging or developing within an already existing one—society functionally differentiates into subsystems, subsystems do not develop independently and fuse into society; (4) in showing how communication, as an independent phenomenal domain, emerges from the interactions of the individual human beings who ultimately underpin it—in leaving out the observer there is nothing to bootstrap the system into operation; (5) his analysis is functionalist, an approach Maturana and Varela reject; and (6) the social is restricted solely to communication. In spite of its rigor and subtlety his candidate autopoietic subject meets very few if any of the formal requirements of autopoiesis theory and his arguments remain unconvincing.

In contrast with Luhmann, Zeleny and Hufford (1992) chose to meet the problem of social autopoiesis head on. Their strategy was to test their candidate subject—the family model—against the six-point key (6PK) of Varela et al. (1974, pp. 192-193). If it satisfied in full each of the six key points it could be considered an autopoietic unity, otherwise it was not. Although Zeleny and Hufford have failed to convince their critics, it has to be said that in using the 6PK to test their claims the cards were stacked against them in advance. The 6PK is almost exclusively concerned with structure-matter-potential. Zeleny and Hufford simply did not have an adequate conception of this in the context of their "family model," hence the increasing sense of desperation one finds in their arguments.

The conclusion that we can draw from the above discussion is that social models of autopoiesis fail if they stick too closely to the physical model because social systems do not follow the same physical laws as organic cells (Zeleny), and that also they fail if they are too distant from the physical model and hence do not to meet the formal requirements of the theory (Luhmann).

THE ENTERPRISE MODEL

In the previous sections we derived the M-A model as a general conceptual model of autopoiesis. We cannot use the 6PK to test the M-A model itself since as a general conceptual model of autopoiesis it assumes the 6PK. Neither, since we take scientific knowledge to be of the universal and not the particular, can it be tested against a particular specimen and success be taken as signalling its universal applicability to all specimens. In the case of Zeleny and Hufford's "family model," what was being tested was not a particular family but the universal family model—that is, just those features that were taken to be common to all families. If the family model satisfied the 6PK in full, then all particular instances of it could be taken as also satisfying it. What we can do is propose what we call the Enterprise model—what Maturana might call a "nonnatural" social system—based on a work relationship and the low autonomy of system components (a characteristic of all autopoietic systems) and test it. We use the term "enterprise" in preference to the more cumbersome "business corporation" or the potentially confusing "business organization" but take it to mean the same thing. The relationship between the Enterprise (and the Organic) model and the general M-A model can be presented diagrammatically as in Figure 8.4.

Figure 8.4
The Generic M-A Model and Its Species

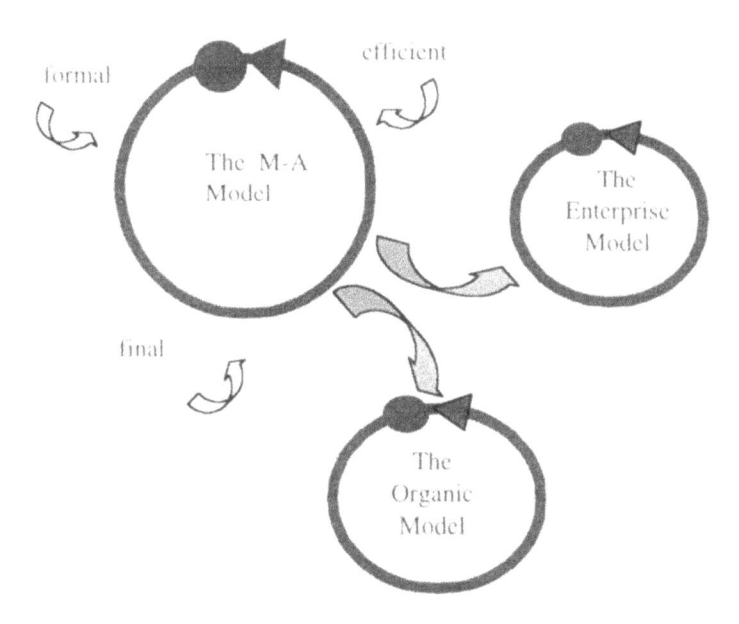

CONCLUSIONS

As we noted earlier, the Enterprise and Organic models are posited as special cases of the more general M-A model and are assumed to share its distinctive generic features. They are separated into different species according to the standard Aristotelian formula of genus + differentiae = species and at the level of the individual specimen the genera and differentiae are realized in the appropriate space (e.g., organic bodies and their components in the physical space, enterprises and their components in the social space) thus avoiding domain confusion. Maturana and Varela claim that if the 6PK is satisfied in full we have an autopoietic unity in the space in which its components exist. Although restrictions on space do not permit a full discussion of the Enterprise model in the context of testing it against the 6PK, the trick to establishing autopoiesis is via the form-matter hierarchy and the perceptible-intelligible distinction. Questions surrounding boundary production and maintenance and component production in general, we argue, can be unproblematically accommodated within the explanatory framework of the M-A model as we have outlined it above.

NOTES

1. All references to Aristotle are from *The Complete Works of Aristotle: Revised Oxford Translation* edited by J. Barnes, Princeton University Press, 1998.

2. Thelonius is a fictitious generic "person" and is for illustrative purpose only.

REFERENCES

Bogen, J. (1996). Fire in the Belly: Aristotelian Elements, Organisms, and Chemical Compounds. In F. Lewis & R. Bolton (Eds), *Form, Matter, and Mixture in Aristotle*. Oxford: Blackwell.

Dougall, C. (1999a). Autopoiesis and Aristotle: Rethinking Organization as Form, *Kybernetes, 28*, 777-791.

Dougall, C. (1999b). The Substantive Subject of IS Research. *In Proceedings of the UKAIS Annual Conference* (pp. 149-158). New York: McGraw-Hill.

Furth, M. (1988). *Substance, Form and Psyche: An Aristotelian Metaphysics*. Cambridge: Cambridge University Press.

Gotthelf, A. & Lennox, J. G. (Eds.) (1987). *Philosophical Issues in Aristotle's Biology*. Cambridge: Cambridge University Press.

Grene, M. (1976). Aristotle and Modern Biology. In M. Grene & E. Mendelsohn (Eds.), *Topics in the Philosophy of Biology* (pp. 3-36). Dordrecht: Reidel.

Heidegger, M. (1978). The Question Concerning Technology. In D. Krell (Ed.), *Martin Heidegger: Basic Writings* (pp. 311-341). London: Routledge.

King, M. (1993). The "Truth" About Autopoiesis. *Journal of Law and Society, 20*(5), 218-236.

Lawson-Tancred, H. (1998). *Aristotle: The Metaphysics.* Harmondsworth: Penguin.

Loux, M. (1998). *Metaphysics: A Contemporary Introduction.* London: Routledge.

Luhmann, N. (1986). The Autopoiesis of Social Systems. In F. Geyer & J. van der Zouwen (Eds.), *Sociocybernetic Paradoxes* (pp. 172-192). London: Sage.

Maturana, H. (1993). Biology of the Aesthetic Experience. In M. Titzmann (Ed.), *Zeichen (Theorie) in der Praxis,* (pp. 37-56). Passau: Wissenschafts Verlag Rottie.

Mingers, J. (1992). The Problems of Social Autopoiesis. *International Journal of General Systems, 21,* 229-236.

Mingers, J. (1995). *Self-Producing Systems: Implications and Applications of Autopoiesis.* London: Plenum.

Moravcsik, J. (1975). Aitia as Generative Factor. *Dialogue, 14,* 622-38.

Touraine, A. (1977). *The Self-Production of Society.* Chicago: University of Chicago Press.

Varela, F., Maturana, H. & Uribe, G. (1974). Autopoiesis: The Organization of Living Systems: Its Characterization and a Model. *Biosystems. 5* 187-196.

Von Glasersfeld, E. (1997). *Distinguishing the Observer: An Attempt at Interpreting Maturana.* <http://www.oikos.org/vonobserv.htm>.

Winograd, T. & Flores, F. (1987). *Understanding Computers and Cognition: A New Foundation for Design.* Wokingham: Addison-Wesley.

Woodbridge, J. (1965). *Aristotle's Vision of Nature.* Westport, CT: Greenwood.

Zeleny, M. & Hufford, K. (1992). The Application of Autopoiesis in Systems Analysis: Are Autopoietic Systems Also Social Systems? *International Journal of General Systems, 21,* 145-160.

Chapter 9

AUTOPOIESIS AND GOVERNANCE: SOCIETAL STEERING AND CONTROL IN DEMOCRATIC SOCIETIES

John H. Little

INTRODUCTION

In the world of government, where goals are multiple, unclear, and often conflicting, top-down systems of accountability too easily lead to systems of constraints that result in government that is inherently less responsive, less effective, and less efficient. What is worse, it produces government that a growing percentage of the public sees as less, rather than more, accountable to them. From the perspective of many citizens of democratic societies, government seems incapable of control by the people, who supposedly are sovereign. Citizens often speak of "the government" as though it is not simply separate from, but is clearly closed and inaccessible to them. This perception helps to delegitimize the actions and actors of government.

Niklas Luhmann's social systems theory (1990a, 1990b, 1995) helps explain this perception of government. There is another, competing theory, however, proposed by Peter Hejl (1993, 1997a, 1997b) which also seems potentially useful for understanding what might be done to change the perception. This chapter explores the usefulness of sociocybernetic concepts, particularly Luhmann's and Hejl's social systems theories, and their possible application to a normative theory of democratic participation in the administration of government.

STEERING SOCIETY WITH SOCIETY STEERING

A central issue of sociocybernetics is the question of societal steering, or to what extent societies can be steered by their governments. Geyer and van der Zouwen (1986) and in 't Veld et al. (1991) explored this issue in some depth.

Kickert (1991, 1993a, 1993b, 1995) and Dunshire (1993, 1996) addressed the question of autopoietic social systems and the implications for societal steering and governance from the perspective of public management and administrative theory. Kickert (1991) rejected the idea of autopoietic (or self-referential) systems as applicable to that purpose because it raises questions rather than solves problems and undermines the whole notion of control. Dunshire (1996) considered the impact of organizational closure and self-referentiality on the possibility for governmental regulation, and suggested several possible strategies for governmental intervention into autopoietic social subsystems. Both Kickert and Dunshire approached their subjects from the perspective of governmental control, either of controlling (managing) governmental organizations, or of controlling social systems external to government.

We have learned over the last half of the twentieth century that our ability to control society is limited. Governments are unable to govern above and apart from society, since societies act as complex networks and not simple machines (Kickert, 1993a). In complex networks governance is a matter of autonomous self-control and not of top-down steering from a central position. In classical, or first-order, cybernetics, there is a separate entity exercising rational control and there the system reflects little uncertainty and little complexity. These assumptions, however, do not hold in the field of public administration, which needs theoretical notions of self-governance and autonomy (Kickert, 1993b, p. 194).

It is not enough, however, to question whether or how governments can steer social systems. We also need to address the inverse question. Are governments, themselves, controllable by the public? Assuming the answer to that question is "yes," the question becomes "how can we accomplish that?" These questions are of special interest to those of us who study the field of public administration from a political rather than managerial perspective. We are concerned, among other things, with normative questions about the role of public officials and public employees in a democratic society (e.g., Wamsley et al., 1990; Fox & Miller, 1995; Little, 1996; Stivers, 1990, 1996; McSwite, 1997). How might public administration as a field of study, and public administrators as members of a profession, act to foster democratic control of the administration of government?

The "democratic administration" school of thought, at least as it applies to the United States, involves two notions as keys to reestablishing administrative and governmental legitimacy. First, we need to find a more democratic approach to administration if government is to be seen as legitimate. "Administrative legitimacy requires active accountability to citizens, from whom the ends of government derive. Accountability, in turn, requires a shared framework for the interpretation of basic values, one that must be developed jointly by bureaucrats and citizens in real-world situations, rather than assumed. The legitimate administrative state, in other words is one inhabited by active citizens" (Stivers, 1990). Democratic administration also involves a focus on "governance" rather than "government." "Governance" is intended to mean "something larger than "administration," a holistic view that includes citizens along with the elected officials and public professionals who are the apparatus of government" (Box, 1995).

The democratic administration movement parallels the growing tendency of citizens to bring questions of values and collective responsibility back into community governance issues, while rejecting technical rationality as the sole basis for actions. Both reflect a movement away from large, bureaucratic government, a turn towards values of local control, and small and responsive government. Both involve the notion of the professional public administrator as a person who helps citizens govern rather than as a person who controls public agencies.

Sociocybernetics encompasses conceptual approaches with considerable potential for informing and supporting normative theories of public administration. The sociocybernetics perspective seems to offer a source of new ideas and insights, and a possible approach towards theoretical grounding of a field that has often seemed to wander aimlessly between the precepts of political science and business administration. Niklas Luhmann's (1990b, 1995) interpretation of social systems as autopoietic is particularly interesting, since it seems to speak particularly to questions of democracy and societal steering. Moreover, Luhmann's early work focused on public administration and organizational theory, which informed his later theoretical work on social systems in general (Brans & Rossbach, 1997). Both sociocybernetics and Luhmann are virtually unknown to public administration theorists in the United States.

HOW CAN WE GOVERN THE GOVERNORS? OR CAN WE?

How democratic forces can effectively influence governmental actions, or even if they should be able to, is an old question. The whole idea of representative government rests, in large part, on the idea that direct democracies should be avoided, and that the public's role should be primarily to elect those who govern them. This may be satisfactory when populations are relatively small and when individuals' exposures to the instruments of governance are rare. As the ratio of citizens to representatives has grown larger while the number of laws and regulations has increased, and the number of unelected people involved in governance has grown, the public's sense that government is, in the words of Abraham Lincoln, "government of the people, by the people, and for the people," seems to have declined. The question is not only how governments can control social systems. The question is also how to control governments, themselves, in a way that fosters effective governance and an increased public sense of government's legitimacy.

The issue can quickly be muddled, since the public's attitudes towards what governments should do and how they should do it is interrelated with what governments already do and how they do it. It is difficult to distinguish the public's influence on governmental decisions, in terms of overall policy, from the influence of government's policy actions on public perceptions and attitudes.

Studies show that public opinion and the political system tend to track each other, although they do so imperfectly. What is not clear is whether it is public opinion that influences the political system or the political system that molds public opinion. According to Dye (1998): "Public policy may accord with mass opinion, but we can never be certain whether mass opinion shaped public policy or public policy shaped mass opinion. The public does not have opinions on many major policy questions, public opinion is unstable, and decision makers can easily misinterpret and manipulate public opinion. Public policy is more likely to conform to elite opinion than to mass opinion" (p. 334). The political scientist V. O. Key, Jr. (1967) wrote: "Government . . . attempts to mold public opinion toward support of the programs and policies it espouses. Given that endeavor, perfect congruence between public policy and public opinion could result from government of public opinion rather than government by public opinion." Although Key was convinced that public opinion does affect public policy, he was never able conclusively to demonstrate that fact. He did, however, find substantial evidence that elections, parties, interest groups, and the like do institutionalize communication channels from citizens to decision makers (Dye, 1998, p. 318).

While governments can be said—at best—to have only a very general tendency to adopt policies that agree with public preferences, political decision-makers, in turn, have little influence over the implementation and enforcement of those policy decisions, and citizens see themselves as unable to influence the day-to-day administrative decisions of a "faceless" bureaucracy, even when those decisions will directly affect their lives. Luhmann's Social Systems Theory suggests how these kinds of things happen.

LUHMANN'S SOCIAL SYSTEMS THEORY

Niklas Luhmann drew on new theoretical ideas from systems theory, notions of self-production, or "autopoiesis," to produce "the most developed and most radical attempt within contemporary sociology to recast completely the theory of society" (Harrison, 1995, p. 65).

Systems of Communication

Luhmann viewed social systems as systems of communication, not of human beings. People are necessary elements for communication, of course, but a person is no more a part of a Luhmannian social system than a neuron is part of a human being's thought processes. Communication is the result of three selections. "Information," what the communication is about, "is a selection from a (known or unknown) repertoire of possibilities" (Mingers, 1995, p. 140). Then a behavior expressing this communication ("utterance") must be chosen either intentionally or unintentionally. Finally there is selection by a receiver, or "understanding," which involves "the sense of meaning that a communication generates (which might include misunderstandings) in the receiver" (Mingers, 1995, pp. 141-142). When information, utterance, and understanding are synthesized, communication emerges.

The notion of self-reference forms the core of Luhmann's systems theory. Social systems are self-referential systems (Luhmann, 1995, p. 437). Self-reference is the means through which a system designates itself as a unity (Luhmann, 1995, p. 33). Self-reference is independent of observations by others, and implies that unity, or "self," can only be produced and maintained through relational operations. This leads to a form of organizationally closed system in which it can interact with its environment only in ways that allow the system to maintain its unity. Eventually, self-reference leads to a paradox, which must be resolved if unity is to be maintained. This can only be done through increased complexity. The whole system restructures itself into subsystems and subsystems' environments, multiplying its own reality. In modern society, the social system incorporates political, economic, scientific, and other subsystems, each with its own environment (including other subsystems) within the entire social system (Luhmann, 1995, p. 191).

Each subsystem is a network of meaningful, coded internal communications, which allow the system to distinguish itself from its environment. These codings are binary expressions of the functionally differentiated nature of that subsystem. Thus, the legal system codes its communications in terms of whether the subject matter is "legal" or "illegal." This internal coding also closes subsystems operationally from their environments. Operational closure means the system's environment (which includes machines, human psyches, and other social systems) cannot directly influence the system, but can only perturb it. The system, not the environment, determines whether it has been perturbed and what structural change will result. Each social system restructures itself in ways that reflect that certain environmental perturbations occur. In this way, subsystems become structurally coupled to each other. Since each subsystem is operationally closed, however, it is the social system, not the environment, that determines what is, or is not, a perturbation, and what changes a perturbation will produce. Social systems, then, can be said to co-evolve. All other social systems influence each system, but the other systems do not determine how that system changes.

This view of society is very different from the traditional one. Subsystems constantly renew and redefine themselves in processes of mutually interdependent but largely autonomous co-evolution and are virtually independent of society's external environment (Mingers, 1995, p. 148).

LUHMANN'S POLITICAL SUBSYSTEM

The constitutional state is a special type of political system involving negative feedback in the form of constraints on the state's actions. The constitutional state evolves into the welfare state, which involves positive comments in the form of demands for more entitlements for more people. This increasing demand for entitlements leads to growth in size and complexity as the political system deals with the paradox of insatiable demands which introduces still more paradox, and so on (Luhmann, 1990a). Eventually the system reaches a situation in which it can only maintain its unity by avoiding decisions, which becomes politics' core value.

The evolution of social subsystems, including political and administrative systems, can never avoid paradox, which is the logical equivalent of self-reference. Politics involves collectively binding decisions, but, since the decision-making occurs inside society, they bind the decision-maker as well. This reduces the capacity to decide and to change decisions. This problem can only be solved through creating greater complexity. Decisions involve more and more distinctions and specifics about whether and how decisions may be changed. Since, however, these solutions must be the result of decisions, the problem simply moves to a higher level. Pessimistically, Luhmann's systems theory implies that there is no alternative to this evolutionary process. Luhmann (1990a) is even more pessimistic about the future of democracy:

Depending on which concept of democracy we choose, the future of democracy appears different. Moreover, each different future creates problems in the present that one believes others do not see or do not take seriously enough. If democracy is about reason and freedom, about emancipation from societally conditioned tutelage, about hunger and need, about political, racist, sexist and religious suppression, about peace and about worldly happiness of any kind, then things, in fact, look pretty bad. And indeed so bad that the probability is great that everything that one does to counter this only makes matters worse.... But even with a narrower concept of democracy, restrictive decisions have to be made if one wants to stand on firm ground. Here too, impossibilities and extreme improbabilities must be excluded from the concept. (pp. 231-232)

Luhmann argued that democracy cannot be the nullification of political power through domination of the people by the people, since this would represent short-circuited self-reference. Neither can it involve the notion of making all decisions in a way that everyone can participate, since this would lead to decisions about decisions, endlessly compounding the decision-making process. Rather, he understood democracy as "the bifurcation of the top of the differentiated political system by the distinction of government and opposition" (Luhmann, 1990a, p. 232). By coding the perturbations caused by its environment in terms of "government" and "opposition," the political system produces internal information about what is advantageous to either governing or opposing parties, both of whom are part of the political system. The political system is further differentiated into "public," "politics," and "government." "Public" refers only to those aspects of the public that are politically relevant, "politics" speaks to the narrow sense of party politics and the legitimization of power; and "government" includes legislation, jurisdiction, and the administrative bureaucracy (Brans & Rossbach, 1997, pp. 428-429).

The political system's three subsystems are operationally closed and are only structurally coupled to each other. The public sees government as unresponsive and popular opinion is interpreted by partisan politics as a demand for more responsiveness by the bureaucracy. The politics subsystem, however, cannot exert direct control over government, but can only perturb or irritate it. Government, in turn, reacts to this perturbation by increasing its bureaucratic control structure in an attempt to increase its internal accountability, thus reducing its ability to respond directly to the public. In other words, public opinion triggers the political system to irritate the administrative system, which restructures itself in ways that reduce its responsiveness, which further alienates the public. Since all of these systems consist only of communications and not human beings, individual psychic motivations and desires are not directly involved in the process.

Various attempts to resolve this accountability dilemma have been tried or proposed, including: devolving governmental functions to lower levels, privatizing some functions, or even breaking nation-states up into smaller entities. These approaches may temporarily reduce system complexity and alleviate the problem but, if Luhmann is correct, they must ultimately fail.

Luhmann's theory tells us that social systems, or subsystems such as government, are operationally closed systems of communications. We can perturb them and—perhaps—provoke some response, but we cannot predict or control that response. Moreover, even if we could exert some degree of control over the action of government acting as a social system, how would we as individuals experience that control? To the extent we experienced it at all, it seems likely we would experience it as top-down control imposed on us as individuals by "the government." In other words, it may be that our previous attempts to increase our control over "the government" as a social system are the source of the alienation of citizens and government we are trying to moderate. We have gained that insight into the problem by looking at theory which takes society as its level of analysis. We need to look for a solution in theory that approaches society from a different level of analysis, such as that of Peter Hejl.

HEJL'S SOCIAL SYSTEMS THEORY

Hejl's (1997b) theory of social systems, called "synreferentiality," reflects his differences with Luhmann's social systems theory and his primary interest in human social phenomena. In his view, it is never "communication" that communicates but individuals in social systems. This leads him to an explanation of social phenomena that recognizes autopoiesis as only a model of living and cognizing systems, such as humans, and not of social systems. This approach, while it may not lead to the explanations of political phenomena that make Luhmannian theory attractive, does focus importance back onto the individual, which is a key conceptual element of democratic administration.

According to Hejl, what sets social systems apart from other types of systems is their synreferentiality, which refers to shared reality constructs, the associated behavioral programs, and the shared norms and values that form a basis for communication and interaction. A social system, then, is "a set of individuals, who (a) participate in the same synreferential domain, and (b) act and interact with respect to the behavior of autonomized systems" (Hejl, 1997b, p. 3). The idea of synreferentiality is compatible with a view of social systems as self-referential, self-organizing, and self-regulating, yet, in Hejl's view, it avoids some theoretical difficulties of Luhmann's conception of social systems. "Autonomization" does not imply "autonomy," but indicates that social systems behave according to the possibilities offered by their synreferential domains and ignore anything that does not match the possible realities and available programs. We cannot control or regulate Luhmann's social systems, but we can regulate Hejl's synreferential systems. We can only do this, however, to the extent that we understand the dynamics of the system and have an accurate model of the possible realities and alternatives that can be achieved within the dynamics of that system (Hejl, 1997, p. 7).

From the perspective of Hejl's systems theory, two factors must be considered if social systems are to be controlled effectively by governmental systems or if governmental systems are to be, themselves, controlled by democratic processes. First, the elements of social systems are human agents, who are, themselves, operationally closed systems, that co-evolve. Second, social systems are synreferential systems whose regulation requires an accurate model of the possible realities and available alternatives.

Both factors offer some clues to ways to regulate the regulators. The first suggests that a focus on individuals, rather than on regulation, accountability, or structure is required. The second suggests that regulating the behavior of governmental organizations is best done not by an outside observer, but from inside those organizations, where change agents are more likely to have some understanding of the organizational realities and alternatives.

RECONCILING LUHMANNIAN AND HEJLIAN APPROACHES

Hejl's theory seems to give us micro-level insights about how individuals, acting as citizens or as public administrators, might influence the behavior of government. Luhmann's theory offers macro-level insight into the behavior of social systems and the difficulties of steering them. How, then, can we choose one theory over the other, or must we?

Sys- versus Synreferentiality

Randall Whitaker (1993) has suggested one approach. He treats the two theories as simply involving different levels of analysis. Luhmann's top-down view of social systems (which Whitaker terms a "sysreferential" approach) focuses our attention on the entire social system as the unit of analysis, while Hejl's bottom-up view focuses attention on the individual participants as units or levels of analysis. This is not surprising in view of recent thinking about linking micro and macro approaches to social analysis (Alexander et al., 1987), and is not necessarily problematic. In practice, the two perspectives are complementary, and we tend to flip back and forth more or less unconsciously between the two. If we believe, as Whitaker suggests, that the current balance is tilted toward one perspective, we can increase the use of the other. This requires human beings to be "capable of interacting with mutual interference upon each other." We can foster this by increasing the ability of people to interact pliably with each other in dyads, rather than in large social groupings.

Hierarchy Theory

One might also consider the two theories from the perspective of Hierarchy Theory. Hierarchy Theory draws from Herbert Simon, Ilya Prigogine, Jean Piaget, ecologists, and cyberneticians such as Gregory Bateson to produce a theory that takes as its substance the "interrelations between observation, perception, and learning" (Ahl & Allen, 1996, p. 13). It focuses on matters of scale and of levels of organization, observation, and explanation, and on the relationships among these levels. The details of lower-level behavior of complex systems profoundly affect the upper level. The notion of "level" according to hierarchy theory, however, does not deal with features of the external world, but with an observer's point of view. In other words, complexity, which comes from the relationships between levels, is not a feature of the external world, but the result of the way we ask questions.

According to hierarchy theory, understanding comes from addressing multiple levels of organization simultaneously. For a given system, there is no singular, "proper" level of explanation, so we must simultaneously consider issues of scale and levels of organization, observation, and explanation and their interrelationships when we attempt to describe a complex system (Ahl & Allen, 1996).

Our traditional approach to taming complex systems has been to try to gain tight control over their behavior. This mechanical, "authoritarian" approach to dealing with complexity ignores chaos theories and the knowledge that the behavior of complex, nonlinear, dynamical systems is largely unpredictable, much less controllable. The uncertainty with which complex social systems may respond to mechanical, top-down attempts to control them helps to explain, among other things, how seemingly "wise" men in government may produce evil in the process of trying to eliminate evil. This complexity and the effects of deterministically chaotic behavior lead us, based on understanding that is always incomplete, to believe we can cause a social system to behave as we would like it to behave, or design a social system for a particular pattern of behavior.

Contemporary systems theory, including sociocybernetics, suggests an alternative approach to taming complex systems. This is to expand the problem domain to include both the observer and the system observed. This approach avoids the mechanistic solution that characterizes the other approach. Hierarchy theory supports this latter approach by focusing on the observer/observed interface, which "gives insights into a new class of solutions based on pragmatic assessment of the limits of understanding rather than on . . . tight control within a limited problem domain" (Ahl & Allen, 1996, p. 11). Whereas the mechanistic approach takes goals and values for granted, this approach includes the observer's goals and motives as part of its investigation.

Higher levels of hierarchical systems maintain their integrity by providing the context for lower levels, as Ahl and Allen (1996) indicate:

By being unresponsive, higher levels constrain and thereby impose general limits on the behavior of small-scale entities. Constraint is therefore achieved not by upper levels actively doing anything but rather by them doing nothing. For example, parents constrain a child's temper tantrum not by shouting back but rather by not reacting, and ignoring all the child's high-frequency thrashing and screaming. It may seem counterintuitive that imposing limits through constraint is passive, absence of behavior, rather than active manipulation. In the parlance of statistics, the upper level is a parameter for the variable behavior of lower levels. Parents are parameters for children's high-frequency developmental change. (p. 103)

CONCLUSION

Both Luhmann's and Hejl's perspectives can inform public administration theory. Luhmann's theory helps us understand that top-down structural changes will not make administration (or government, for that matter) more directly democratic. Such changes *might* facilitate one-to-one government at a lower level of analysis, but we have no way of accurately predicting what the actual result of the projected change might be. At the level of the political system or of government, the whole idea of management as it is normally conceived is meaningless. Moreover, there appears to be no direct way to reverse the growing sense of separation between individuals and "the government," or to foster a public belief that government is really, as Abraham Lincoln put it, "government by the people."

Even seemingly democratic movements like political pluralism, or the growing use of technological advances such as scientific polling and the Internet, only make the problem worse. These approaches represent increases in environmental complexity, to which the political system responds by increasing its own complexity. The result is government and its administrative subsystems that are even less directly controllable by the public.

At the lower level of analysis, the level encompassed by Hejl's theory, we can more clearly understand that democratic administration must be focused on dealing with individuals, not with social systems. Attitudes about government's legitimacy must change one at a time, through one-to-one encounters between individual citizens and individuals in government. To the extent possible, people must be dealt with as individuals, not as members of stakeholder or interest groups. This suggests that New Public Management approaches, based on concepts of "efficiency" and measures of "customer satisfaction," are on the wrong track, although they may experience some short-term success, since they remove citizens even further from any sense of participation in governance and convert them simply into government's *customers*.

Perhaps we should stop thinking in terms of democratic control of government in any but the most general or abstract terms and concentrate, instead, on linking the psychic systems of individuals both within and without government via authentic one-to-one or small group exchanges between administrators and citizens. In these situations, full operational closure is less likely and systems are more Hejlian and less Luhmannian. This does not imply that smaller organizations are somehow better than larger ones, but that we have more hope of understanding the dynamics and possible eigenbehaviors of small, comparatively simple subsystems, and thus of steering them, than of larger, more complex organizations.

REFERENCES

Ahl, V. & Allen, T.F.H. (1996). *Hierarchy Theory: A Vision, Vocabulary, and Epistemology*. New York: Columbia University Press.

Alexander, J.C., Giesen, B., Munch, R. & Smelser, N.J. (1987). *The Micro-Macro Link*. Berkeley: University of California Press.

Box, R. (1995). The Future Is Not What It Seemed. *Administrative Theory & Praxis, 17*, 87-91.

Brans, M. & Rossbach, S. (1997). Autopoiesis of Administrative Systems: Niklas Luhmann on Public Administration and Public Policy. *Public Administration, 75*, 417-440.

Dunshire, A. (1993). Modes of Governance. In J. Kooiman (Ed.), *Modern Governance*, (pp. 21-34). London: Sage.

Dunshire, A. (1996). Tipping the Balance: Autopoiesis and Governance. *Administration and Society 28*, 299-334.

Dye, T.R. (1998). *Understanding Public Policy*, 9th ed. Upper Saddle River, NJ: Prentice-Hall.

Fox, C. & Miller, H. (1995). *Postmodern Public Administration*, Thousand Oaks, CA: Sage.

Geyer, F. & van der Zouwen, J. (1986). *Sociocybernetic Paradoxes*. London: Sage.

Harrison, P.R. (1995). Niklas Luhmann and the Theory of Social Systems. In D. Roberts (Ed.), *Reconstructing Theory: Gadamer, Habermas, Luhmann* (pp. 65-90). Victoria, Australia: Melbourne University Press.

Hejl, P.M. (1993). Culture as a Network of Socially Constructed Realities. In A. Rigney & D. Fokkema (Eds.), *Cultural Participation: Trends Since the Middle Ages* (pp. 227-250). Amsterdam: J. Benjamins.

Hejl, P.M. (1997a). Communication and Social Systems: Evolutionary and Developmental Aspects. In P. Sweigart et al. (Eds.), *Human by Nature: Between Biology and the Social Sciences* (pp. 407-421). Mahwah, NJ: Erlbaum.

Hejl, P. (1997b). Social Phenomena and Law: What Kind of Systems? In *Workbook: Biology, Language, Cognition, & Society*. International Symposium on Autopoiesis. Belo Horizonte, Brazil, November, 1997.

Key, V.O. Jr. (1967). *Public Opinion and American Democracy*. New York: Knopf.

Kickert, W. (1991). Applicability of Autopoiesis to Administrative Science. In R.J. in 't Veld, J.A. Schaap et al. (Eds.), *Autopoiesis and Configuration Theory: New Approaches to Societal Steering* (pp. 193-206). Dordrecht, Netherlands: Kluwer.

Kickert, W. (1993a). Autopoiesis and the Science of (Public) Administration: Essence, Sense and Nonsense. *Organizational Studies, 14*, 261-278.

Kickert, W. (1993b). Complexity, Governance and Dynamics: Conceptual Explorations of Public Network Management. In J. Kooiman (Ed.), *Modern Governance: New Government-Society Interactions* (pp. 191-204). London: Sage.

Kickert, W. (1995). Steering at a Distance: A New Paradigm of Governance in Dutch Higher Education. *Governance, 8*, 135-157.

Little, J.H. (1996). Thinking Government: Bringing Democratic Awareness to Public Administration. In G. Wamsley & J. Wolf (Eds.), *Refounding Democratic Public Administration* (pp. 327-350). Thousand Oaks, CA: Sage.

Luhmann, N. (1990a). *Political Theory in the Welfare State*. New York: de Gruyter.

Luhmann, N. (1990b). *Essays on Self-Reference*. New York: Columbia University Press.

Luhmann, N. (1995). *Social Systems* (translated by John Bednarz, Jr. and Dirk Baecker, originally published in German in 1984). Stanford, CA: Stanford Press.

McSwite, O.C. (1997). *Legitimacy in Public Administration*. Thousand Oaks, CA: Sage.

Mingers, J. (1995). *Self-Producing Systems: Implications and Applications of Autopoiesis*. New York: Plenum.

Stivers, C. (1990). Active Citizenship and Public Administration. In G.L. Wamsley et. al. (Eds.), *Refounding Public Administration* (pp. 246-273). Newbury Park, CA: Sage.

Stivers, C. (1996). Refusing to Get It Right: Citizenship, Difference, and the Refounding Project. In G.L. Wamsley & J. Wolf (Eds.), *Refounding Democratic Public Administration* (pp. 260-278). Thousand Oaks, CA: Sage.

in 't Veld, R.J., Schaap, C.J., Termeer, A.M. & van Twist, M.J.W. (Eds.) (1991). *Autopoiesis and Configuration Theory: New Approaches to Societal Steering*. Dordrecht, Netherlands: Kluwer

Wamsley, G.L. et al. (Eds.) (1990). *Refounding Public Administration*. Newbury Park, CA: Sage.

Wamsley, G. & Wolf, J. (Eds.) (1996). *Refounding Democratic Public Administration*. Thousand Oaks, CA: Sage.

Whitaker, R. (1993). Interactional Models for Collective Support Systems: An Application of Autopoietic Theory. In R. Glanville & G. de Zeeuw (Eds.), *Interactive Interfaces and Human Networks* (pp. 119-135). Amsterdam: Thesis Publishers.

PART III

OBSERVATION OF SOCIAL SYSTEMS

Chapter 10

IMPLICATIONS OF AUTOPOIESIS AND COGNITIVE MAPPING FOR A METHODOLOGY OF COMPARATIVE CROSS-CULTURAL RESEARCH

Bernd R. Hornung & Charo Hornung

FEMININITY, MASCULINITY, ANDROGYNY, AND CROSS-CULTURAL RESEARCH

The background of this attempt to outline a methodology for comparative cross-cultural studies taking into account autopoiesis and cognitive mapping is a small empirical replication study done by the second author of this chapter (C. Hornung, 1999). This study dealt with androgyny and achievement motivation in cross-cultural comparisons, looking at university students in Germany and Peru.

Androgyny is a combination of feminine and masculine properties in the same person. Both feminine and masculine properties can be positive or negative. The positive properties can be considered to have a high survival value for a person in her or his role as a woman or man in the particular cultural context. To the extent that feminine and masculine properties and roles are not clearly defined and not fully mutually exclusive, a person who has both sets of positive properties (i.e., an androgynous person) can be considered to have the combined skills and advantages of both women and men.

This concept promises to lead to both emancipation by bridging the femininity/masculinity gap and to psychologically healthier or at least better adapted individuals, as an androgynous person would have both feminine and masculine characteristics, which are each advantageous to cope with problems in different types of situations.

This makes androgyny a highly political issue in the context of feminism and emancipation (Friedan, 1997). It also makes it a highly fascinating research topic with regard to its relation to achievement motivation, as achievement is one of the great idols of modern society. This double relationship of the concept of androgyny with modern society along with the claim of psychology to be a universal science (i.e., to be valid for all mankind) raises the question to what extent such claims truly hold in intercultural comparisons.

The types of gender [1] relevant for this endeavor are four. There are the two traditional ones, femininity and masculinity, and in addition androgyny, which characterizes persons rating high both on masculinity *and* femininity scales. There is, however, a fourth group of those who rate low on both scales, the "undifferentiated."

SOCIOCYBERNETIC PREMISES FOR CROSS-CULTURAL THEORY BUILDING

One central (and highly ethnocentric) problem of androgyny research has been that many researchers did not consider it necessary to define clearly what to understand under femininity and masculinity. This seemed to be self-evident, although, at a closer look, these are highly culturally dependent categories.

A second problem, in spite of the fact that most of these studies were done by psychologists, is the inadequate model of the underlying psychological systems. In some research and in some measuring instruments it is quite clear that a trait-oriented personality model is used. In others this is mixed with the use of the concepts of instrumentality versus expressivity as developed by Talcott Parsons and Robert Bales in the context of their four function model of social systems. The Bem Sex Role Inventory (BSRI) and the Personal Attributes Questionnaire (PAQ), also used in the study reported here, have been constructed on the basis of the dimension of "instrumentalism" vs. "expressivity" as originally developed by Parsons and Bales in their sociological context (Spence & Buckner, 1995, p. 108). Still other scales try to measure a mix of traits, behaviors, self-assessments, social desirability, and the like. Only recently, a theoretical effort has been made to dishinguish all the different aspects related to masculinity and femininity but not necessarily correlating nicely (Betz, 1995, pp. 120, 127-130; Spence & Buckner, 1995, p. 119; Spence, 1985, pp. 71, 75). In addition, scales which were developed for measuring femininity, masculinity, and androgyny in one context were also transferred to different social and cultural contexts, like from the United States to Germany, Mexico, Peru, and elsewhere (Betz, 1995, pp. 126, 137f).

The tools also were validated, at least to some extent, in these new contexts. Nevertheless, "culture" remained in these studies a more or less undefined category, a catch-all or residual. And yet the authors of such studies undertook many pains attempting to arrive at meaningful conclusions from their unclear and contradictory data by using some of the most sophisticated and refined statistical procedures, before finding out that first of all a viable theory is needed.

These substantial, methodological, and theoretical problems had been worked through by the authors of this chapter in an attempt to replicate a study on relations between femininity, masculinity, and achievement motivation comparing students of economics at Marburg University, Germany, and the Universidad del Pacífico in Lima, Peru. The only possibility to advance seemed to be the use of concepts from general systems theory and sociocybernetics in order to arrive at a clear theoretical framework for cross-cultural comparisons in the field of androgyny studies.

A first important premise for such a framework is the postulate of the unity of science, which is basic to systems theory. This implies that after all there is only one science to investigate all cultures. Even if at present we may not yet have the appropriate theories and tools available, the unity of science means that cross-cultural comparisons and research are possible in principle.

Several other premises which appear necessary and useful for a sociocybernetic approach to cultural, social, and psychological systems have been elaborated elsewhere in some detail (Hornung, 1995):

1. Everything which is the case, is the case within the time-space continuum of relativity theory. The elementary component of the space-time continuum is the event. Structure and process are derived categories. They designate particular kinds of sequences of events.
2. All sequences of events follow the irreversible arrow of time.
3. Basic ontological categories (i.e., the "substance" of the universe of events) are the classical couple of matter/energy and, with the advent of information physics, information.
4. The empirical world is a structure of emergent hierarchical layers, reaching from the physical to the social and the cultural/informational.
5. The theoretical world or a theoretical conceptualization of the empirical world is a structure of layers in two dimensions:
    A. Aggregation (i.e., system, subsystem, etc. [empirical and theoretical objects])
    B. Abstraction (i.e., classes, subclasses, etc. [theoretical objects only])
6. The psychological system is an information processing system in which we have to distinguish at least three major subsystems: cognitive, normative, and affective.

These subsystems work intimately together to process information and to produce decisions and ultimately (social) actions.

The individual cognitive system corresponds most directly to the idea of information processing by individuals. The concept of cognitive systems (Axelrod, 1976; Bossel et al., 1982) implies information and knowledge, just like the "cultural stuctures" of Lévi-Strauss (1958, 1973, 1962). This concept is, however, more flexible, richer in content, and avoids the problematic connotations of "structures." Moreover, it can be used at both the individual level of the psychological system and the collective level (e.g. of groups, organizations, and societies).

In a sociocybernetic context, therefore, and taking into account that information is a basic ontological category, "culture" need not remain a vague and ambiguous concept. Rather it can be defined as a collective, intergenerational, cognitive (and normative) system (Hornung, 1995), as "the information, i.e., experience, knowledge, beliefs, norms and values, contained in the collective memory of a group or population that have been collected and retained in the course of the history of that group (or system). It is an encompassing system of knowledge and symbols which is passed from generation to generation by means of socialization" (p. 870).

Seen in this way, culture is a system of symbols and information, including values, which constitutes the core of collective cognitive systems at different levels of a society. Depending on the case, such cultures at lower levels of aggregation can be considered as subcultures (e.g., of particular social classes, groups, or also organizations).

THE PROBLEM OF UNDERSTANDING

Postulating the Unity of Science—along with the existence of different individual (psychological) and social (cultural) cognitive systems and with the claim to be able to make valid cross-cultural comparisons—implies the assertion that communication and understanding between such systems, as well as by scientists as external observers, is possible. From a naïve point of view there is certainly no problem. At a closer look, however, several developments in the social sciences and humanities have clearly shown that the possibility of understanding meaning or semantics—two concepts which also play a central role in Luhmann's version of systems theory (Luhmann, 1987, especially pp. 224, 382)—and hence communication, is not self-evident.

In this section, the following developments are described: hermeneutics which, in theology and philosophy, is about two thousand years old and has recently become fashionable in sociology; cultural relativism in cultural anthropology; the work on Emics and Etics in linguistics and cultural anthropology; cognitive mapping in cognitive science and systems theory; and finally autopoiesis in biology and autopoietic systems theory.

The Problem of Hermeneutics

The classical problem of hermeneutics is the problem of understanding and interpreting texts. It deals with the problem of finding out "what the author really wanted to say with this text." Sometimes there is also the question "What is the objective meaning of a text,"—for example, according to "objective hermeneutics" as developed by Oevermann (Reichertz, 1997). "Text" in this context can have a very wide meaning (Hitzler & Honer, 1997b, pp. 8-12). In this respect, there are two particular problems. First, the authors of, say, biblical texts have passed away long since. We cannot ask them. Second, we have good reasons to assume that the context (i.e., the historical and cultural situation in which those texts were written), was very different from what we know from our contemporary world.

Hitzler and Honer (1997a) give an overview of hermeneutic techniques currently in use in empirical social research. Hermeneutics proposes three basic methods to overcome these problems:

1. Iterative study of the text in its own right, until the reader obtains some understanding by empathy and intuitive understanding, "reliving" the suspected situation of the author and maybe relating it to personal experience.
2. The Delphi-method—asking other experts about the text and finding consensus.
3. Careful study of the context and environment of the text—of other texts permitting comparisons, of other information about the author and his or her work, and the historical and cultural situation in which it was written.

The first method relies on "introspection," the subjective belief and conviction of the reader to have understood the text correctly. The second method resorts to "intersubjectivity," which, if combined with proper scientific methods, is perfectly acceptable for producing reliable results. This at least to the extent that one follows Thomas S. Kuhn's change of paradigm from scientific objectivity to scientific intersubjectivity (Kuhn, 1962). The third method works along the same lines—that is, to exclude possible interpretations as contradictory and unlikely on the basis of a broader and more detailed picture of the intellectual and social environment of the text. The most promising strategy, of course, would be to combine the three methods. This would make an erroneous interpretation relatively unlikely, but still the readers could not be perfectly sure "what the author really meant."

Hermeneutics is clearly aware of the basic difficulties of understanding and proposes a solution based on careful analysis of context and consensus.

The Problem of Cultural Relativism

The issue of cultural relativism, in the wake of the school of Franz Boas in the 1920s (Benedict, 1959; Tennekes, 1971; Hildebrandt, 1978), raised the question to what extent cultures, conceived as coherent systems, are unique—that is, unique responses of human populations to the challenge of how to organize their life. The uniqueness implied that different cultures could not be comparable after all. At a more philosophical or also ideological level it also implied that each culture, being a unique and workable way of life for its respective population, has the same status as any other culture. It has to be considered just as "good" as any other culture without being placed in some sequence of "progress" or evolution.

Taken to the last consequence, this position, ethically and morally desirable as it might be, would mean to give up the postulate of the Unity of Science. Strictly speaking, and also as a consequence of Kuhn's change of paradigm towards "intersubjectivity," no science can be free of culture. Consequent cultural relativism would therefore imply that each culture could and should have its own science which cannot be valid in another culture.

The important issue for the present purpose is, how a member of another culture, an outsider, can grasp the insider's view and understand the insider. This involves three problems:

1. How can the outsider (the anthropologist) understand the insider?
2. How and to what extent, if at all, is the insider's view of one culture comparable to the insider's view of another culture?
3. If the anthropologist can grasp the insider's view of a given culture, how can he communicate his findings to the other members of his own scientific community?

Cultural relativism itself points towards two solutions to the problem of understanding. Only one of them, however, is really acceptable from its own point of view. One solution is to "understand" only superficially and to interpret what the others are saying as in a children's game "... let's play..., but of course we know better!" We might say this is the ethnocentric approach of playing the role of the other. The second approach is "taking" the role of the other—that is, submerging oneself in the other culture and "going native." By anthropology this is expressed in terms of transculturation and acculturation of individuals. In this process true and deep understanding can be gained, but it also implies at least a partial loss of the culture of origin. The more this second solution to understanding is taken, however, the more it aggravates the problem of communication with one's own original scientific community.

The Problem of Emics and Etics

The three questions of cultural relativism along with the two strategies proposed for a solution have been brought much closer to an answer and to a clear theoretical and methodological conceptualization by the concepts of etics and emics. These terms, which have Greek roots and are derived from phon*emics* and phon*etics*, were developed by Kenneth L. Pike. He first introduced these concepts in 1954 in the field of linguistics (Headland, 1990, see p. 15). Marvin Harris (1964, 1968) then expanded their use to wider applications in cultural anthropology and the study of the development and evolution of societies and cultures. It is in particular this latter approach which is of interest and value in the present context.

Previously we have talked about "insiders vs. outsiders." Although this distinction is useful, it does not permit the precision required for an adequate theory and methodology, the way the concepts of "emics" and "etics" do, although there is also terminological confusion about emics, etics, and related terms (Harris, 1990a, pp. 50-52; Headland, 1990, pp. 15, 20-21). Emics and etics are defined by Harris (1990a) as follows:

Emic statements refer to logico-empirical systems whose phenomenal distinctions or "things" are built up out of contrasts and discriminations significant, meaningful, real, accurate, or in some other fashion regarded as appropriate by the actors themselves. An emic statement can be falsified if it can be shown that it contradicts the cognitive calculus by which relevant actors judge that entities are similar or different, real, meaningful, significant, or in some other sense "appropriate" or "acceptable".... Etic statements depend upon phenomenal distinctions judged appropriate by the community of scientific observers. Etic statements cannot be falsified if they do not conform to the actor's notion of what is significant, real, meaningful, or appropriate. (p. 48)

The concepts of emics and etics are already considered as an important contribution to anthropology and related sciences in their present form (Headland, 1990, p. 17). Harris (1990a, p. 50) states about their use that "it is absolutely essential to the success of a nomothetic science of sociocultural systems." The argument to be supported in this chapter is that the use of these concepts will develop their full potential in the context of sociocybernetics.

In addition to the implicit systemic character, it is important to point out that emics-etics is not a characteristic of the object of investigation (i.e., not an ontological property), but a characteristic of the methodological access to an object of investigation and of the knowledge such an access produces. This means it is an epistemological characteristic.

The distinction of emics and etics results in four different kinds of descriptions which also reflect the ontological categories of matter/energy and information (Harris, 1990a, p. 53, originally developed in Harris, 1979): emics of mental life; emics of behavior stream; etics of mental life; etics of behavior stream; where "mental life" is thinking and mental behavior, and "behavior stream" is bodily activity and verbal behavior.

In analogy to the problem of translation between two languages (Feleppa, 1990, p. 116), the understanding of another person's thinking and mental processes can be considered correct or successful to the extent that the persons involved succeed to coordinate their (manifest and verbal) behavior and actions and succeed to produce effective interpersonal behavior.

In concluding we can say that the concepts of emics and etics are also applicable to thinking and mental behavior. While making explicit the problems of understanding, they permit us to formulate possibilities of understanding explicitely covering thinking, mental behavior, verbal behavior, and physical action. In this respect, the concepts of emics and etics go beyond classical hermeneutics. Also, in this approach understanding is based on context, coherence, and consensus. In addition, however, practical success of behavior and behavior coordination plays a crucial role.

From Etics to Emics and Back

If one expands the perspective of investigation from components and elements of beliefs and cultures to entire systems, it is hardly possible to avoid the concept of "function" which is a key concept of sociocybernetics (Luhmann, 1974; Thompson et al., 1990, pp. 104-107). It permits us to establish an aspect under which otherwise uncomparable things do become comparable, in case they are equivalent in providing the respective function (Luhmann, 1973, pp. 236-256). Berry (1990, p. 89) states that "it has been suggested by Frijda and Jahoda ... quite independently of Goldschmidt ... that functional equivalence is a prerequisite for the cross-cultural comparison of behavior. ... Without this equivalence, it is suggested, no valid cross-cultural behavioral comparisons may be made."

Berry (1990, p. 88) indicates that comparing behaviors from "different behavior settings" is not really possible. This problem, which is at the root of cultural relativism, can be resolved in analogy to the corresponding linguistic problem, if function and functional equivalence are used in a way similar to semantics. If behavior and behavior settings correspond to the literal surface of sentences and their contexts, functions can be conceived similar to the deeper semantic meaning of such literal sentences, expressing what behavior is "really" about. Given functions can be performed also by certain other, functionally equivalent behaviors. Apart from functional equivalence, referring primarily to what Harris calls the behavior stream, and conceptual equivalence, referring to meanings in mental life of the observed or of the observers (i.e., of scientific concepts), a third equivalence is necessary if we aim at cross-cultural comparison in terms of quantitative studies. This is metric equivalence of the tools of measurement used in the cultures to be compared (Berry, 1990, p. 88; Hui & Triandis, 1985, pp. 133-135).

On the basis of such considerations Berry proposes a three-step procedure for cross-cultural research (Berry, 1990, italics in the original):

The initial step is usually taken armed with a concept or instrument rooted in the researcher's own culture (one that is really an emic concept or instrument for that culture) but that is used as an etic orientation in two senses: It is assumed by the researcher to be a valid basis for *studying* a phenomenon in another culture (the tools for this being brought in from outside for that purpose); and it is assumed by the researcher to be a valid basis for *comparing* the phenomenon in the two cultures. This pair of assumptions about one's own initial position led Berry to refer to the approach as an *imposed etic* one.

Unless one subscribes to total subjectivity in science ... then a researcher is in a position to do *emic* work. It involves setting aside one's own cultural baggage ... Once this is accomplished, the researchers have two conceptual systems at their disposal, and the act of comparison demands that they be brought into touch with each other. If they remain totally mutually exclusive, there is no possibility of comparison. However, if there are some features in common, comparison *is* possible, but only for these shared features; the common aspects for which comparison takes place were indicated by the term *derived* etic. (pp. 90-91)

This means it is possible to move back and forth between etic and emic analysis, as also Pike and Harris agree (Harris, 1990b, p. 77). In the course of such a movement from *imposed etics* to *emics* and back to *derived etics* the researcher can identify those components in two or more cultures which these cultures do have in common. Such common components can be compared also quantitatively, if in addition to their *functional equivalence* and *conceptual equivalence* their *metric equivalence* can be established.

The Problem of Cognitive Systems

Cognitive systems in a wider sense (Hornung, 1982, 1990; Hornung & Adilova, 1997) include cognitions about facts, concepts about norms and values, as well as cognitions concerning connections between facts and norms or values. The latter correspond in cognitive systems analysis to what is usually called attitudes in psychology. In a more narrow sense, the term "cognitive system" may refer to the cognitions about facts only. At any rate, cognitive systems at this level of abstraction are neither etic nor emic, but simply subjective. They consist of concepts and relations between concepts which together represent the view of a reality as seen by some actor (i.e., the actor's cognitive map). To the extent that individuals constitute collective actors like groups and share their cognitions, we can talk of collective cognitive systems. Culture as defined above can be conceived as a particular type of cognitive system. That emic and etic analysis in cultural anthropology after all aims at this collective level above the individual is indicated by Reiss (1990, p. 182).

The cognitive systems approach has been widely used in Artificial Intelligence for the construction of knowledge bases and expert systems. In this field, however, the same problems of understanding as between human beings and their psychological systems appear, when the different paradigms involved in constructing certain kinds of Artifical Intelligence (AI) systems—e.g., expert systems, are taken into consideration. The first paradigm is mapping domain knowledge—knowledge about a particular topic. Understanding the system is no problem, as it simply represents the knowledge as stated by a human expert— the expert's cognitive map. A difficulty may lie, however, in the quantity of information which needs to be traced in order to "understand" a result produced by such a system.

In many cases the explicit knowledge of a human expert is not sufficient to reproduce the conclusions this expert would draw. Therefore modelling developed as a second paradigm for the construction of expert systems. This second paradigm includes the implicit and tacit knowledge of the human expert. It now implies an observer who knows the human expert better than the human expert himself, like a psychologist analyzing her client. In this case there is a problem of understanding between modeller and human expert, as well as a double problem of validity. The first question is whether the model constructed corresponds to the functioning of the human expert modelled. If that is the case, a second problem is whether the knowledge of the human expert corresponds to reality. The user of the expert system does not only have to follow and accept the knowledge of the human expert as it is mapped, but also the constructed part and the assumptions made by the modeller, which may be more or less implicit (Studer et al., 1999).

A third paradigm, finally, could be called the generative one. Here aspects of learning and creativity are included, thus bringing expert systems even closer to reality but also closer to the same level of incomprehensibility we have between human beings.

This means, on the one hand, that the cognitive systems approach as applied to technical systems encounters the same ambiguity with regard to understanding/no understanding as the other approaches outlined. On the other hand, however, the concept of cognitive systems indicates—and the computer implementation of cognitive systems requires—a well-defined and specified structure (e.g., as a semantic network). It is this kind of specified structure which is important in the present context.

Combining the idea of semantic networks with the cognitive systems approach, we obtain a conceptual framework for differentiating literal semantic meaning, deep meaning, and contextual meaning within a system-subsystem hierarchy of contexts.

The Problem of Autopoiesis

As autopoiesis has been widely discussed in both the tradition of Maturana and in sociology in the context of Luhmann's theories, a few remarks shall suffice here. Autopoietic systems are self-reproductive systems based on circular processes. They are operationally and, at least in Maturana's and Varela's tradition, informationally closed systems. A key sentence for autopoietic theory is that "anything said is said by an observer" (Maturana, 1980, p. 8). In a way, this implies that real understanding is not possible, only something like the kind of superficial ethnocentric observation as mentioned in the context of cultural relativism. However, like some other theories, autopoietic theory admits the possibility of some kind of deeper understanding. This is essentially based on the phenomenon of practical success, which already has been pointed out as an important criterion in the context of emics and etics.

Autopoietic theory admits basically three mechanisms of openness which in some way convey information without "real" information exchange. These are, first, *structural coupling*, which is a kind of exchange of independent actions or triggering events between two systems, which in the long run lead to structural change and mutual adaptation of the systems involved. A second mechanism according to Luhmann is *interpenetration*, which is a special, very stable kind of structural coupling between two systems which are not only interacting but mutually dependent on each other, like psychological and social systems. Finally there is *self-observation* registering practical success and failure of the system. In a most radical way, success and failure mean for an autopoietic system either to be able to continue autopoiesis or to disintegrate.

All three mechanisms of openness permit in a way an "understanding" of what is going on, but only by testing self-generated information against the practical success and failure of actions taken. Although understanding in autopoietic theory seems to be somewhat impoverished, autopoietic theory goes beyond the other approaches by explicitly linking it to an evolutionary context in the case of structural coupling.

THE PROCESS OF UNDERSTANDING

The previous analyses in very different fields show that understanding is difficult but, at least to some extent, possible. The elements and tools for understanding as proposed by these different approaches can serve as a basis for a methodology of cross-cultural research. These are:

Procedures: iterative processes; intuition; analogy; peer consensus (social or scientific context); inference from verbal or behavioral data and artefacts
Methods of Data Collection: communication, reports; observation; interaction
Levels of Understanding: literal meaning; semantic meaning; contextual meaning
Control of Understanding: contexts and hierarchies of contexts (systems)
Criteria for Correct Understanding: back-translation; successful coordination of action/behavior; a culture "works"; structural coupling; interpenetration; practical success; evolutionary success.

TOWARDS A METHODOLOGY OF CROSS-CULTURAL RESEARCH

Considering the serious theoretical deficits mentioned in the beginning, cross-cultural research concerning human behavior and hence psychology in general and the issue of femininity and masculinity in particular, requires both a better and more explicitly specified model of the psychological system and its relevant environment. It also needs a more differentiated view of femininity/ masculinity.

Several aspects of gender have to be clearly distinguished, if meaningful empirical cross-cultural comparisons are to be made. The main aspects are those of identity, those of self, and those of social roles. While identity can be considered in a way as a culture-free introspective experience of the individual (cf. Erikson's (1966, 1968) concept of ego-identity), aspects related to self are psychological-cognitive and in their contents strongly influenced by culture. Role-related aspects are clearly sociocultural. Although roles do not concern identity in its proper sense, in literature often the term "identity" is used nevertheless referring to role aspects (Spence, 1985, p. 81).

Gender identity is defined by Spence "as a fundamental existential sense of one's maleness or femaleness, an acceptance of one's gender on a psychological level that, with rare exceptions, parallels and complements awareness and acceptance of one's biological sex" (Spence, 1985, p. 79f).

Taking into account the issues of etics and emics as well as the characteristics of cognitive systems and the model of personality as outlined above, the question of what is femininity/masculinity as the basis for the construction of measuring scales has to be differentiated into three research questions on androgyny:

1. What *is* femininity/masculinity the way the individual experiences it? (experienced psychological gender)
2. What is femininity/masculinity the way it *should* be and is *accepted* by the individual? (desirable and accepted psychological gender)
3. What is femininity/masculinity the way society prescribes it according to *cultural* definitions? (culturally defined gender stereotypes and roles)

Furthermore, *gender identity* has to be distinguished from psychological gender and cultural stereotypes and roles.

Cross-cultural research requires comparisons of individuals, groups, or cultures with regard to these aspects. Two concrete individuals (or objects), however, are never fully comparable, not least because of their systemic properties. They become comparable only to the extent that they are not unique (i.e., to the extent that they have properties in common). Usually this implies abstraction, which is precisely one of the strengths of sociocybernetics and systems theory. At an abstract level, according to orientation theory (Bossel, 1996a, pp. 195-204; 1996b, pp. 153-164; 1998; 1999), each living system has to resolve the same basic and universal problems. To do this, it has to perform a series of functions. At an abstract level (metabolism, information processing, etc.) these functions may be considered the same across systems. At a concrete level, however, they are very likely to be different. To perform a function, mechanisms (i.e., combinations of structures and processes) are necessary. To perform a specific function, however, quite different but functionally equivalent mechanisms can be used.

Since in the present case the interest is a comparison related to a theoretical concept at a lower level of abstraction (i.e., femininity/masculinity resp. psychological gender) this concept has to be included into the framework. Below the level of the basic problems/orientors, this results in a sequence of functions; theoretical constructs (masculinity/femininity) in their functional context; and functionally equivalent mechanisms (to be operationalized by means of items).

In cross-cultural comparisons, which in addition intend an emic analysis of cognitive systems and cultures, the dimension of concepts has to be considered too. In fact, taking up some of the ideas of the etics-emics discussion, a parallel sequence appears:
1. Contextual meaning (context of other concepts, values, attitudes, references to other concepts) ---> Semantic Network
2. Semantic meaning (concept, definition) ---> Semantic Space
3. Literal meaning (vocabulary, dictionary) ---> Concept Definition

With regard to concepts, comparability and the possibility to clearly identify differences and similarities in semantic meanings can be nicely established, if an appropriate semantic space can be defined. Such a semantic space consists of a set of dimensions representing the relevant properties of the concepts investigated. Different concepts or the "same" concept in two different languages can then be compared with regard to their similarity and distance on the different dimensions. If no comparable concept exists in the other language, at least the place in the semantic space can be indicated where it would be needed.

The contextual meaning can be analyzed by means of semantic networks or cognitive maps indicating the connections between different concepts. Creating semantic networks for two different cultures may reveal that a concept which is the same according to its location in semantic space has a quite different position in the semantic networks of the two cultures. Yet also two different concepts may have the same position in both networks—that is, they are "functionally" equivalent.

This means that in the case of androgyny research it would be necessary to find out whether the concepts of femininity and masculinity in the German and Peruvian context are really the same in a joint semantic space. In a second step their relations to other concepts would need to be investigated. This would reveal to what extent these connections are the same or different in Peru and Germany. On the basis of such information it would be possible to judge the conceptual equivalence of the concepts in both cultures.

Only if the conceptual equivalence is sufficient, functional equivalence can be analyzed meaningfully and functional equivalences can be identified. In that case, the conditions for meaningful cross-cultural comparison would be fulfilled.

THE PROCESS OF CROSS-CULTURAL RESEARCH

In an overall fashion, the process of cross-cultural research should follow the sequence proposed by Berry (1990) as discussed above. The previous discussions, however, have also shown that, at least in the case of psychological research on androgyny involving emic aspects, a purely psychological approach is not feasible. Cross-cultural research of this type requires a psychological approach complemented by cognitive systems analysis, functional analysis, and a cultural anthropological access. Such a combination, for which sociocybernetics provides an ideal framework and for which the elements have been developed in the previous sections, permits an effective and productive use of the etic and emic perspectives. As we have argued, these are indispensable for meaningful cross-cultural research.

In the following, the steps of such a process are listed.

The Process of Cross-Cultural Research on Androgyny

1. Selection of a group of individuals representative for culture A.
2. Selection of those individuals scoring high on gender identity.
3. Investigation of what traits make up their psychological gender.
4. Investigation of the sociocultural concepts.
5. Synthesizing the emic view to a still culturally specific etic view.
6. Development of an etic concept of femininity/masculinity.

7. Transfer to the international scientific discourse and international cognitive system.
8. Development of a preliminary etic concept (Imposed Etics).
9. Establishing conceptual equivalence with concepts of culture B (semantic space).
10. Establishing cognitive functional equivalence (semantic network).
11. Investigation of the relevant part of the sociocultural field (functional sociocultural context of the construct femininity/masculinity).
12. Operationalization of functional core concepts.
13. Specification of items (not necessarily literal but functional equivalence).
14. Emic study culture B.
15. Generalization into cross-cultural concepts, interpretations, and theory (Derived Etics).
16. Establishing metric equivalence for statistical comparisons.

The development of the procedure proposed here was guided by the concern of being able to provide a sound methodological basis for statistical computations and comparisons in cross-cultural research on androgyny. The interest in statistical methods is apparently a key concern of virtually all researchers in this field. Yet it is also a concern limiting the perspective in a dangerous way. As we have tried to show, by sophisticated psychological and sociocultural systems analysis, it should be possible to identify segments of cognitive systems and sociocultural systems which are similar or roughly the same in different cultures. In this case statistical analysis is legitimate. But as a consequence of the previous efforts in identifying similarities, statistical differences cannot really be expected anymore. Under these conditions statistics can be used to confirm similarity, hardly to analyze differences. If there are differences in the results, these can be due either to residuals not analyzed (i.e., factors and functions which have not been included in the scientific model used and which may constitute undetected cultural differences) or they can be due to faults in the measuring instruments or the research approach. If both sources of differences can be excluded, such statistical differences still remain quantitative only, while cultural differences are likely to be qualitative according to all that cultural anthropology and ethnology have to tell us. This problem is probably the more serious the smaller are the "core areas" investigated.

This amounts to the caution that sophisticated statistical procedures should be used only in combination with an appropriate and explicit theoretical approach and only after the field of investigation has become clear and well-structured by a more "ethnographic" type of qualitative and descriptive research. Such research provides excellent tools not only to investigate and document "universalities" but in particular cultural differences within a joint etic framework.

The overall procedure developed here can be understood as a set of hermeneutic circles. A first circle in the culture of origin, a second circle in the other culture to be compared, and both circles together integrated into a third overall circle from etics to emics and back again to etics.

NOTE

1. Some authors suggest to reserve "sex" for biological and "gender" for psychological differences (cf. footnote in Spence & Buckner, 1995, p. 105).

REFERENCES

Axelrod, R. (Ed.). (1976). *Structures of Decision, The Cognitive Maps of Political Elites.* Princeton, NJ: Princeton University Press.

Benedict, R. (1959). *Patterns of Culture.* Boston: Houghton Mifflin.

Berry, J.W. (1990). Imposed Etics, Emics, and Derived Etics, Their Conceptual and Operational Status in Cross-Cultural Psychology. In T.N. Headland, K.L. Pike & M. Harris (Eds.), *Emics and Etics* (pp. 84-99). London: Sage.

Betz, N.E. (1995). Gender-Related Individual Differences Variables, New Concepts, Methods, and Measures. In D. Lubinski & R. Dawis (Eds.), *Assessing Individual Differences in Human Behavior* (pp. 119-143). Palo Alto, CA: Davis Black.

Bossel, H. (1996a). Deriving Indicators of Sustainable Development. *Environmental Modelling and Assessment. 1,* 193-218.

Bossel, H. (1996b). Ecosystems and Society, Implications for Sustainable Development. *World Futures, 47,* 143-213.

Bossel, H. (1998). *Earth at a Crossroads: Paths to a Sustainable Future.* Cambridge: Cambridge University Press.

Bossel, H. (1999). *Indicators for Sustainable Development, Theory, Method, Applications*, A Report to the Balaton Group. Winnipeg, Canada: International Institute for Sustainable Development.

Bossel, H., Hornung, B.R. & Müller-Reissmann, K.F. (1982). *Kognitive Systemanalyse.* 4 vols. Hannover, Germany: Institut für angewandte Systemforschung und Prognose.

Erikson, E.H. (1966). *Identität und Lebenszyklus; Drei Aufsätze (Orig.: Identity and the Life Cycle),* Frankfurt/Main: Suhrkamp.

Erikson, E.H. (1968). *Identity, Youth and Crisis.* London: Faber & Faber.

Feleppa, R. (1990). Emic Analysis and the Limits of Cognitive Diversity. In T.H. Headland, K.L. Pike & M. Harris (Eds.), *Emics and Etics* (pp. 100-119). London: Sage.

Friedan, B. (1997). *Beyond Gender: The New Politics of Work and Family.* Washington, DC: The Woodrow Wilson Center Press.

Harris, M. (1964). *The Nature of Cultural Things.* New York: Random House.

Harris, M. (1968). *The Rise of Anthropological Theory.* New York: Thomas Y. Crowell.

Harris, M. (1979). *Cultural Materialism: The Struggle for a Science of Culture.* New York: Vintage Books.

Harris, M. (1990a). Emics and Etics Revisited. In T.N. Headland, K.L. Pike & M. Harris (Eds.), *Emics and Etics* (pp. 48-61). London: Sage.

Harris, M. (1990b). Harris's Reply to Pike. In T.N. Headland, K.L. Pike & M. Harris (Eds.), *Emics and Etics.* London: Sage.

Headland, T.N. (1990). Introduction: A Dialogue Between Kenneth Pike and Marvin Harris on Emics and Etics. In T.N. Headland, K.L. Pike & M. Harris (Eds.), *Emics and Etics* (pp. 13-27). London: Sage.

Headland, T.N., Pike, K.L. & Harris, M. (Eds.). (1990). *Emics and Etics, The Insider/Outsider Debate.* London: Sage.

Hildebrandt, H.J. (1978). Kritische Bemerkungen zum Kulturrelativismus und seiner Rezeption in der deutschen Ethnologie. *Kölner Zeitschrift für Soziologie und Sozialpsychologie 30*, 136-157.

Hitzler, R. & Honer, A. (Eds.). (1997a). *Sozialwissenschaftliche Hermeneutik.* Opladen: Leske + Budrich.

Hitzler, R. & Honer, A. (1997b). Hermeneutik in der deutschsprachigen Soziologie heute. In R. Hitzler & A. Honer (Eds.), *Sozialwissenschaftliche Hermeneutik* (pp. 7-27). Opladen: Leske + Budrich.

Hornung, B.R. (1982). Qualitative Systems Analysis as a Tool for Development Studies. In R.F. Geyer & J. van der Zouwen (Eds.), *Dependence and Inequality* (pp. 187-219). Oxford: Pergamon Press.

Hornung, B.R. (1990). The Construction of Knowledge Based Systems for the Analysis of Development Problems in Health Care Systems. In F. Geyer & J. van der Zouwen (Eds.), *Self-Referencing in Social Systems* (pp. 115-141). Salinas, CA: Intersystems Publications.

Hornung, B.R. (1995). Sociocultural Evolution. In *Association Internationale de Cybernétique* (Ed.), 14th International Congress on Cybernetics, Namur (Belgium), August 21-25, 1995, Proceedings, pp. 867-872. Namur: Association Internationale de Cybernétique.

Hornung, B.R. & Adilova, F.T. (1997). Conceptual Modelling for Technology Assessment of IT Systems, Smart Cards and Health Information Systems. In F. Geyer (Ed.), *Sociocybernetics: Complexity, Dynamics and Emergence in Social Science, Special Issue, Kybernetes 26* (6/7), 787-800.

Hornung, C. (1999). *Die Beziehung zwischen Androgynie und Leistungsmotivation, Ein interkultureller Vergleich*, Marburg: Fachbereich Psychologie, Universität Marburg.

Hui, C.H. & Triandis, H.C. (1985). Measurement in Cross-Cultural Psychology. *Journal of Cross-Cultural Psychology, 16*, 131-153.

Kuhn, T.S. (1962). *The Structure of Scientific Revolutions.* Chicago: University of Chicago Press.

Lévy-Strauss, C. (1958, 1973). *Anthropologie structurale*, 2 vols. Paris: Plon.

Lévy-Strauss, C. (1962). *La pensée sauvage.* Paris: Plon.

Luhmann, N. (1973). *Zweckbegriff und Systemrationalität.* Frankfurt/Main: Suhrkamp Verlag.

Luhmann, N. (1974). Funktionale Methode und Systemtheorie. In N. Luhmann, *Soziologische Aufklärung.* Bd. 1, (pp. 31-53). Opladen: Westdeutscher Verlag.

Luhmann, N. (1987). *Soziale Systeme.* Frankfurt/Main: Suhrkamp Verlag.

Maturana, H.R. (1980). Biology of Cognition. In H.R. Maturana & F.J. Varela (Eds.), *Autopoiesis and Cognition.* Dordrecht, Netherlands: D. Reidel Publishing Company.

Reichertz, J. (1997). Objektive Hermeneutik. In R. Hitzler & A. Honer (Eds.), *Sozialwissenschaftliche Hermeneutik* (pp. 31-55). Opladen: Leske + Budrich.

Reiss, N. (1990). The Emic-Etic Distinction as Applied to Language. In T.N. Headland, K.L. Pike & M. Harris (Eds.), *Emics and Etics* (pp. 168-183). London: Sage.

Spence, J.T. (1985). Gender Identity and Its Implications for the Concepts of Masculinity and Femininity. In T.B. Sanderegger (Ed.), *Pychology and Gender* (pp. 59-95). Lincoln: University of Nebraska Press.

Spence, J.T. & Buckner, C. (1995). Masculinity and Femininity, Defining the Undefinable. In P.J. Kalbfleisch & M.J. Cody (Eds.), *Gender, Power, and Communication in Human Relationships* (pp. 105-138). Hillsdale, NJ: Erlbaum.

Studer, R., Fensel, D., Decker, S. & Benjamins, V.R. (1999). Knowledge Engineering, Survey and Future Directions. In F. Puppe (Ed.), *Knowledge-based Systems*. Vienna: Springer. Also <http://www.aifb.uni-karlsruhe.de/WBS/publications/pub99.html>.

Tennekes, J. (1971). *Anthropology, Relativism and Method*. Assen: Van Gorcum.

Thompson, M., Ellis, R. & Wildavsky, A. (1990). *Cultural Theory*. Boulder, CO: Westview Press.

Chapter 11

SOCIAL DIFFERENTIATION AS THE UNFOLDING OF DIMENSIONS OF SOCIAL SYSTEMS

Jürgen Klüver & Jörn Schmidt

THE PROBLEM: SOCIAL EVOLUTION AND THE GEOMETRY OF SOCIAL SPACES

Social network and group analysis have shown frequently that it is possible in several ways to define topological and metrical relations within social systems. One approach is to define *social distance* between two persons as the number of intermediating persons the first two persons need to get into contact with each other (Milgram, 1967; Freeman, 1989). By replacing the concept of "person" with that of "social role," it is easy to conceptualize a metrical space of interactions between persons who are acting according to their specific roles and to define the distance between roles as the number of necessary social contacts with several intermediating roles. This definition constitutes a metrical space, as can be easily demonstrated, and because each metrical space of course is a topological space too, we get this way a topology of social interactions by which it is possible to define mathematically concepts like social nearness, degrees of social cohesion, and so forth.

Another possibility of defining the topological concept of social proximity goes back to the classical definitions of group memberships of Homans (1951) and defines, roughly speaking, the degree of social proximity by the number of contacts a person has with members of different groups (Freeman, 1993). Thus, an individual belongs to one group if its number of contacts to the members of this group is greater than the number of contacts to members of other groups; topologically speaking the members of the first group are nearer to our individual than the members of other groups. By generalizing this concept one obviously gets a topology of social nearness defined by the mean number of contacts to the members of different groups. Which one of these two approaches is more suited is of course a question of the particular problems one has to deal with. In this chapter we prefer the first definition.

Accordingly, it can be demonstrated that the concept of geometrical dimensions can be introduced into social systems theory so that social systems can be viewed as a network of rule-governed interactions which constitute a space of interactions with one, two, or three dimensions. It is important to note that dimensions of social space do not mean the dimensions of the physical space in which the different persons interact, but mathematical characteristics of a *social* space. In this chapter we refer only to the concept of dimension as it is used in vector algebra and physics; the topological concept of dimension is more complicated and not necessary for our purposes.

In the theory of vector spaces, the number of dimensions of a space is defined as the number of *linear independent* unit vectors which are needed to express each vector of the space in terms of linear combinations of the unit vectors. When this rather abstract concept is translated, for example, into the well-known (physical) space of our daily perceptions, we see that we perceive this space as one with three dimensions because there are three *independent* options to describe each perception: left - right, in front – behind, and below - above. Thus, the reason why we think of physical space as three-dimensional lies in the fact that we can describe each experience in terms of the three options: something is (left of, behind, above) me. Obviously these options are independent from another as it is not possible to define one by combinations of the other two. As we usually have to add the concept of time for any complete description of an experience, we have to introduce a four dimensional "space" of physical space and time: Something happened to me (several hours ago, left, behind, above). The number of dimensions of a "space of experiences" is then nothing else than the number of independent options one has to take into consideration for a *complete* description of any experience.[1]

Accordingly, the number of dimensions of a social space of interactions must be defined as the number of independent options which are needed to describe each *social* experience. This may be done of course in different ways; little children, for example, live probably in a social space of one dimension as they have just the option "parents versus not parents." As we are looking for general descriptions of social experiences (i.e., manners of description which are not dependent on the particularities of specific social groups or cultures), it seems reasonable to use general theories of societies, namely the well-known theory of social evolution, as the originating of different forms of social differentiation: social segments (i.e., families), social strata (e.g., classes), and social functional systems (Luhmann, 1984; Habermas, 1981).

These three different levels of social differentiation constitute three independent options for describing each social experience, especially each social role another person holds: "belonging to one's own group" versus "strange" (segmentary differentiation), "below" versus "above" (stratificatory differentiation), and "action role" versus "client role" (functional differentiation). These options are clearly independent as it is not possible to substitute one by a combination of the others; they are complete in the sense that each other person can be described *socially* completely in terms of these options. The completeness cannot be demonstrated in a strict sense in this chapter; Luhmann (e.g., 1984) and Habermas (1981) deal with this question rather thoroughly.

As these options constitute dimensions of the social space of interactions—of a social system, see below—we can represent each level of differentiation as a specific dimension in a formal geometrical space. So we can characterize each social system by the number of its dimensions; in particular we see from the theory of social differentiation that early tribe societies are one-dimensional systems; class societies form two-dimensional systems, because both segmentary and stratificatory differentiation constitute these societies; and modern societies can be described as a three-dimensional space of interactions. It is worthwhile to note that the theory of social differentiation, if reformulated in geometrical terms, postulates an unfolding of dimensions as a fundamental feature of social evolution.[2]

THE LOGICAL CHARACTERISTICS OF SOCIAL SYSTEMS

So far the introduction of geometrical concepts into the theory of social differentiation is nothing more than a *structural* precision of this theory. Yet social systems are of course dynamical systems and must therefore be analyzed above all in regard to their particular dynamics and evolution. The classical way of physics (and chemistry) to analyze system dynamics by using differential or difference equations is only rarely possible for studying dynamical social systems—with the exception of comparatively simple cases. The reason for this is particularly the fact that social systems are adaptive (see below): social actors are able to change the rules which determine their actions (Mayntz, 1990), which of course the elements of physical systems cannot do. Therefore one has to go back to the classical and basic concept of *social rules* and define the logics of social systems by it: social systems are to be understood as sets of social actors whose interactions are determined by specific rules; these rules generate the dynamics of social systems. Following this approach the dynamics of social systems—the succession of the system states, respectively the trajectories in their state space—is nothing else than the intended or unintended consequences of social actions (Klüver, 1999). To analyze the dynamics of social systems mathematically, it is therefore necessary to construct computer programs which are based on specific rules—the formal counterpart of the social rules of the "real" social systems. Only the methodical tool of computer simulations allows a precise analysis of the complex dynamics of social processes.

Another important aspect of social systems must be taken into consideration: social systems are not only self-organizing systems, as has been stressed for example by Luhmann (1984); they are also *adaptive* systems, which means that they are able to change their rules of interaction according to particular demands of their environment. The term of adaptation is to be understood in this context rather generally and not as an antithesis to self-organization: each adaptive system is also self-organizing in the sense that it always operates according to its own logics. The environment can force an adaptive system to change its rules of interaction; yet the manner of changing is *part of the self-organization* of the system and not a simple reaction to the environment.

An adaptive system therefore has not only one set of rules by which the interactions are constituted and the dynamics of the system is generated, but at least two sets of rules: the rules of interactions and *meta rules* by which the rules of interactions—the base rules—are changed if the environment makes these changes necessary. In a logical sense adaptive systems are *hybrid systems* because they are combined of two or more different sets of rules (Klüver et al., 1997). We call the rules of interaction *base rules* and the rules which change the base rules *meta rules* because they operate *upon* the base rules. The term meta rules of course is borrowed from logical semantics (Tarski, 1956) and its famous distinction between object languages and meta languages. Yet, though meta rules may seem to be rather artificial concepts, it is easy to see that each social system contains meta rules. Well-known examples are the rules of procedure of parliaments which define among other subjects the manner of changing the modes of interactions between the parliamentarians; other examples are given by Schwartzman (1978) for play-groups of children which have well defined rules for altering the rules of the different games.

As an adaptive system generates its dynamics in two ways—namely by following particular rules of interactions *and* by changing these rules via the meta rules and generating sometimes quite another dynamics—it seems appropriate to speak of the *metadynamics* of adaptive systems (Farmer, 1990), meaning with this term a dynamics generated by rules and meta rules. For the sake of simplicity we usually use only the term of system dynamics when it would be more accurate to speak of metadynamics.

By concentrating upon the concept of social rules, by the way, we get an interesting theoretical by-product for the problem of social evolution. Theorists of social evolution are not always very clear about the question of which social units correspond to the genes in biological evolution. Biological evolution, as is well-known, operates directly only upon the genome and only indirectly upon the organisms via selection. If there is a social evolution, what are the social genes? Some theorists like Giesen (1980) postulate that these are intellectual products like ideas, beliefs, and so on and refer to the Third World of Popper where social evolution has its place. Other proposals are the infamous "memes" of Dawkins (1976) which are neither well defined nor sociologically grounded.

By defining adaptive systems by their capacity to change their rules and by considering the trivial fact that only adaptive systems can evolve, the question above is rather simply solved: social evolution occurs by varying, eliminating, and enlarging social rules and therefore the social genes are nothing else than the social rules which constitute a social system at a particular time.[3] No mysterious entities like memes are needed and no excursions into a third world of ideas are necessary, only the good old concept of social rules (cf. also

Skvoretz and Fararo, 1995). Sometimes seemingly difficult questions turn out to be rather simple.

THE COMPUTER MODEL

In order to model social evolution as the unfolding of dimensions in social space, we constructed a formal hybrid system (TRISOC = 3-dimensional society) which consists of a stochastic cellular automaton (CA) and a genetic algorithm (GA). In this model the CA represents the "real" system (i.e., a particular social system with its rules of interaction); the GA defines the meta rules of the system. Our intention was not to build a realistic model of the corresponding historical processes but to demonstrate logical and mathematical restrictions underlying their dynamics. We have therefore considerably simplified the model down to the very principles of dimensional dispersion.

Usually CA are nothing else than a grid of cells which are in one of several possible states, symbolized for example by one particular integer; the CA rules are "transition rules" which define the transitions of one cell state to other states depending on the states of the cells in the "neighborhood" of the cell. That is why CA modeling is done "bottom up": The dynamics of the system is generated by rules of strict local interactions (i.e., one cell interacting with its immediate neighbors on the grid). That is why CA are very well suited for modeling approaches which are based on the concept of social actions and social rules. A (discrete) metric d of a social system can be defined according to the grid logic of the CA model. Such a definition would be:

For any cells x and y
$d(x, x) = 0$
$d(x, y) = 1$ if and only if y belongs to the (Moore) neighborhood of x,
$d(x, y) = c + 1$, if c is the number of cells between x and y on the grid (the "Milgram definition").

It is easy to see that d fulfills all the characteristics of a metrical space. The hybrid system described here applies only to the first two definitions in connection with the evaluation function of the GA.

The CA of the hybrid system consists of 1,000 to 4,000 cells, the state of which is defined by a triple (γ,κ,φ) denoting the cell states in each of the social dimensions: segmentary, stratificatory, and functional differentiation. The cells can adopt five values in each dimension, denoting the membership in one of five social groups (families), one of five classes, and one of five functions, respectively. The CA starts with five groups; all cells belong to class 1 and function 1 (only segmentary differentiation). The cells' states within each of the three dimensions can be transformed independently with each time step provided the environmental (Moore neighborhood) conditions are given. Thus there are three independent sets of transformation rules which are executed in the following order:

1. If the average of class indices in the environment is lower than the class index ι of the cell diminished by a certain constant (usually about 0.9), the class index is changed ("descent" or "ascent"). The transformation is, however, stochastic in the sense that it takes place with a limited probability specific for each transformation from a class κ into a class λ; these probabilities are expressed by a class transformation probability matrix $C(\kappa,\lambda)$.
2. If the environment of a certain cell with function index i contains more than two cells with a certain, different function index φ, its index is transformed to φ—the cell "joins another function"—with a probability given by a matrix $F(\kappa,\varphi)$. Note the class dependence of those probabilities.[4]
3. For transformation of the group membership of a cell with a certain class index κ the nearest class index ν of all cells with the most frequent group index γ in the neighborhood is determined; then the cell transforms to group index γ with a probability given by the corresponding element of a group transformation probability matrix $G(\kappa,\nu)$. This rule intends to model certain marriage schemes between groups: the probability of a marriage increases (a) with the frequency of social contacts, and (b) with class vicinity.

The meta rules of our whole system are given by the "genetic operators" of a GA which uses the logics of biological evolution (cf. Michalewicz, 1994). So the rules of the CA can be changed by mutation (i.e., random processes) and crossover, which is a formal counterpart to heterosexual reproduction. We prefer GAs for constructing meta rules because they are very efficient and model evolutionary processes which stem from cultural transitions (crossover) and from accidental innovations within the system (mutation). Of course we do not assume by using these formal techniques that social evolution is an exact mirror-image of biological evolution. For example, social evolution obviously is more "Lamarckian" than "Darwinian" because social systems are able to transmit characteristics which have been acquired.

The GA operates on 20 sets of these CA rules in the following way: The elements of the three probability matrices C, F, and G can be increased or decreased by a certain increment. In addition, the class transitions for the five classes can be changed from ascent to descent or can be totally forbidden. Finally, the length of the vector segment which is object to crossing over can be varied.

The evaluation function for the selection of the rule sets, which have turned out to be the "fittest" within an interval of time steps, is essentially the distance between a system's performance vector and a predefined target vector. The vectors describe the output of the system as a whole, applying five different categories of output; these categories can be interpreted as analogs for certain output categories of real societies, like production of food, production of technical goods, educational achievements, and so on. In TRISOC the contribution of a cell of a certain class κ and function φ to an output category ω is given by two output matrices $OK(\kappa,\omega)$ and $OF(\varphi,\omega)$, which have to be defined in advance; the contributions of individual cells are simply summed up.

Additional contributions arise from cells which share their neighborhood with cells of the same social group, class, or function, respectively, thus rewarding social coherence.[5]

Thus, the social cohesion of a segment or a social class is measured by the metrical distance between individuals—cells of the CA—of the same segment or class. According to "real" sociocultural evolution, our system always starts with only one level of differentiation, namely the level of social segments which means an agricultural society, divided into different families.

The whole formal system is obviously self-organizing and adaptive in the sense defined above; in addition to the simple definition of adaptation, it is to be noted that not only the rules of the CA are changed by the operations of the GA but in specific cases the operations of the GA also can be changed by the CA. For example the CA can switch off the operating of the GA if specific demands of the environment are fulfilled. Therefore the concepts of base rules and meta rules have to be understood in a "dialectical" manner: the different sets of rules form levels which interact in both ways and not only in one direction. The GA is even capable to operate on itself which has been done by a "meta meta rule." Whether the GA changes itself or the rules of the CA, or whether the CA changes the operations of the GA depends only upon the "progress" the CA makes (i.e., the success in reacting to particular environmental criteria). The theoretical idea behind this is of course the assumption that social evolution—as any evolution—occurs only if there is an environmental pressure which forces the social system to change its traditional structure (for the transition from tribe societies to class societies cf. Eder, 1976; Habermas, 1981 I).

DISCUSSION OF THE MODEL

We mentioned above that the CA approach has a great advantage, namely the possibility to base modeling approaches directly upon the concepts of social actors and social rules which govern social interactions. That is certainly why CA are used more frequently now in the attempts to model social dynamics and evolution (Nowak & Lewenstein, 1996; Hegselmann, 1996; Passerini & Bahr, 1997). Apparently this also may be an advantage for the natural sciences (Toffoli, 1997). Thus, adaptive social systems and their evolution may be modeled by introducing social actors and the particular social rules they follow directly into the models as well as the adaptation of these systems by their rule-changing capacity. That is basically the same theoretical approach as that of Skvoretz and Fararo (1995) who use a GA for changing the rules of production systems, an idea developed by Holland with the concept of classifier systems (Holland et al., 1986).[6]

In contrast to this action- and rule-based approach, many mathematical models and computer simulations of social dynamics follow the classical paradigm of the natural sciences—that is, the modeling of social dynamics by the use of differential or difference equations. Rather common is the use of equations of the Lotka-Volterra type. Nowadays sometimes equations also are used which are borrowed from the famous model of the hypercycle by Eigen and Schuster (e.g., Leinfellner, 1995).

Whether these more classical lines of research are able to capture the problems of social evolution and complexity remains to be seen. The approach we favor has one great advantage though, namely the possibility of translating the concepts and ways of thinking of the mainstream of sociology directly into formal models. Concepts like social role or social actors in relation to social situations can be translated directly into formal systems like CA or the related Boolean networks. This is not possible with the classical approaches borrowed from the natural sciences, and that may be one of the reasons why mathematical and/or computational sociology still has difficulties getting accepted by most theoretical sociologists (Fararo, 1997). CA modeling is probably more suited to capture the ways of thinking which most theoretical sociologists are used to.

RESULTS AND INTERPRETATIONS

The most important results are:

1. Social differentiation, understood as the evolution of different levels of social structures and rules, is very improbable because a lot of different parameter values must be balanced at the same time. This explains the well-known historical fact that the evolution of different social levels happened only very seldom in human history. In our formal system often the evolution from the first level to the second level of stratificatory differentiation began to unfold but then the system stagnated or even regressed: it either did not reach full stratificatory differentiation but stayed in a state between the first and second level of differentiation or it went back to the state of only segmentary differentiation. This corresponds very well with the empirical results known from human history: most of the known social systems did not pass into the level of stratificatory differentiation but remained in the state of segmentary differentiation or in states between the two levels or they regressed (i.e., they went back to the simple state of segmentary differentiation). Habermas (1981 I) cites many cases where social systems "did not make it" (i.e., they just could not pass this threshold of sociocultural evolution). These observations are even more valid for the transition from the second level to the third.

Our model suggests the mathematical reasons for these results: only very narrow regions of parameters—in our case, above all the values of the two output matrices and the additional values gained for social coherence—lead to the desired evolution. Most combinations are not suited for the evolution of different social dimensions. In other words: if the systems are not able to change the values they define for the different functions a system has to fulfill in order to maintain its existence, then social evolution will not occur. These rather simple mathematical considerations may help to understand why the unfolding of social dimensions happened so seldom in history: the social systems were just not pressed enough to change some of their basic values.

2. The more different levels a system contains, the more sensitive the system is to external perturbations and the more difficult it becomes for the system to reach and maintain simple attractor states (this is not exactly the same as the well-known results about chaotic systems). This might explain the also well-known fact about the problems modern societies have to maintain social stability. To be more precise: these difficulties are a consequence of the fact that social systems, as well as our formal system, are adaptive and therefore rather *variable* systems. Their variability enables these systems to react adequately to different environments, especially by unfolding different dimensions of their space of interactions. Thus, the system on the one hand is able to reach favorable states which are well suited for solving environmental problems; on the other hand the same capability produces complex rule systems in order to reach such favorable states, but these rule systems generate trajectories which lead the system quickly away from the favorable states. Therefore the rules have to be changed again and so forth; the system becomes extremely sensitive to external perturbations and is in itself usually far away from simple attractors. Each view upon modern societies confirms the results we got from our experiments: modern societies obviously have to pay for their adaptive efficiency with permanent unrest.

3. Social relations on one level of differentiation—for example, family relations on the first level—are disturbed and partly dissolved when the system evolves to the next levels of differentiation. It is apparently nearly impossible for our system to develop different levels of differentiation *and* maintain social cohesion on all levels simultaneously. The mathematical reason for this is again the problem mentioned above of combining different values of the system. This is also a fact which is well-known from complex and especially modern societies, a classical topic of sociological theories since Marx, Durkheim, and critical theory. Consequently, there may be mathematical reasons for the fact that in modern societies traditional relations are permanently changed and dissolved—a fact which was predicted by Marx and Engels in the *Communist Manifesto*:

The bourgeoisie, wherever it has got the upper hand, has put an end to all feudal, patriarchal, idyllic relations. It has pitilessly torn asunder the motley feudal ties that bound man to his "natural superiors," and has left no other nexus between man and man than naked self-interest, than callous "cash payment." It has drowned out the most heavenly ecstacies of religious fervor, of chivalrous enthusiasm, of philistine sentimentalism, in the icy water of egotistical calculation.... All that is solid melts into air, all that is holy is profaned, and man is at last compelled to face with sober senses his real condition of life and his relations with his kind. (Marx/Engels, Manifesto of the Communist Party)[7]

Obviously, Marx and Engels explained this by the revolutionary role of the bourgeoisie. Our experiments demonstrate that this "dissolving of social relations" may be a necessary consequence of the unfolding of more than one dimension of social space—in other words, an emergent consequence of the particular evolutions of social complexity.

CONCLUSIONS

Two fundamental consequences may be drawn from our results. On the one hand it is apparently possible to define several main concepts of theoretical sociology in geometrical terms and to make geometrical models of social actors and interactions the base of theoretically grounded computer simulations. Of course, the concept of the geometry of social space which we introduced in this chapter is rather rough, as we used only very basic geometrical concepts. Further research may show the fertility of more advanced concepts like the dimensions of fractal spaces. On the other hand, our experiments hint at the possibility that there are *mathematical* reasons for the particular paths human history has taken. It is neither necessary to speculate about the influence of human nature upon history and thus reduce sociology to biology like sociobiology tried, nor to introduce particular "interests" of social groups like the interests of the bourgeoisie or the proletariat in the tradition of Marx. Perhaps human history went the way it did because social systems are constrained—as each complex system is—by the mathematical possibilities and thresholds each level of complexity necessarily introduces. But these are questions for the future.

Yet, even now it is possible to say a few words about the characteristics of social laws—if there are any. As mentioned above it seems not very useful to employ the classical mathematical tools of theoretical physics and chemistry for the analysis of social complexity. Accordingly, it seems not very useful either to look for social laws like the laws of nature the natural sciences have discovered so far. In our opinion, there are no master equations which may describe the dynamics of social systems—there is no social $E = mc^2$. The reason for this is again the fact that social actors and therefore social systems can change their rules, their dynamics, and even of course their meta rules. In particular, social systems are, like the mind, self-referential systems which can model themselves and anticipate their possible future (Klüver, 1999). Therefore one has to look for other mathematical modes of description which may be called a mathematics of self-referentiality. Social laws must contain these basic characteristics of social reality; that is why such laws are probably more similar to the well-known "implicative universals" from theoretical linguistics (cf. Pinker, 1994): if a social system moves from the level of stratificatory differentiation to the level of functional differentiation—it unfolds a third dimension—*then* it will get problems with social cohesion and tradition. But of course there are absolute universals also—formal universals in the terms of Chomsky (1965): unfolding more than one dimension of social interactions is rather improbable because a lot of different values must be combined at the same time.

Our models are based upon the theory of social evolution as expressed particularly by Habermas and Luhmann. In this sense we follow a tradition which has been aptly described by Fararo (1997, p. 95): "Mathematical sociology always meant reworking the practice of theorizing in sociology, putting it on a more rigorous basis." Yet "reworking" also means to transcend the theories the models are based upon: neither Habermas nor Luhmann gives an explanation for the fact that the unfolding of social dimensions happened so rarely in history. Our model at least hints at an explanation, namely that this process is mathematically speaking very improbable. Thus, the model gives more than the original theory offered, and that is of course the only reason for the technically often difficult construction of formal models. The same holds, by the way, for explaining the fact that in modern societies traditional relations are permanently dissolved and the dynamics of modern societies are extremely complex.

Despite this gain, our model of course does not capture the richness of the original theories and it did not intend to. The formal reconstruction or reworking of complex theories is a task which can be accomplished only by combining very different modeling approaches. In the computer project at our institute at the university of Essen we are experimenting with several techniques of formal modeling (Klüver, 1995; Stoica, 1999)—for example, expert systems, artificial neural nets or Boolean networks, combined with GA. Which combination of these techniques will be sufficient to model social complexity as expressed for example in the theories of Luhmann and Habermas will be a question of the future.

Finally, are mathematical models like ours a tool for predicting the future of modern societies? In the classical sense of prognosis certainly not, because our system allows only predictions about *possible* paths of development—more or less probable—on the one hand and the analysis of the consequences of particular paths on the other. We can say that a fourth level of differentiation is not very probable because it would enforce the systemic problems mentioned above. Yet one never knows with complex systems, and therefore the introduction of geometrical concepts into theoretical sociology gives at least precise insights into the reasons of the problems modern societies have to cope with as well as first assumptions why human history was determined by the improbability of social differentiation in the sense of unfolding social dimensions.

ACKNOWLEDGMENT

This chapter is a slightly revised version of an article with the same title which originally appeared in the *Journal of Mathematical Sociology*, Vol. 23, issue 4, 1999. The editors wish to thank the copyright holder, Gordon & Breach Publishers, for the permission to use the original text.

NOTES

1. That is, by the way, exactly the manner in which the dimensions of state or phase spaces are defined in physics or chemistry: the number of

dimensions of a state space is the number of *independent* variables needed to give a complete description of the state of a system.

2. This notion has an interesting counterpart in contemporary physical theories: The so-called superstring theory claims that the physical space-time originally had 10, or according to another mathematical model 26, dimensions (Peat, 1988). These dimensions, however, remained mostly in the regions of the elementary particles; only four of them unfolded themselves during the early evolution of the universe. Perhaps evolution of complex systems is also an unfolding of dimensions.

3. Obviously biological genes are from a logical point of view also nothing else than rules which generate a particular dynamics, namely the ontogenesis of the organism. Biological evolution constitutes logical hybrid systems insofar as the biological operators of mutation, heterosexual reproduction, and selection may be seen as meta rules which constantly change the rules of the ontogenesis—the genes (see below).

4. To provide for functional differentiation starting with an undifferentiated society, it was assumed that classes have a specific affinity to certain functions; for the sake of simplicity it was assumed that a class κ prefers function κ. Thus an additional rule prescribes that, whenever a functional transformation takes place, the cell with the class κ takes with 10% probability the function κ, regardless of the actual neighborhood condition.

5. The dynamics of the model system TRISOC can be observed separately in the three dimensions mentioned above, or combined in a three-dimensional representation; in addition, the program offers several tools by which the results (e.g., certain trajectories) can be visualized.

6. Other examples for using GA for social problems can be found in Freeman (1993) or Axelrod (1987).

7. Die Bourgeoisie, wo sie zur Herrschaft gekommen ist, hat alle feudalen, patriarchalischen, idyllischen Verhältnisse zerstört. Sie hat die buntscheckigen Feudalbande, die den Menschen an seinen natürlichen Vorgesetzten knüpften, unbarmherzig zerrissen ... Alles Ständische und Stehende verdampft, alles Heilige wird entweiht, und die Menschen sind endlich gezwungen, ihre Lebensstellung, ihre gegenseitigen Beziehungen mit nüchternen Augen zu betrachten. (MEW 4, 464 f.) Translation from the German original by Jürgen Klüver.

REFERENCES

Axelrod, R. (1987). The Evolution of Strategies in the Iterated Prisoner's Dilemma. In L. Davis (Ed.), *Genetic Algorithms and Simulated Annealing* (pp. 32-41). Los Altos, CA: Morgan Kaufmann.

Chomsky, N. (1965). *Aspects of the Theory of Syntax*. Cambridge, MA: MIT Press.

Dawkins, R. (1976). *The Selfish Gene*. Oxford: Oxford University Press.

Eder, K. (1976). *Die Entstehung staatlich organisierter Gesellschaften*. Frankfurt: Suhrkamp.

Fararo, T.J. (1997). Reflections on Mathematical Sociology. *Sociological Forum 12*, 73-101.
Farmer, D.J. (1990). A Rosetta Stone for Connectionism. In S. Forrest (Ed.), *Emergent Computation.* Physica D 42, (pp. 1-3). Amsterdam: North Holland.
Freeman, L. C. (1989). Social Networks and the Structure Experiment. In L.C. Freeman (Ed.), *Research Methods in Social Network Analysis.* Fairfax, VA: George Mason University Press.
Freeman, L.C. (1993). Finding Groups with a Simple Genetic Algorithm. *Journal of Mathematical Sociology, 17,* 227 – 241.
Giesen, B. (1980). *Makrosoziologie. Eine evolutionstheoretische Einführung.* Hamburg: Hoffmann und Campe.
Habermas, J. (1981). *Theorie des kommunikativen Handelns I and II.* Frankfurt: Suhrkamp.
Hegselmann, R. (1996). Cellular Automata in the Social Sciences. Perspectives, Restrictions and Artefacts. In R. Hegselmann, U. Mueller & K. Troitzsch (Eds.), *Modeling and Simulation in the Social Sciences from the Philosophy of Science Point of View.* Dordrecht, Netherlands: Kluwer.
Holland, J.H., Holyoak, K.J., Nisbett, R.E. & Thagard, P.R. (1986). *Induction.* Cambridge, MA: MIT Press
Homans, G.C. (1951). *The Human Group.* New York: Harcourt, Brace and Company.
Klüver, J. (1995). *Soziologie als Computerexperiment.* Braunschweig-Wiesbaden: Vieweg.
Klüver, J. (1999). *The Dynamics and Evolution of Social Systems.* Dordrecht, Netherlands: Kluwer.
Klüver, J., Stoica, C. & Schmidt, J. (1997). Simulations of the Self Modeling of Social Systems by a Hybrid System. In F. Faulbaum & W. Bandilla (Eds.), *SoftStat 97. Advances in Statistical Software.* Stuttgart: Lucius.
Leinfellner, W. (1995). Neuere mathematische Modelle der Kulturevolution. In K. Johannesen & T. Nordenstam (Eds.), *Culture and Value.* Vienna: Springer.
Luhmann, N. (1984). *Soziale Systeme.* Frankfurt: Suhrkamp.
Mayntz, R. (1990). *The Influence of Natural Science Theories on Contemporary Social Science.* MPIFG Discussion Paper. Cologne: Max-Planck-Institut für Gesellschaftsforschung.
Michalewicz, Z. (1994). *Genetic Algorithms + Data Structures = Evolution Programs.* Berlin: Springer.
Milgram, S. (1967). The small world problem. *Psychology Today, 1,* 61-67.
Nowak, A. & Lewenstein, M. (1996). Modeling Social Change with Cellular Automata. In R. Hegselmann, U. Mueller & K. Troitzsch (Eds.), *Modeling and Simulation in the Social Sciences from the Philosophy of Science Point of View.* Dordrecht, Netherlands: Kluwer.
Passerini, E. & Bahr, D. (1997). Collective Behaviour Following Disasters: A Cellular Automaton Model. In R.A. Eve, S. Horsfall & M.E. Lee (Eds.), *Chaos, Complexity, and Sociology. Myths, Models, and Theories.* London: Sage.
Peat, D. (1988). *Superstrings and the Search for the Theory of Everything.* Chicago: Contemporary Books.

Pinker, S. (1994). *The Language Instinct*. New York: Morrow.

Schwartzman, H. (1978). *Transformations. The Anthropology of Children's Play*. New York: Plenum.

Skvoretz, J. & Fararo, T.J. (1995). The Evolution of Systems of Social Interaction. *Current Perspectives in Social Theory, 15*, 275-299.

Stoica, C. (1999). *Die Vernetzung sozialer Einheiten. Hybride interaktive neuronale Netzwerke in den Kommunikations- und Sozialwissenschaften*. Wiesbaden: Deutscher Universitätsverlag.

Tarski, A. (1956). *Logics, Semantics, Metamathematics*. Oxford: Oxford University Press.

Toffoli, T. (1997). How Much Can You Get for How Little? A Conceptual Introduction to Cellular Automata. *Interjournal*. Boston: New England Complex Systems Institute.

Chapter 12

THE DYNAMICS OF EDUCATIONAL EXPANSION: A SIMULATION MODEL

Cor van Dijkum, Niek Lam & Harry B.G. Ganzeboom

INTRODUCTION

Human societies generally do not develop according to a linear evolutionary pattern. Whether we look at wealth, inequality, or political institutions, a universal pattern of societal development is hardly discernible. However, there appears to be one major exception to the lack of a universal pattern: in all societies and at all times, the educational distribution seems to be expanding upward. Wherever we go and whenever we look, more recently born cohorts always have a higher level of education than previous ones. For example, in a previous study by one of the authors, comparing educational distributions of cohorts in thirty countries throughout the twentieth century (Ganzeboom & Treiman, 1993), it was found that in each society the trend in educational levels was generally upward, with very few exceptions for wartime cohorts in lower developed countries like Turkey and India.

In this chapter, we set out to investigate the mechanisms behind educational expansion. Several mechanisms can be suggested. At the macrolevel, there are two competing views of the causes of educational expansion. Neoclassical theories in economics as well as functionalistic theories in sociology tend to attribute the rising levels of education to a rising demand in the labor market for higher educated, more productive workers. According to these theories, one would expect a strong and causal relationship between industrial and economic restructuring on the one hand, and educational expansion on the other, while educational expansion should follow patterns of industrial development. This "modernism thesis" has been criticized by many: ample research shows that occupational distributions tend to react to variations in the educational stock (instead of the other way around), and even that only at some distance.

There is strong evidence for the existence of an autonomous mechanism of educational expansion, which is not directly related to demand in the labor market. Radical suggestions allude to status competition between countries and imitation between countries as the primary drives behind educational expansion. While such suggestions have their merits, they are difficult to test quantitatively. At the microlevel, a more acceptable view holds that educational expansion is the unintended consequence of what economists (Thurow, 1975) refer to as job competition, and sociologists as status competition. In each version, the basic underlying mechanism is that students observe the economic or social value of certain diplomas in society, and decide that it is rational for them to push on to a subsequent level in order to compete effectively with the existing educational stock. Whether this explanation is phrased in terms of job competition or status competition makes very little difference for the result that for members of the next cohort it is always rational to continue school longer than for the previous cohort.

Our long-term project aims to investigate and understand the mechanics of educational expansion. Research on educational expansion should address the main explanatory questions on the development of the educational distribution. Three main issues stand out in this context. First, countries—and episodes—vary in the speed of educational expansion. In some countries educational expansion takes place rapidly, in others it emerges more slowly. Under which conditions can a high speed of development or near stability be expected? Second, an important observation is that as the distribution of the population over educational levels in a society expands, the form—and in particular the dispersion—of the distribution may change. In some countries, educational expansion implies that the distribution rolls up from the bottom (i.e., in each new cohort a smaller number of lower educated appears, while the number of higher educated does not rise proportionally). In other countries, the pattern is the opposite: educational expansion implies that the number of higher educated expands faster than the number of lower educated. As a consequence, the dispersion of the educational distribution declines in the first case, and increases in the second case. A model of educational expansion should be able to account for these different patterns of development. Finally, there is the issue about who gets better access to higher education when education expands. A general pattern, found around the world, is that the children of higher status background (often best indicated by parental education) are better equipped to make a grade. An obvious question then is, does educational expansion change the chances of success of children from high-status background relative to those of less-privileged background?

Our long-term aim is to elucidate and cover all these issues by following a dual-track analytic strategy. First, variations in educational expansion are assessed in a data-analytical model by comparing survey results from a large number of countries and by relating the cohort-wise differences to empirical macroindicators. Second, we want to understand the underlying mechanics of educational expansion in a simulation model that mimics the real world closely, but introduces only a limited number of simple assumptions to reproduce the real world. While our final aim is to combine data-analytic and simulation models into one analysis and use this model to deal with all three issues on educational expansion outline above, the aim of this chapter is much more modest. We build a simulation model for educational expansion that exploits the simple assumption that expansion occurs because students, who are in school, compare their expected final outcomes to the existing stock in their society, and try to compete with the older cohorts by staying in school for a longer period. The basic drive behind educational expansion is a simple process of status comparison. The aim of this chapter is to codify this assumption in a simulation model that can account for at least one empirical result, namely the changes in the educational distribution of the Netherlands over the past century.

The data we use to calibrate our model are taken from some twenty surveys that are part of the International Stratification and Mobility File (ISMF) (Ganzeboom & Treiman, 1993). This "superfile" collects and standardizes survey data on social mobility (i.e., data on occupations and educations of parents and children) from countries around the world. The subsample for the Netherlands in the ISMF is particularly large, due to the fact that more than twenty surveys have become available for comparison. These surveys were conducted between 1958 and 1997. However, the birth cohorts contained in the

Table 12.1
Percentage of Achieved Education in Different Birth-Cohorts in The Netherlands, 1900-1975

Cohort	Primary %	Presecondary %	Secondary %	Tertiary %	N
1900 – 1904	67.1	18.9	8.4	5.6	579
1905 – 1909	61.0	20.0	10.9	8.0	792
1910 - 1914	61.1	23.9	8.5	6.5	1,268
1915 – 1919	49.8	28.6	12.6	9.1	1,675
1920 – 1924	44.6	29.8	15.5	10.1	2,479
1925 – 1929	38.0	32.2	18.8	11.0	2,998
1930 – 1934	33.6	34.1	18.8	13.5	3,386
1935 – 1939	27.8	35.6	21.4	15.2	3,619
1940 – 1944	20.2	39.4	23.4	17.0	3,923
1945 – 1949	14.5	40.4	25.5	19.6	5,170
1950 – 1954	13.5	36.1	27.7	22.7	5,308
1955 – 1959	10.3	33.3	31.7	24.7	4,987
1960 – 1964	6.8	28.8	39.0	25.5	3,602
1965 – 1969	4.8	26.7	43.5	25.0	2,406
1970 – 1974	2.9	21.2	45.8	30.0	1,170
1975 – 1979	2.5	17.8	44.8	35.0	326
N	10,043	14,389	11,232	8,023	43,687

survey cover the whole period, as the older interviewees in the older surveys were in school even as early as 1910. After standardizing the educations, categorizing them in four classes (primary, presecondary, secondary, and tertiary), and organizing the birth cohorts by five year widths, Table 12.1 shows the pattern of educational expansion for the Netherlands in this century (for men): we see a sharp decline in the number of lower educated and a considerable increase of the number of higher educated. These simple data are our main benchmark here: how can we account for the specific pattern of educational expansion that has occurred in the Netherlands in the twentieth century?

A SYSTEM DYNAMICS MODEL

By simulating social phenomena researchers in the social sciences make fruitful use of the idea of systems science (Von Bertalanffy, 1952; Boulding, 1956; Klir, 1991) that social phenomena can be analyzed as (social) systems. Especially the time-dependent interaction between the parts of a system can be made explicit in this way. To deal with the complexity of this interaction system, researchers make use of computer-aided model building. The logical basic for such tools is laid down in the theory of dynamic systems. In this theory the concept of feedback (Wiener, 1948) is used to express the idea that the interaction between parts of a system is reciprocal—that is, that a part of a system influences at time t_0 another part, and at time t_1 the other way around. These feedback-regulated models can be mathematically expressed in recursive difference (i.e., differential) equations and then formalized in computer algorithm's (Forrester, 1968; Hanneman, 1988; Levine & Fitzgerald, 1992; Van Dijkum, 1997; Haefner, 1996). User-friendly software such as ITHINK (Peterson & Richmond, 1994) can be used to handle the computer models, while software like MADONNA (Zahnley, 1996) makes it possible to engage in advanced simulation experiments.

With the aid of this software we can thus develop a sophisticated dynamic model of educational expansion which seems to respect its complexity. Our system dynamics model in Figure 12.1 consists of three submodels which mimic the population system, the education system, and the choice system. A set of starting values of parameters represents the state of affairs (of the society) at the macro level. In the simulation model, four levels of education are distinguished: primary, presecondary, secondary, and tertiary. The levels are elements of the population submodel, the education submodel and the choice submodel. In the next sections the submodels are explained.

Society Parameters

To start with: the society parameters represent preset starting values. The population of the Netherlands in 1900 was, for example, four million people.

The Dynamics of Educational Expansion

Figure 12.1
The Population Submodel, the Education Submodel, and the Choice Submodel

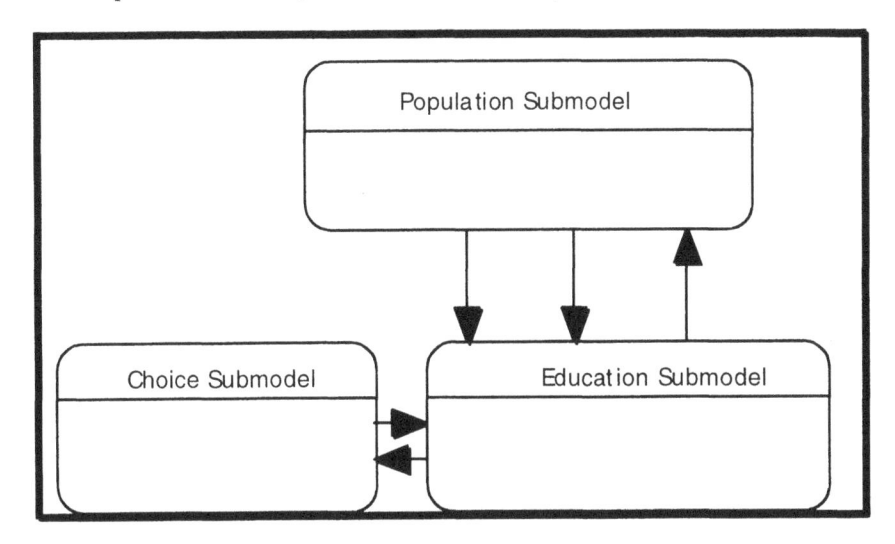

The simulation covers the period from 1900 to 2020. In this period the compulsory primary education in the Netherlands is supposed to be six school years. The average duration of the primary, presecondary, secondary, and tertiary education are 6, 3, 3 and 6 years, respectively. As a consequence the average ages on which one leaves school receptively are 12 (primary), 15 (high school), 18 (college), and 24 (university). The last (highly artificial model) assumption was that nobody has a child before the age of 25. In this way the minimal duration of the period people live without a child is determined: 13 years for people with only primary education, 10 years for people with presecondary education, 7 years for the college student, and 1 year for a university student.

The Population and Education Submodels

The population and education submodels form the core of the simulation model, also because of the interaction between these submodels. The population model is the input for the education model, whereas the output of the education model is the input for the population model. Figure 12.2 is used to describe these submodels in detail.

In this figure three parts are to be identified: the population submodel, the education submodel, and in-between the six years of age (four ellipses). Viewed in more detail the figure consists of many rectangles and arrows. Each numbered rectangle represents a category of a group. As an example: number 21 represents a group of children (of a primary educated father) leaving school with only

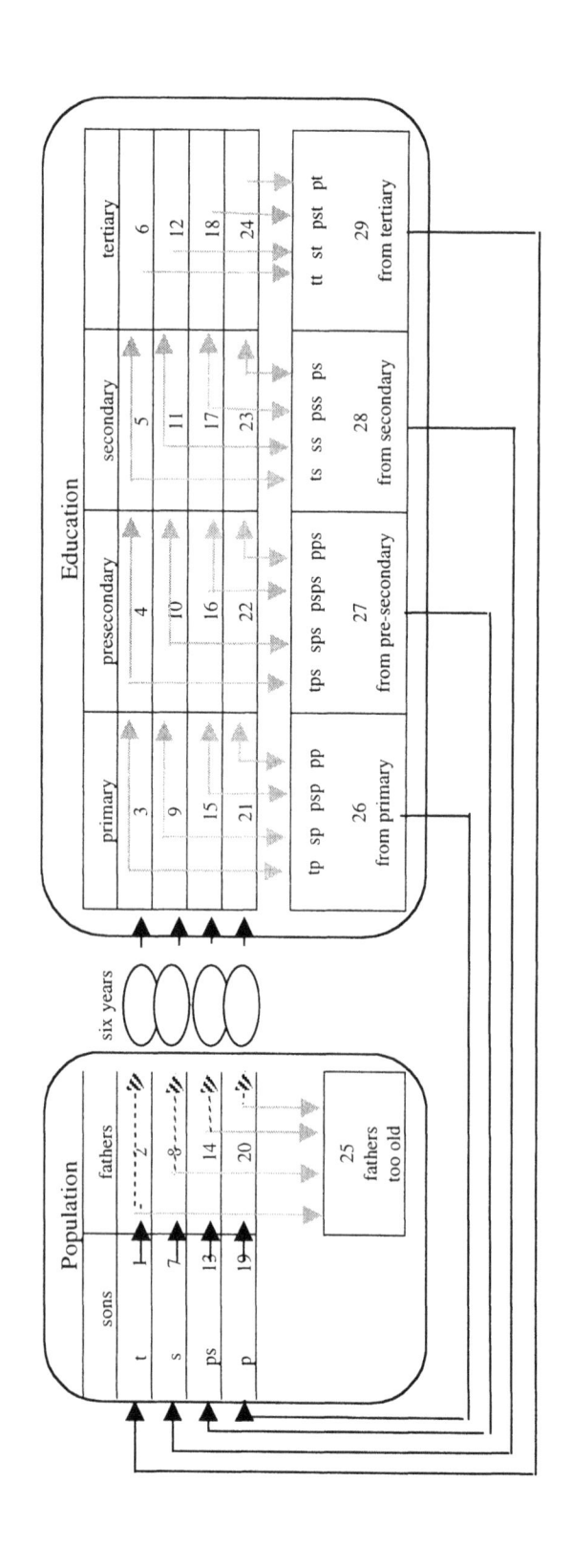

Figure 12.2
The Population and Education Submodels in Detail

primary school as a qualification. In this rectangle one can also find abbreviations of subgroups in each category. For example tp stands for those children who have a father with tertiary education, who themselves did not reach further than primary education. These subgroups are important to analyze mobility between classes.

There are three kinds of arrows: solid, shaded and dashed. Solid and shaded arrows represents throughputs. A solid arrow indicates that the whole group flows from one group to another (for example group 1 to group 2). A shaded arrow indicates a splitting, one part flows to group A, another part flows to group B. Dashed arrows represent the origin of a fiow.

The Population Submodel

We start with the description of the population submodel. Three groups are to be distinguished in this model: sons, fathers, and "fathers who are too old to give birth to a son." The groups of fathers and sons are split into four education classes: primary, presecondary, secondary, and tertiary. In between these classes function three flows: (1) the inflow from the education model; (2) the throughput from sons to fathers; (3) the outflow of fathers to "fathers who are too old."

The first inflow, from the education model, feeds the population model with sons of different degrees of education. Those sons will mature, and after their childless period they will become fathers in turn. The duration of this period is determined by the preset society parameters. When sons become fathers they move a column to the right and then belong to the population of fathers.

From each category of fathers two arrows start. The shaded arrow refers to the group of "fathers too old," because there will be a time that fathers do not get a son anymore. The dashed arrows are the sons of the fathers who are six years of age, and represent the input of the education system.

The number of fathers together with the degree of their fertility determine the number of six-year olds. Our (arbitrary) assumption is that the average number of sons a father has, is the same for each level and is to be estimated by 1.82, that is each year (during the twenty years fathers do get sons) the chance to get a son is 0.09.

The Education Submodel

These sons mature and will enter the education system at age six. This means that the education system is coupled to the population system with a delay of six years.

Mobility between classes is in our model only possible in the education system. At birth sons belong to their father's class, but after leaving the education system their achieved class depends solely on their highest diploma. Thus, for instance, sons from the highest class may achieve less education than their fathers, and drop out of their class (e.g., from tertiary born to presecondary educated).

At the age of six they enroll in the education system. Their first opportunity for leaving it is after graduating primary school at the age of twelve. In Dutch history, this graduation produced for a long period the difference between classes. However, because of the long period of compulsory education in the Netherlands, the majority nowadays will seek further education. Thus, after finishing presecondary education at age fifteen one has to choose again. Graduating from secondary education gives the opportunity to enroll in tertiary education levels at age eighteen. At the age of twenty-four students (in this model) leave the education system. There are no opportunities for further education, which reflects the structure of the Dutch education system.

The outflows of the education system are the inflows of the population system. For example, students who stop after a secondary education are the inflow of the secondary class of the education system, and will after some delay become fathers. The same is true for the other types of education, and thus the circle will be closed: the education system influences the population system and the population system influences the education system.

The Choice Submodel

There are three moments of choice in the simulation model: (1) after primary education the choice for presecondary education; (2) after presecondary

Figure 12.3
Proportion of Throughput Related to the Throughput Three Years Ago for Sons of Fathers with Primary Education and for Sons of Fathers with Tertiary Education

Actual proportion of throughput to tertiary education

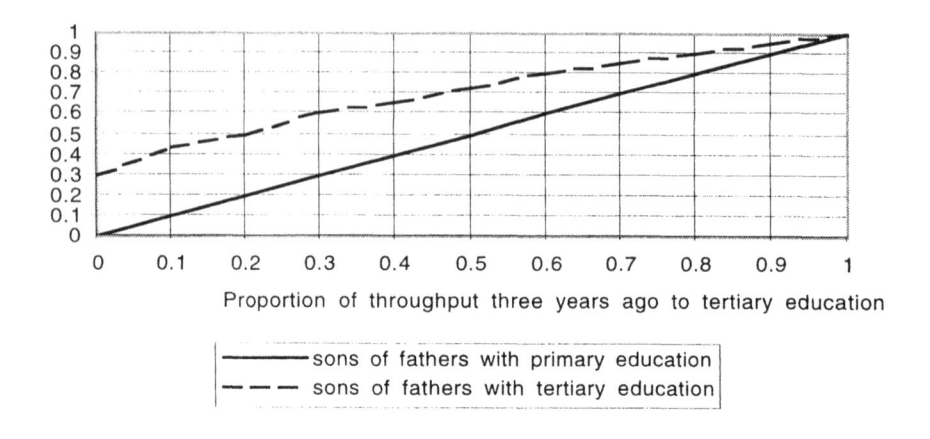

Proportion of throughput three years ago to tertiary education

——— sons of fathers with primary education
— — — sons of fathers with tertiary education

education the choice for secondary education; (3) and finally after secondary education the choice for tertiary education.

Our first assumption is that there are differences in throughput for each education class. Probably more sons of high class will enter tertiary education than sons belonging to low classes. That assumption leads to 3 (choices) x 4 (educational classes) = 12 choice submodels. Our second assumption is that former cohorts will influence the choice of the next cohort. That assumption can be entered in these submodels as shown in Figure 12.3.

The parameter which is modeled is the proportion (in Figure 12.3 "throughput to tertiary school") that "flows" in a year to the next level of education. Our first assumption implicates that for each class a different graph has to be used. As a consequence two class graphs are plotted in Figure 12.3: one for the primary class and one for the tertiary class. The second assumption has as a consequence that from the (throughput) proportion of a former cohort (arbitrarily determined as three years ago) plotted on the horizontal dimension, the graph will determine what (throughput) proportion will result for the current cohort. For the primary class we have plotted, as an example, that the throughput will remain the same. In the graph for tertiary education our third assumption is pictured. That assumption is that the next cohort will try to reach as far or farther than the former cohort.

WHICH CHOICE MODEL IS ADEQUATE?

Figure 12.4
Proportion with Only Primary Education of Birth Cohorts in the Netherlands, 1900-1975

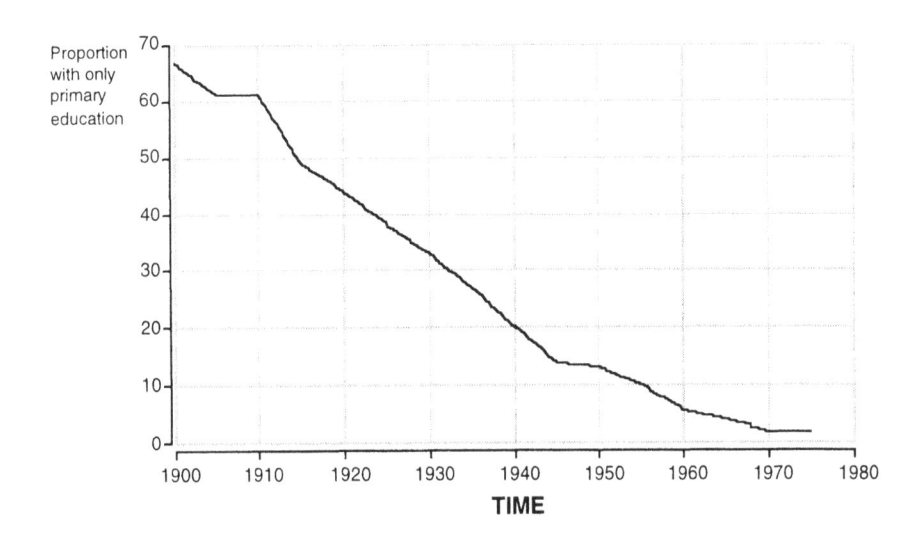

Figure 12.5

Proportion with Only Presecondary Education of Birth Cohorts in the Netherlands, 1900-1975

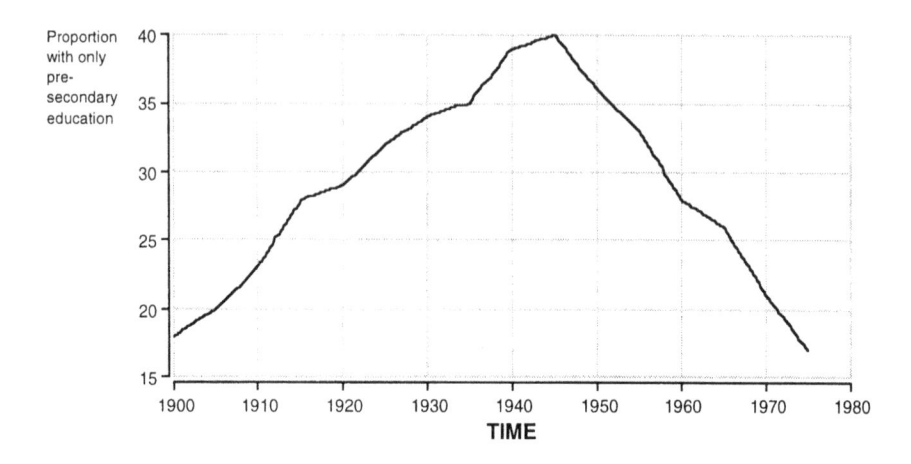

It is of course crucial which graphs we select for our choice model. To get a realistic model we confront the outcome of the selected choice model with empirical date from the Netherlands. For the period 1900-1975 these data represent the distribution of education levels and are characterized with graphs such as are shown in Figures 12.4 and 12.5 (these figures are based on the numbers as presented in Table 12.1).

Fitting with a Linear Model

In a first series of experiments we selected the most simple type of graph: a linear relation between the "proportions of throughput." That linear relation can vary, as is shown in Figure 12.6.

If the throughput stays the same we can use the graph in the diagonal (y=x). But we assume that in most of the cases the next cohort is reaching higher than the former cohort. That means that graphs are selected in the upper diagonal area of the rectangle {(0,0),(1,0),(1,1),(0,1)}. Moreover, we assumed that the higher the class the stronger the drive to reach farther—that is, for a higher class we took the graph which started higher in the vertical dimension, and as a consequence was less steep. Finally, we have done experiments with the rule that coming higher in the level of education makes the drive stronger to move up.

THE DYNAMICS OF EDUCATIONAL EXPANSION 215

Figure 12.6
Several Linear Relations Between New and Old Throughput

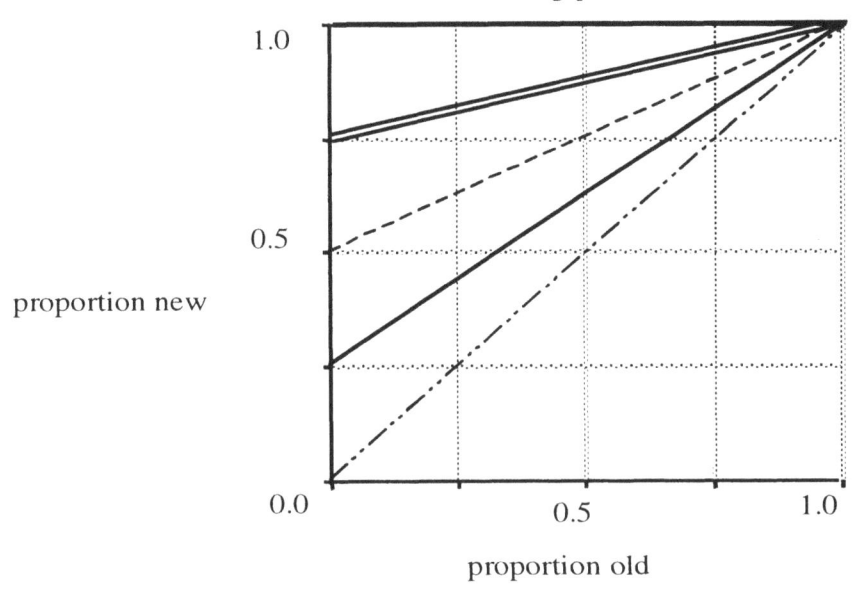

Figure 12.7
Fitting Presecondary Education with a Linear Choice Model

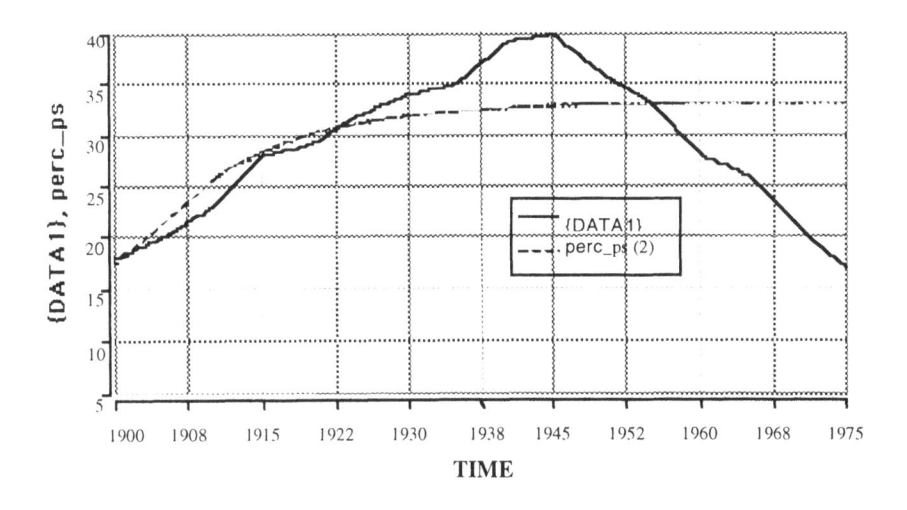

To test all these assumptions we compared the outcome of those experiments with the portrayed empirical data. A typical outcome of such comparisons is given in Figure 12.7.

It is at the same time the most difficult data to fit. Contrary to the other time-dependent proportions, which are monotonously decreasing or increasing, this proportion is going up and down (i.e., is passing a maximum). To choose values of parameters which produce outcomes (shown as perc_ps) which are reasonably close to the data (DATA1) seems possible. However one cannot realize with those values that the model passes *a maximum*[1]. Moreover, the fit between data and other proportion variables, such as the participation in primary education, is poor and can only be optimized at the expense of the fit between other data and variables. Besides, this conclusion does not take into account a possible ordering between the different parameters, such as has been discussed in the section "The Choice Submodel." But that is not necessary: It can be shown whatever ordering is presupposed between parameters, the optimum of combination of values of parameters cannot produce the passing of a maximum such as has been found in the data. Herewith our linear model is falsified in a qualitative way.

Fitting with a Logistic Relation

That leads us to the idea that the graphs in our choice model have to be nonlinear. Reasoning about the dynamics of our model, in which the growth of the population is exponential, we thought that the most adequate graph is the logistic one (see Figure 12.8).

The development of the logistic curve can be seen in the rectangle {(-1,0),(1,0),(1,1),(-1,1)}. We use the right part of this rectangle and in this area we prefer those graphs which are located above the diagonal between (0,0) and (1,1). For those logistic graphs two parameters are used: (1) s is an indication of the slope s^* of the graph; (2) i is an indication of the point of intersection i^* of the graph. With these parameters our logistic graph can be calculated by the next formula:

$$\text{proportion\_new} = \frac{1}{\left(e^{(s*\text{proportion\_old}+i)}+1\right)}$$

For each flow from one education group to another a different graph can be used as well as different values of the related two parameters. This results in twenty-four parameters.

With these parameters experiments are done to minimize the distance between the outcome of our model and the mentioned data. However, the values of the parameters cannot be arbitrarily chosen. Some values make sense for our reasoning about the model; other parameter values which could minimize the

THE DYNAMICS OF EDUCATIONAL EXPANSION

Figure 12.8
A Logistic Relation Between Old and New Proportion of Throughput

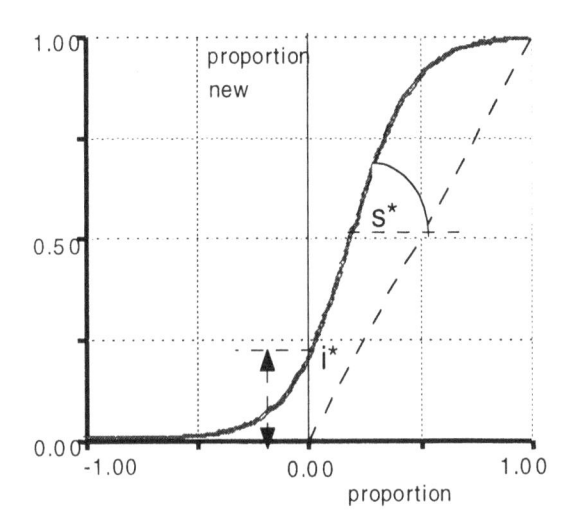

distance cannot be justified so easily, for example, because there is no throughput at all during the simulation period, and thus have to be rejected. According to the fitting experiments, and in line with acceptable graphs, the best parameters give rise to the following fitting situations, as shown in two examples, pictured in Figures 12.9 and 12.10.

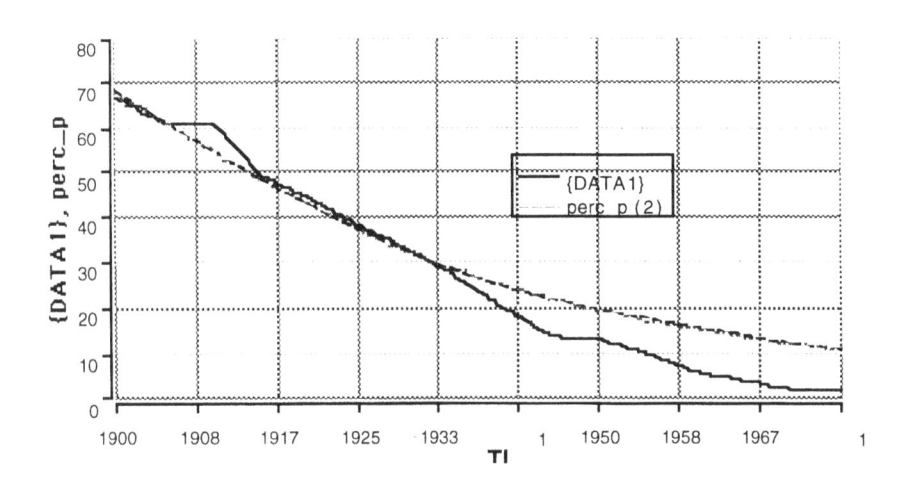

Figure 12.9
Proportion Primary Throughput in Model (perc_p) and Data (data1)

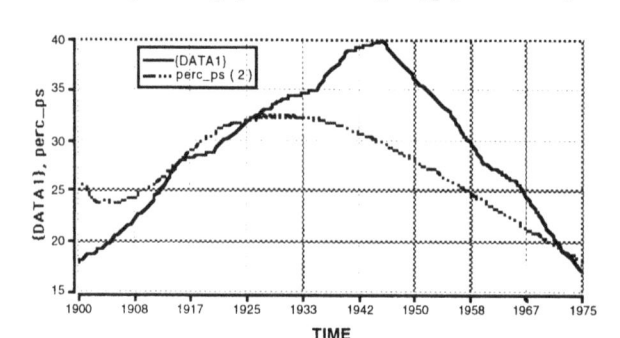

Figure 12.10
Proportion Presecondary Throughput in Model (perc_ps) and Data (data1)

Different values of parameters lead to a set of choice graphs. Most of these graphs are according to our idea that each generation tries to come further than the previous generation. The graphs are located in the area above the diagonal in Figure 12.8. Moreover, there seems to be a system in the ordering of the graphs. The slope of the graphs (its indicator s, respectively -9, -13, -41, -70)^2 representing the throughput to presecondary is steeper the higher the class of the father. That can be interpreted as the idea that the higher the class the more chance to reach presecondary education. For the next education level the same interpretation can be used. However in this case it is not because of the slope of the graphs (s is constant at -12), but because of the moving of the graph to a more favorable area (i as indicator, respectively 4, 2, 1.4, 0). For the tertiary education level the point of intersection also moves more to the right (i as indicator, respectively -3, -2, 2.7, 5), thus also in this stage of an education career, the higher the class the higher the chance to attain a university education.

However there are two interesting exceptions to our line of reasoning so far: the graph of the throughput of primary to secondary; and the graph of the throughput of tertiary to tertiary (see Figure 12.11). Here are periods in which the throughput is less than it was before.

The first hypothesis to explain this result is: it is an artifact of our model. It seems unlikely, but we cannot completely eliminate this possibility. However, another system-dynamics-oriented hypothesis is thinkable. To come to a system in which an in-between-class—such as the presecondary class—at first rises to a maximum and subsequently goes down to a lower stationary value, negative feedback is necessary. An empirical interpretation of the result is that for the lowest class the achievement of the presecondary level is historically viewed successful, but for the next step, to the secondary level, the educational career is initially inhibited because a threshold is working. However, when enough members of the primary class have overcome that barrier, the educational career will be enhanced by positive feedback. For the highest class the interpretation can be that, historically viewed, achieving the tertiary level was initially not stimulated.

THE DYNAMICS OF EDUCATIONAL EXPANSION 219

Figure 12.11
Two Exceptions to the Rule that Each Cohort Tries to Reach Further Than the Previous Cohort

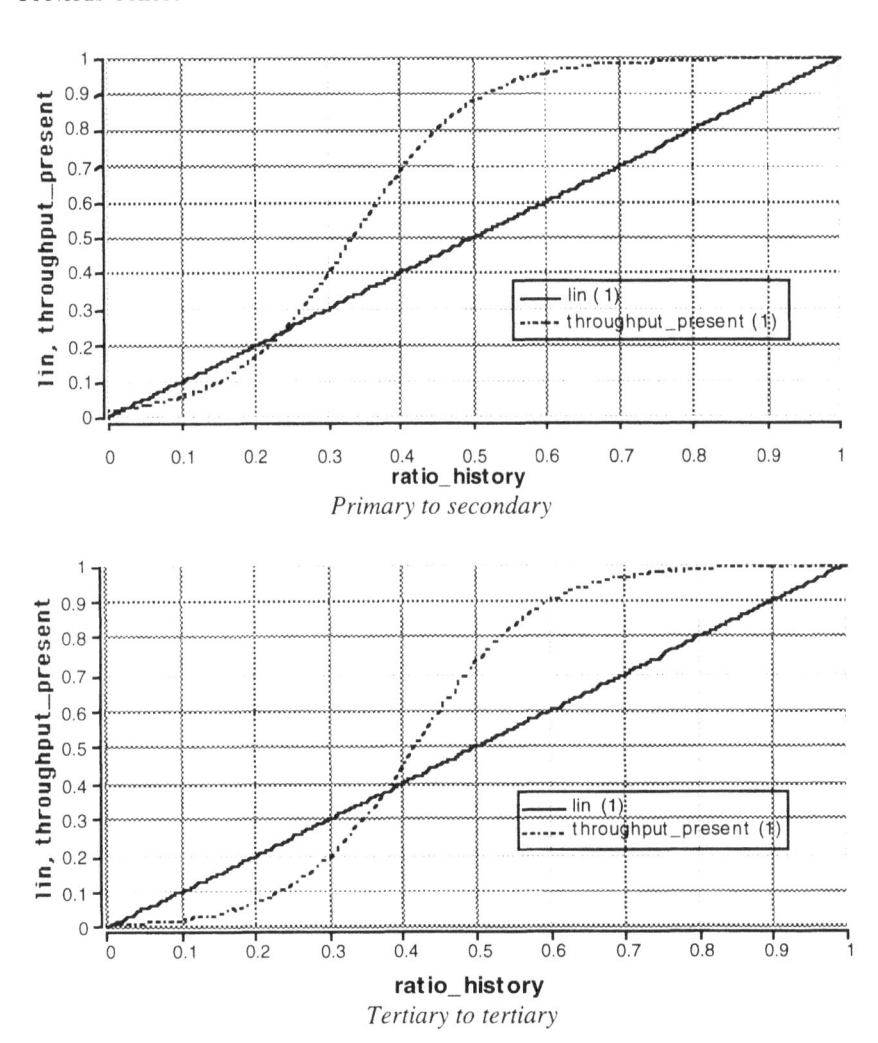

Primary to secondary

Tertiary to tertiary

Other Relevant Outcomes of the Model

There are other relevant outcomes of the model. One of these is the achieved average education in years (Figure 12.12). The increase is between seven and fourteen years, according to the empirical study of Ganzeboom & Treiman (1993). In this way our model adequately produces the speed of educational expansion.

Figure 12.12
Average Achieved Education in Years for Sons, 1900-1975

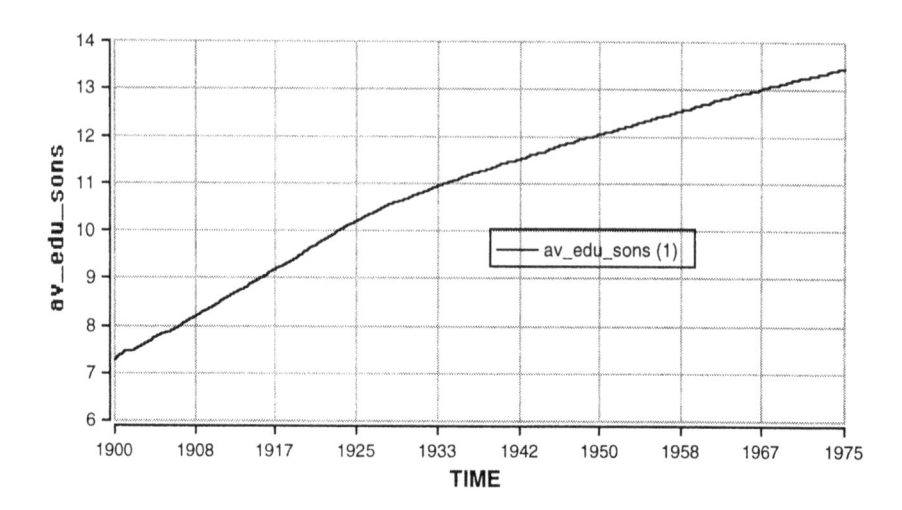

Another aspect of educational expansion is the dispersion of the achieved education in the course of time. Concerning that variable our fitted model produces the outcome such as has been pictured in Figure 12.13. As a pattern it gives the rise and fall of the standard deviation and in this way it adequately represents the empirically found educational inequality (Ganzeboom & Treiman, 1993). Our model is thus verified in a qualitative way.

Figure 12.13
Development of the Standard Deviation of the Achieved Education in Years, 1900-1975

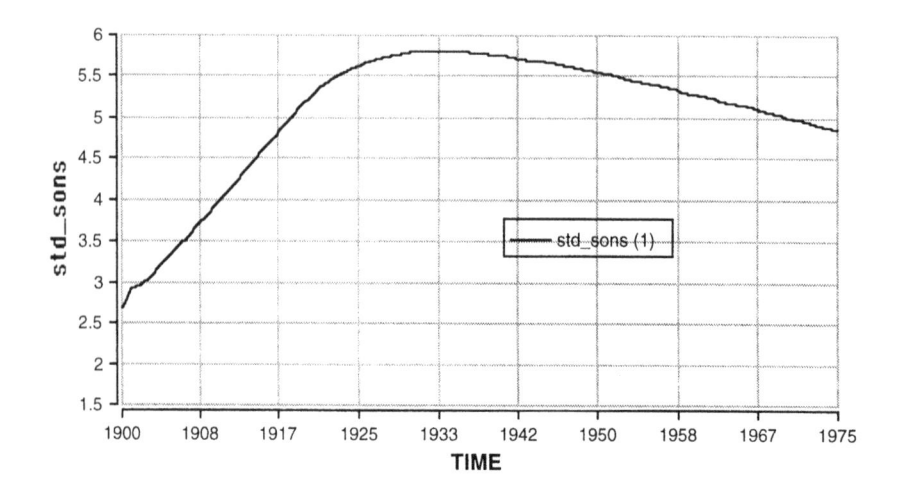

WHAT NEXT?

Our model can be viewed as a qualitative step towards understanding the mechanism of educational expansion and its complexity. However, some of our ideas are still rather speculative and have to be explored by better simulation studies. More empirical reference is needed and the model has to be falsified or verified with the aid of quantitative measures of fit—measures which allow a better discussion of the parsimony of a model than was possible in this chapter.

The next step in our study is also to include more than one country in our empirical data as well as other variables of interest. We are optimistic about the possibility to generate with our model the empirically found variety in (the speed of) educational expansion of other countries. We also think it possible with our simulation model to produce other variables of interest, such as realistic mobility tables.

NOTES

1. The software we used for those fitting experiments, MADONNA, can automatically adjust the values of selected parameters—in our case the slope of the linear function—to reach an optimal fit. The algorithm which achieves that is the Down-Hill Simplex Algorithm (see Press et al., 1992).

2. The intersection point is about the same and does not make a difference.

REFERENCES

Bertalanffy, L. von (1952). *Problems of Life*. London: Watts.

Boulding, K.E. (1956). General Systems Theory: The Skeleton of Science. *Management Science, 2*, 197-208.

Dijkum, C. van (1997). From Cybernetics to the Science of Complexity. *Kybernetes, 26*, 725-738.

Forrester, J. (1968). *Principles of Systems*. Cambridge: Wright Allen Press.

Ganzeboom, H.B.G. & Treiman, D.J. (1993). Preliminary Results on Educational Expansion and Educational Achievement in Comparative Perspective. Unpublished Paper, Utrecht University.

Haefner, J.W. (1996). *Modeling Biological Systems: Principles and Applications*. New York: Chapman & Hall.

Hanneman, R.A (1988). *Computer-assisted Theory Building: Modeling Dynamic Social Systems*. Newbury Park, CA: Sage.

Klir, G. (1991). *Facets of Systems Science*. New York: Plenum Press.

Levine, R.L. & Fitzgerald, H.E. (Eds.) (1992). *Analysis of Dynamical Psychological Systems and Cybernetics*. New York: Plenum Press.

Peterson, S. & Richmond B. (1994). *Introduction to System Dynamics Modeling. ITHINK: the Visual Tool for the 90's. Software from High Performance Systems*. Hanover: High Performance Systems.

Press, H., Flannery, B.P., Teukolsky, S.A. & Vetterling, W.T. (Eds.) (1992). *Numerical Recipes, the Art of Scientific Computing*. Cambridge: Cambridge University Press.

Thurow, L. (1975). *Generating Inequality: Mechanism of Distribution in the U.S. Economy*. New York: Basic Books.

Wiener, N. (1948). *Cybernetics or Control and Communication in the Animal and the Machine*. Cambridge, MA: MIT Press.

Zahnley, T. (1996). MADONNA Software. Berkeley: University of California.

Chapter 13

TOWARDS A METHODOLOGY FOR THE EMPIRICAL TESTING OF COMPLEX SOCIAL CYBERNETIC MODELS

Johannes van der Zouwen & Cor van Dijkum

CYBERNETICS AND SOCIAL SCIENCE

The First Applications of Cybernetics in Social Science

From the beginning of general systems theory—or its twin, cybernetics—attempts were made to apply its concepts and ideas to the study of social processes. The "father of cybernetics," Norbert Wiener, wrote his book on *The Human Use of Human Beings: Cybernetics and Society* (1950), only two years after the publication of his foundational work *Cybernetics, or Control and Communication in the Animal and the Machine* (1948; cf. Geyer and van der Zouwen, 1994). Other well-known early applications of cybernetics and systems theory are those of Talcott Parsons (1952) in sociology and Karl Deutsch (1963) in political science.

One of the criticisms voiced against these early applications of cybernetics, was that the authors did not sufficiently take into account the specific nature of social systems, systems that are essentially different from equilibrium-maintaining systems like the thermostat. One of the first applications of ideas from general systems theory in which the particular characteristics of social systems are explicitly reckoned with, is Walter Buckley's book *Sociology and Modern Systems Theory*, published in 1967.

Since the publication of this book, over thirty years have passed. Classical, or first-order, cybernetics is succeeded by a modern, second-order cybernetics. And analogous to this development, the classical "social cybernetics" is succeeded by the modern "sociocybernetics" (Geyer & van der Zouwen, 1991). In modern sociocybernetics it is well understood that social systems are more than boundary-maintaining, goal-seeking, input-output machines. We all know that social systems can observe themselves, may learn from their experiences, can organize and steer themselves, change their structure in order to better cope with challenges coming from their environment, and even reproduce themselves.

The Growing Sophistication of Sociocybernetic Theories

The growing sophistication of sociocybernetic theories has led to a kind of paradoxical situation: The more sociocyberneticians reckon in their theoretical work with the specific characteristics of social systems, the more their theories become realistic and plausible. Over the years there is a gain in "validity" or "truth" indeed. But at the same time, these sophisticated theories lead to complex models, models that cannot, or only with great difficulty, be tested empirically. It is sometimes even difficult to see which testable hypotheses can be derived from these models.

Sophisticated sociocybernetic theories no longer generate hypotheses about bivariate distributions, which can easily be tested. The theories involved have to be translated into simulation models and run on a computer in order to see which predictions can be derived from the theory. Insofar as the predictions concern social processes, the output of the computer will consist of generated time-series, or trajectories. These computed trajectories have to be compared with the observed time-series, and the degree of fit between both trajectories has to be established.

However, it turns out in practice that the outcome of the comparison between both trajectories is often not univocal, at least not as univocal as the outcome of the test of a classical "bivariate hypothesis" against the data. For example, with complex models, a minor change in one of the model parameters can lead to a completely different behavior. And on the other hand, trajectories describing about the same behavior can be generated by completely different models (van der Zouwen, 1997). This makes the validation of models that are derived from complex theories a hot issue in methodology.

The Problem of Model Validation

In this chapter we will explore the issue of "model validation" by showing how the introduction of, as such plausible, statements about the structure of social systems, leads to models with complex and sometimes unexpected behavior. Next, we will investigate what possibilities and procedures researchers can use to empirically validate these models. The problem of this chapter can be summarized in the following, general, question: "What problems and solutions can sociocyberneticians and social scientists share when they both try to construct empirically testable models, and validate these models in a scientifically acceptable way?"

(SOCIO) CYBERNETIC CONCEPTS AND SYSTEM BEHAVIOR

Characteristics of Social Systems

The first question we have to answer is: "what are the common characteristics of social systems?" A social system—that is, a system in which actors, their actions and/or their communications form the elements (like marriages, organizations, nation states, but also conversations)—is, by definition, a set of *interacting elements* separated from its *environment* by a boundary.

To an increasing degree the following characteristics are specific for social systems:

1. *Openness of the system*. Social systems are *open* systems: they receive inputs from their environment and send output into their environment. The variables describing the actual state {S(t)} and the output of a system {O(t)} are thus dependent on its input {I(t)}. Or, S(t), O(t) = f[I(t)].

2. *Delays in input-output transformation*. During the transformation of inputs into outputs *delays* may occur, which means that a change in the input may have an effect on the output only after a certain period of time has elapsed. For example, a sudden increase of undergraduate students will result in an increase of doctoral dissertations after only a couple of years. If the actual state of the system is dependent on previous inputs, the relationship between actual input and output of a system may become rather complex, and quite often nonlinear. Or, O(t), S(t) = f[I(t), I(t-1), I(t-2), ...].

3. *Homeostatic/goal-seeking behavior via negative feedback loops*. Social systems are able to maintain themselves within a turbulent, unpredictable, and uncontrollable environment. They are able to keep their state variables at about constant values, in spite of unexpected fluctuations of the input from the environment. So one could say that social systems are equilibrium-maintaining or *homeostatic*. One could even say that they are *goal-seeking*. From their reactions to external disturbances it appears that they have desired values on the state variables {S(g)} and output variables {O(g)}, values which they try to reach and maintain. If changes in the environment of a social system lead to deviations from the desired values, countermeasures are taken. Usually these countermeasures are aimed at changing the input: a *feedback loop* emerges between variables describing input and output of the system. Stated otherwise, the causal relationship between input variables and output variables now has two different directions: a positive relationship from input to output, and a negative relationship from output to input. Or, I(t) = f[{S(t) - S(g)}, {O(t) - O(g)}].

These two causal relations together form a negative feedback loop. The presence of such a feedback loop appears from the time-series characterizing the alterations of input variables, state variables, and output variables: after a disturbance, they will return to the goal values S(g) and O(g).

4. *Positive feedback loops and coupling of subsystems*. A feedback loop between input, state, and output is not necessarily a negative one. It is also possible that it consists of two negative or two positive relationships. In such a

positive feedback loop a small deviation from the goal value is not dampened, but amplified instead. The arms race is an example of a process in which two subsystems, the power blocks 1 and 2, are coupled in such a way that a state variable of one block (the level of armament, S) is positively connected with the input of the other subsystem (the acquisition of weaponry, I). Or, $I1(t+1) = f1[S2]$; $I2(t+1) = f2[S1]$; $S1(t+1) = f3[I1]$; and $S2(t+1) = f4[I1]$. The resulting vicious circles, or positive feedback loops, can be recognized by the nonlinear (i.e., exponential), course of the time-series concerning the state variables of these subsystems.

5. *Reflexivity and anticipation via feedforward loops.* Social systems are able to make observations about their state, input, and output. Not only are they self-observing, but they are also *reflexive*. They can reflect on themselves and generate expectations about future situations. Moreover, they can anticipate future developments and problems, and react accordingly by taking countermeasures. If this happens, a *feedforward loop* is acting. Because the system expects a disturbance with respect to the state of the system or its environment, a measure is taken which, in the ideal case, falsifies the expectation on which it is based. Here we have a self-denying prophecy. But there are also feedforward loops producing self-fulfilling prophecies (Henshel, 1990, 1997). A classical example is the expected insolvency of a bank, causing a run on the bank, which makes the bank bankrupt.

Feedforward loops generate difficult-to-analyze, often cyclical, time-series, because here the state and output of the system are not only dependent on the actual input of the system, but also on expectations about the future inputs of the system. Or, $I(t) = f1[\hat{O}(t+1), S(t+1)]$ and $O(t), S(t) = f2[I(t), \hat{I}(t+1)]$.

The well-known "hog cycle" illustrates that not only analysts have problems with feedforward loops but also the actors within the system. The combination of different time delays regarding the processes of breeding pigs and selling pork, together with anticipations regarding expected developments, sets the hog breeders on the wrong foot. To breed many pigs when pork prices are high seems a rational strategy, but when the piglets are ready for slaughtering the same strategy turns out to be a disaster due to strongly decreased pork prices.

6. *Goal adaptation and morphogenesis.* To the arsenal of measures systems can take to maintain themselves in their rapidly changing environment, also belongs the capability to *adapt their goals* or even change their structure (*morphogenesis*), in order to increase the chances of survival. The processes of goal adaptation and morphogenesis are often based on former experience and on the self-observation and reflection mentioned earlier. Social systems are thus learning systems. This means that the processes characterizing the behavior of a social system are themselves changing: the goals of the system are changing and the relationships between the elements of the system are changing too. Or: $Sg(t) = f [\{S-Sg\}(t-1)]$ and $f(t1) \neq f(t2) \neq ft(3)$.

These processes cause nightmares for people who try to investigate the structure which has determined the state transformation—that is, the "state transition structure" or "generative system" in the terminology of George Klir

(1975; see also Cavallo, 1979). The more complex the state transition structure is, the longer time-series one needs to identify this structure; ultimately the number of unknown parameters exceeds the number of data points.

Conclusions

We could proceed with adding to this list more characteristics of social systems. For example, the fact that social systems can organize themselves, steer themselves, and reproduce themselves means that, in the jargon of sociocybernetics, social systems are, or at least look like, *autopoietic* systems. However, the main message from the sequence of characteristics presented above will be clear by now. The more we leave the domain of classical social cybernetics and move into the direction of modern sociocybernetics, the more problems we will face with the operationalization of our concepts and propositions in the "variable language" as used in the social sciences.

Even the less sophisticated application of cybernetics—that is, a restriction to delays, feedback loops, feedforward loops, and morphogenesis only—brings along so many methodological problems that we will restrict ourselves to these smaller problems.

These problems may be called "smaller," but they are not small. Because as soon as we introduce in our models the notion of feedback loop, the usual assumptions behind the use of linear equations and unidirectional causality no longer hold. Moreover, the classical procedures for model construction in the social sciences, like using sets of regression equations, or linear structural models, differential equations and survival analysis, only fit with models of systems which do not take into account the possibility that systems anticipate their future state and change their goals, their behavior, or their structure, accordingly.

The sociocybernetic models we want to construct and validate empirically, bring us into a conflict with classical methodological thinking in the social sciences—that is, with its preference for unidirectional causality and for simple theories. Thus, our first task is to see what the historical background is of these preferences which by now dominate the methodology of the social sciences.

A STRUGGLE FOR RATIONALITY

Karl Popper

The beginning of modern social science is reflected in the statement of Auguste Comte (1830/1842) that society has reached a new era in which the dark ages of feudal regulation of society are fading away and make place for rational decisions supported by positive scientific knowledge.

Members of the Vienna Circle like Morris Schlick, Otto von Neurath, and Rudolf Carnap elaborated this positive idea of science. Their contributions to a program for the rationality of science, in which truth is to be found with the help of arguments in a free discussion between subjects, were gradually transformed into a "logic of science." According to the Vienna Circle (1929), arguments in the scientific discussion have to be grounded in facts about the world and explanations of these facts by theory. Statements in a theory have to correspond with these facts. This *principle of correspondence* was seen as essential for generating valid scientific knowledge.

Popper (1934/1959, 1967) continued this struggle against irrationality, especially against the idleness of modern belief systems which were camouflaged as science. In his quest he took the ideas of the Vienna Circle for granted, but he tried to establish the rules of the logic of science more precisely. To specify the correspondence theory of truth of the Vienna Circle, he used Tarski's effort (1936) to lay the foundation for a theory of truth. Popper followed Tarski's idea that, in between the world and a (grand) theory, a model has to be constructed. According to Tarski, a model is a vehicle by which it can be demonstrated that aspects of a theory are true or not.

Popper had the opinion that with such models, theories could be compared, and that it could be determined which theories are more closely approaching truth (i.e., are more valid). According to Tarski, the language most suited to reveal the truthfulness of a model is the artificial language of logic. But logic was a field in which different formal languages existed. There was the enterprise of Hilbert (Hilbert & Bernays, 1934/1938) to reduce these different formal languages into one computable formal logic. But the fundamental analysis of Gödel (1931) indicated that there are severe limits to this program of simplification of logic to computable first-order predicate logic. Popper, however, was attracted by the simplicity of Hilbert's program and tried to reduce the language in which valid scientific statements are to be expressed, to first-order predicate logic.

Simplicity

Popper preferred finite chains of simple predicative arguments (van Dijkum, 1988). This preference influenced his search for concepts and rules of reasoning that could establish the validity of scientific statements. In general, he made a plea for "parsimony" in the use of concepts in models. If a simple model and a more complicated model can both describe and explain the same facts, then the simple model is preferable. The simple model does more with less concepts and thus grasps more information. Consequently, scientific statements with simple linear relations between variables give more information than more complex statements with nonlinear relations.

Causality

Causal statements represent a class of substantial theories in science. Thus it is important to clarify how those statements can be formulated in a logically correct way. Popper (1967) formulated his understanding of causality as follows: "An event A is the cause of an effect B only then when there exists *a language* in which statements can be formulated, such that: u is a universal law, a is a description of A, b is a description of B and b is a *logical consequence* of u and a" (p. 362, note 7).

Valid statements of causality have to be expressed in the simple terms of first-order predicate logic. The relation between cause and effect, as stated in a universal law, could be either deterministic or stochastic.

Next, according to Popper's preference for working with simple statements, researchers in the social sciences followed Reichenbach (1956) in limiting the interaction between causes and effects. Interaction was restricted to the action of a cause and the reaction of an effect. Would one allow that the effect in return influences the cause, then a logical inconsistency would arise.

The Rise of Myths about Falsification, Simplicity, and Causality

About Falsification

Popper's program gradually dominated the ideas of social scientists. Lakatos (1970) has shown that some followers misunderstood Popper's carefully balanced ideas of objectivity, deduction, and falsification, and turned them into dogmas. For example, Popper's naive falsification principle, in which just one theory is available and, as a consequence, falsification is the only strategy left, had a great appeal to social scientists.

About Simplicity

Another source of misunderstanding was Popper's preference for simplicity. "Simple statements, if knowledge is our object, are to be prized more highly than the less simple ones because they tell us more; because their empirical content is greater; and because they are better testable" (Popper 1934/1959, p. 142). In Popper's days, the natural sciences and the social sciences were restricted to the use of simple linear models, because the mathematics of the calculation otherwise very soon became too complex to understand. It even became an *art* to explain phenomena with those linear models, an art that was later transformed into a habit in many scientific disciplines. But with the aid of new hardware and new software, developed in the 1960s, one could go beyond that fixation and explore nonlinear models in those cases where their usefulness is indicated by the theory. In this way many fruitful nonlinear models were developed by the natural sciences. However, in the social sciences the myth that linear models are always better, no matter what subjects or circumstances are modelled, still has lost little ground.

About Causality

The third myth developed from following the same ideological track of simplification. Reichenbach's idea of causality became dominant in the methodology of social sciences. According to Maruyama (1963) this idea became a myth in textbooks and it became even a taboo to discuss. For decades this myth blocked the development of alternative research programs into the causality in the social sciences. In the practice of social science, an overwhelming majority of the researchers analyzed causality only in a one-way direction. That there are occasions where a cause in its turn can be influenced by its effect was not accepted as a valid scientific statement. Moreover, in quantifying the strength of the relation between cause and effect, the preference for simplicity made that only models were analyzed based on a linear relation between cause and effect (van Dijkum, 1988). Statistics used to formulate stochastic relationships resulted in models in which Pearson correlation coefficients expressed the linear relations. In general, with these models the linear paths that exist between several variables are mapped (see Figure 13.1).

Figure 13.1
Paths for Unidirectional Causality

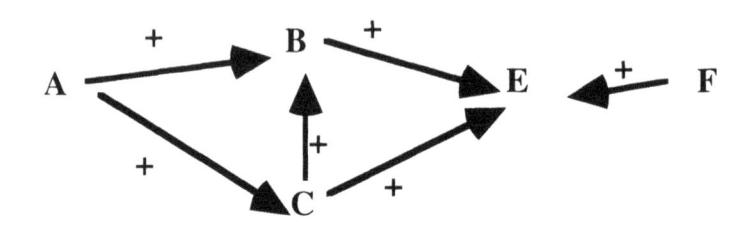

By using partial correlation coefficients one can determine which relation is in fact indirectly produced by other paths. But no feedback relations are allowed in those models and the myth has been consolidated that such analyses are sufficient to express meaningful causal relations.

RULES FOR VALIDATION

Standard Rules in the Social Sciences

The rules for validation in contemporary social science are in line with the above-mentioned simplification of Popper's methodology and the three associated myths. In the well-known book by Campbell and Stanley (1966), which for a long time laid down for many social scientists the rules of "how to do research in social science in the right way," it is stated:

It is by now generally understood that the "null hypothesis" often employed for convenience in stating the hypothesis of an experiment can never be "accepted" by the data obtained; it can only be "rejected," or "fail to be rejected." Similarly with hypotheses more generally—they are technically never "confirmed": where we for convenience use that term we imply rather that the hypothesis was exposed to disconfirmation and was not disconfirmed. This point of view is compatible with all Humean philosophies of science which emphasize the impossibility of deductive proof for inductive laws. Recently Hanson (1958) and (Popper 1959) have been particularly explicit upon this point. (p. 35)

As a consequence, Campbell and Stanley propagated the hypothetico-deductive method. In this method, a hypothesis is inferred from a theory. From that hypothesis a prediction is derived, and an attempt is made to falsify this hypothesis. It is preferred to falsify a causal hypothesis (H_1), and as a result to verify a hypothesis (H₀) which states the nonexistence of a causal relation. The causal hypothesis should be falsified in the most pure way—that is, in a situation where the researcher has control over all variables which are causes of the effects. This can be done in an experiment by varying the independent variables (causes) and observing the influence of that variation on the relevant dependent variables (effects). However, there remains a problem to be solved: alternative causes may jeopardize the conclusion that there is a causal relation between those variables. Following the strategy of the statistician Fisher (1925), efforts are made to control (i.e., to "filter out") those disturbing factors by using all kinds of research settings (experimental designs).

However, for disciplines like social psychology, anthropology, economy, and sociology, it is often not possible to conduct those kinds of experiments. As a substitute for the control of variables that could jeopardize the presupposed unidirectional causality, efforts are made to control the research situation in another way. This is done by standardization of the collection of data, by using standardized interviews and observation-schemes. After the data collection, threats to the validity of the reconstruction of unidirectional causality by disturbing variables are reduced as much as possible. This is done by using designs of data-analysis, such as elaboration of cross-tabulations, partial correlation, and path analysis. Again, in those approaches, for reasons of parsimony, linear models are preferred.

The Introduction of Causal Recursion

Although the focus in mainstream methodology was on unidirectional causality, this did not prevent researchers like Forrester (1968), Meadows et al. (1974), Hanneman (1988), Richardson & Pugh (1981), and Blalock (1969) to stand for the possibility of a mutual interaction between cause and effect. Both cause and effect are viewed as variables and the logical contradiction Reichenbach was afraid of, is eliminated by the concept of causal recursion (Figure 13.2).

Figure 13.2
Causal Recursion

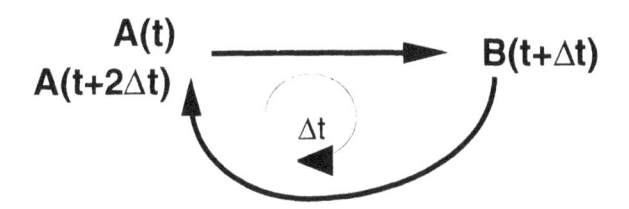

$$A(t) \longrightarrow B(t+\Delta t)$$
$$A(t+2\Delta t) \xleftarrow{\Delta t}$$

At time t, A has a certain value, which has as a consequence at time t+Δt a certain value of B, and that value of B has as a consequence a new value of A at time $t+2\Delta t$. That means a self-reference of A, thus $A=f(A,t)$. This self-reference of variable A is expressed by the equation: $\Delta A/\Delta t = f(A)$.

A recursive difference equation implies causal recursion. Using this type of equation one can also model the concept of feedforward. This implies that the future state of a variable is represented in an "anticipation model." In this way self-fulfilling and self-denying prophecies can be modelled.

It is even possible to construct models which themselves can restructure the causal relations between variables. In this way the morphogenesis of sociocybernetic models can be simulated, by introducing a meta-model that models the parameters of a causal relation in another equation (cf. van der Zouwen, 1997).

Another step ahead is the introduction of nonlinear feedback models whose patterns of outcomes can be described on a meta-level with nonlinear mathematics and can introduce in this way the complexity of self-organizing systems (van Dijkum, 1997).

Validation of Models in System Dynamics

However, feedback models as mentioned above cannot be validated with the "classical" routines of model validation of the social sciences. That is why "system dynamics" developed other procedures for validating its feedback models. Bearing in mind the idea that causal relations have to be expressed in a nomological network of statements, those procedures are aimed at two different levels of validation: validation at the level of the theory, and validation at the level of the facts.

First, the theory, together with the hypotheses derived from that theory, and the structure of the relations between the variables implied by these hypotheses, has to be investigated by answering questions like: Are all relevant variables and feedback loops included in the model? Do the (difference) equations make sense? Are the parameters of these equations meaningful and do they relate to realistic values in the real system? Do the dimensions of the variables in the equations fit both sides of the equation, without introducing fudge factors?

Next, the behavior of the model has to be validated by confronting it with facts (i.e., observed events): Is the model reproducing the sequence of events as observed in the real system? Can the model predict events that are relevant to the problem the model is built for and which are observed in reality? Is the model free of anomalies (i.e., free of the production of events that are too extreme to be observed)? Is the model "economical" with respect to the included feedback loops (i.e., are all these loops necessary to produce all relevant events)? Do plausible changes in parameters lead to observed changes in the events of the real system?

Finally, the behavior of the model has to be validated with respect to possible future events: If values of variables are changed, reflecting actions in the real system, does that lead to behavior that can be observed in the real system? And is the effect of such changes invariant for small, plausible, changes of the values of parameters (Richardson & Pugh, 1981)?

TOWARDS A NEW METHODOLOGY FOR MODEL VALIDATION

We have seen that social scientists need new procedures to validate more complex models. The systematic approach of Popper to come to a theory of validity, grounded in logically sound reasoning, still remains relevant. But the new challenge of concepts like feedback and nonlinearity has to be accepted to produce an adequate methodology for modern social science.

Criteria for the Evaluation of Models

According to Lakatos (1970), Popper's falsification principle has to be understood in a sophisticated way. One has to compare at least *two* models and to choose that model which best describes and explains the data. To judge which model is best, one needs a standard, or rather a measure. According to the idea of sophisticated falsification, one component of the measure has to take into account the facts which falsify the model, and the other component has to deal with the facts which verify the model. A conceptual framework to construct such a measure is presented in Figure 13.3.

Figure 13.3
Comparing Model-Output with Observations

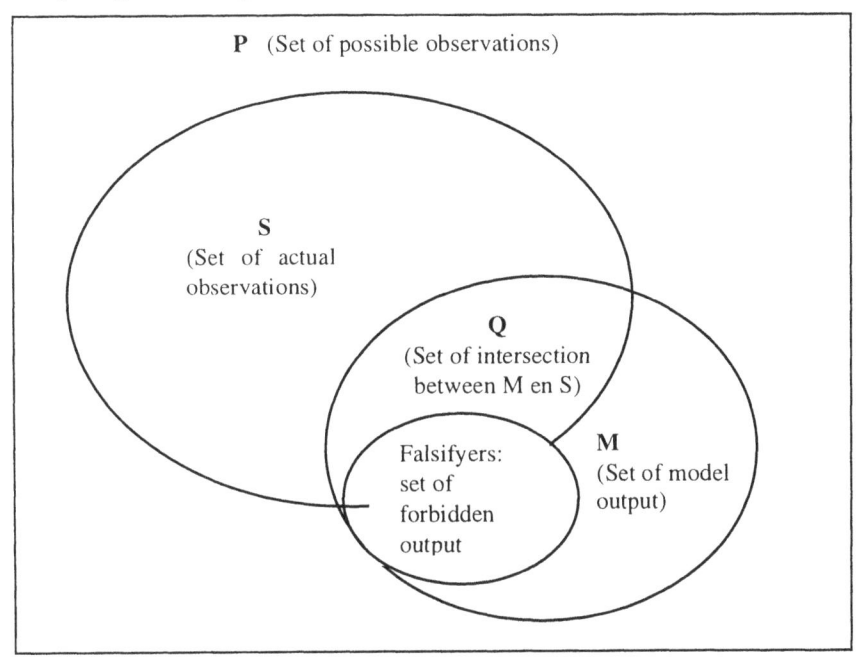

P (Set of possible observations)
S (Set of actual observations)
Q (Set of intersection between M en S)
M (Set of model output)
Falsifyers: set of forbidden output

In this figure the letter P indicates the set of all possible observations, relevant to the problem for which the model is constructed. S represents the set of actual observations (i.e., the available data). M is the set of output generated by the model. Q is the intersection between generated and observed data.

For each model one has also to define a subset of possible observations which would contradict the model (i.e., a set of "forbidden" outputs of the model). If this set of "falsifiers," or part thereof, is part of the set of actual observations S, then the model is falsified by these observations, and left out of further consideration.

The remaining models are judged according to: (1) *model adequacy*, which is the ratio of the size of set Q to the size of set S; and (2) *model reliability*, which is the ratio of the size of Q to the size of M (see Mankin et al., 1977).

In scientific practice, the possible observations P are limited by available instruments of observation and by the research question. Not all facts about the world are observed; only those that are relevant for this research project. Having a "guiding" research question makes it possible to observe relevant facts (relatively) independent of the model and the theory on the background.

Dynamic Evaluation and Validation of Models

There is a relationship between: (1) the *theory* about the world, or rather the model which represents aspects of the theory; (2) and *observations* which are made and compacted within a system of observation. But it is assumed that the coupling between these two components is pretty loose. That idea gives rise to another (dynamic) rule of evaluation of a theory, or rather of a model. A model has to be *progressive* with respect to new facts (S', a subset of S) coming into the scientific game. The set Q, the data that are both observed and predicted by the model, has to grow during the execution of a research program.

Mature science is characterized by not using only one theory, but by letting at least two theories and related models compete with one another. This implies that the standard of validation presented above has to be used in a *comparative* way. This idea is pictured in Figure 13.4.

In this comparison, models are preferred which are at the same time more adequate and more reliable, like model M_1 in Figure 13.4. However, one can easily imagine another situation, namely that M_1 is more adequate than M_2 but less reliable. Usually one will prefer the more adequate one, because the aim of modeling is to explain as many facts as possible. However, if one has to take a decision on the basis of the prediction derived from a model, as often occurs in test psychology, one has to look at the risk one takes by assuming that the prediction is right, while in reality the forecasting is wrong. If the model is not very reliable, the chance is quite high that a prediction derived from the model is wrong. Of course, one tries to minimize such errors, errors that are more likely when the model is less reliable. Statistics can help to avoid getting stuck in a highly adequate but extremely unreliable model, or to avoid the pitfall to end up with a completely reliable, but inadequate model.

Figure 13.4
Comparing Two Models

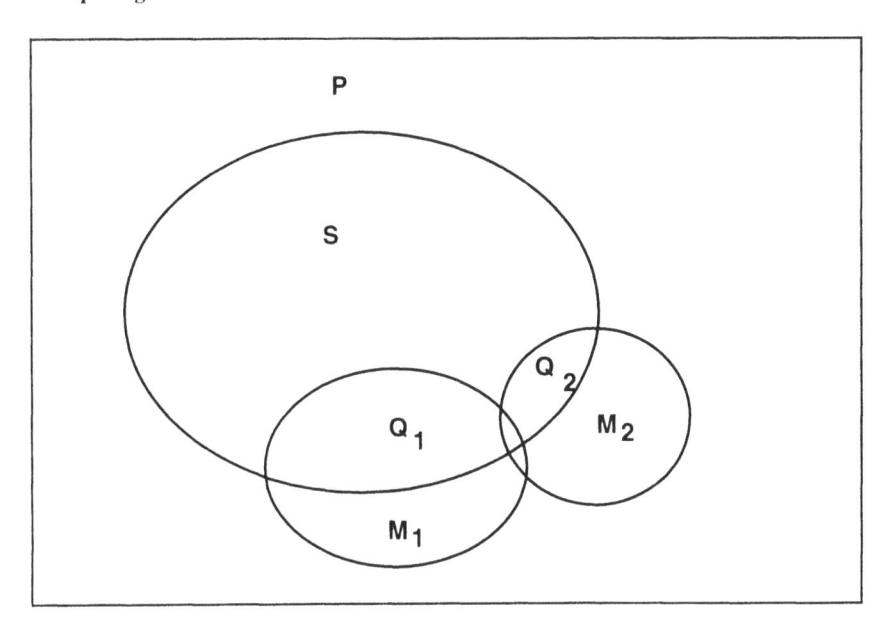

[Figure: Venn diagram showing set P containing set S, with overlapping sets M₁ and M₂; intersections labeled Q₁ (S ∩ M₁) and Q₂ (S ∩ M₂)]

Necessary Extensions of the Validating Framework

In this section we have presented a sketch for a validating framework, to be used when complex models have to be validated and evaluated. The examples used are still too simple for sociocybernetics, because often sociocybernetic models consist of more than one output variable and related trajectories. Nevertheless, with the above reasoning a framework is introduced, a framework which can be used when developing techniques for the validation of simulation models. In this framework, (1) more output variables have to be included, and (2) more mathematical sophisticated validation procedures have to be developed in order to handle nonlinearity.

SIMILARITY BETWEEN DATA AND MODEL OUTPUT

Similarity Between Data and Output of Linear Models

Fortunately one does not have to construct such procedures from scratch. There are a number of operational techniques that can be used for the construction of sound validation procedures for linear models. In these procedures the predictions derived from the model are confronted with relevant facts: the data at hand.

A rather classical procedure is to express the similarity between the observed and the generated trajectories, in the distance between both. Statistics can be introduced by interpreting the model outcomes as expected values of the variables and the data as the observed values. One has to assume errors in the measurement of the data, leading to a known distribution of values of the variables. This distribution can be used to calculate the probability of finding a certain value in the data that differs from the mean outcome of the model.

A rather simple method is to plot in a scatter diagram, for each time point t_i, the actual observation and the related outcome of the model, and to draw a line that fits best with the resulting "scatter plot." For a valid model, one might expect that the slope of this line is 1, and its intercept is 0. The correct approach here is to simultaneously test for both values and to use F Statistics (Dent & Blackie, 1979; for warnings against fallacies threatening this procedure, see Kleijnen, 1999).

If we have more variables, and if there is stochastic variation in the model outcome, other multivariate techniques can be tried. If the data represent repeated measurements and if one can assume that linear correlations between variables are constant, the designs of ANOVA and MANOVA can be used to test the similarity between data and model (Winer, 1971). As has been shown by van der Zouwen (1997) this method can be useful to review the validity of sociocybernetic models. However, if no assumptions can be made about the variance or covariance relationships of the variables, other methods such as profile analysis (Timm, 1975) and cross-correlation techniques (Steinhorst, 1979) should be considered. Both approaches, however, require large data sets: In the case of profile analysis because many replicated measurements are needed; in the case of cross-correlation because long data sets are to be correlated with long model sets.

Comparisons Between Different Linear Models

All techniques mentioned in the preceding subsection validate separate models in an "absolute" way. Working simultaneously with more than one model requires another approach. In the simplest way the distance between data and the outcome of the different models can be used to discriminate between the models. Because models can be artificially made to come closer to the data by manipulating values of variables, the concept of least square distance has to be used: What set of parameter-values minimizes the sum of the square of the (vertical) distance between the model output and the data? That model is preferred which comes closest to the data. For models that include metamodels, the number of degrees of freedom is larger and, as a consequence, the identification of the best model is more difficult. Probably one has to validate the models first in a qualitative way before quantitative validation makes sense.

Statistics will enter if one can express the probability that the model will produce a particular value of a variable. This is the case with models with stochastic variation. If the distribution of the measurement errors is known too, the concept of *likelihood* can be used, and the maximum likelihood value of each model can be computed. This measure makes explicit the distance of each model to the data, taking into account the variation of the parameters, and can be used to select the most likely model. However, there is one problem here: a model with a large number of parameters is more easily fitted to the data than a model with a small number of parameters. In line with Popper's ideas, one should then take into account the parsimony of a model. That is a rather unexplored, but nevertheless important, topic in statistics, which makes it worthwhile to build on the rare studies in which efforts are made to combine in one (information) measure the *parsimony* of the model, with the *likelihood* of the model in relation to the observed data. Again, the inclusion of meta-models makes the question even more difficult, but also more interesting (Spriet & van Steenkiste, 1982).

Statistical Measures of Similarity for Nonlinear Models

The mathematical exploration of nonlinear models is still in its infancy. But for the validation of nonlinear models with time-series data, workable techniques have been developed. An important theorem for those techniques is that of the mathematician Takens (1981). This theorem states that the behavior of a nonlinear function with n variables can be reconstructed by a limited set of data. More precisely, the topology of the nonlinear function is mirrored in the (re)construction of the data space by projecting lagged (with period n) values of one of the involved variables.

QUALITATIVE MODEL VALIDATION

The theorem of Takens (1981) shows that qualitative information about the topology is important to validate nonlinear models. That such qualitative mathematical knowledge is useful can also be demonstrated by means of the falsification of linear models.

If for a particular variable a maximum value is identified as characteristic for the phenomenon under investigation, and this is confirmed by the theory, then the model has to reproduce this maximum. That means that a simple linear function in the model does not any more suffice to describe that phenomenon. With simple mathematics it can be proved that in that case one has to use at least a quadratic function.

When more variables are involved, the data can introduce other qualitative constraints. If, for example, for some variables it is argued that they have to increase monotonously over time, and that for other variables they have to decrease monotonously, and for still other variables that there are minima or maxima, while all these variables are interrelated, then qualitative constraints are set on the interrelations between the variables in the model. These constraints make it easy to eliminate a number of potential models. Stated a bit more precisely, a qualitative strategy may result in the identification of nullclines and equilibria which put constraints on the set of (differential) equations and make it possible that whole sets of models are falsified and others verified. It can be easily demonstrated that also users of linear models can benefit from such qualitative validation (van Dijkum, Lam & Ganzeboom, this volume, chapter 12, section "Fitting with a Linear Model").

Social scientists constructing nonlinear models can also take advantage of sensitivity analysis and error analysis. With these analyses, characteristics like stability, instability, and meta-stability can be explored. There was a time when modelers tended to view the sensitivity of the model for small changes more as a defect and an artifact than as an interesting virtue. However, when it was shown in natural science that such very sensitive behavior can be observed in the real world, these "artifacts" of models were transformed into fundamental theoretical qualities. For sociocybernetics the same qualities are essential for understanding phenomena like self-steering.

A qualitative validation procedure that has to be used when no recognizable patterns are generated by the model, but nevertheless—for human beings—meaningful behavior is expressed by the model, is the Turing Test. It is in fact an ultimate test for computer models. Can human beings discriminate between the outcomes of a computer model and the outcomes of the real system? A well-known practice is to model the knowledge of a (human) expert and let other subjects try to distinguish the answers the real expert gives, from the answers to the same questions that are produced by the computer model. If the experts are not able to discriminate between the model and the real system, the model is validated in an absolute way. However, that does not suffice: more than one model has to be compared and the Turing Test has to result in a rank order of validity.

EPILOGUE

In the past, social scientists have accused cyberneticians who applied their theories and methods to social processes that they did not sufficiently take into account the particular characteristics of social phenomena. Meanwhile, sociocyberneticians have done their very best to account for these characteristics, in all their complexity, flexibility, and unpredictability. Now sociocyberneticians face the problem that the models derived from their theories are very hard to validate empirically with the standard techniques of social science. This chapter is an attempt to foster a dialogue between methodologists in the social sciences and sociocyberneticians, a dialogue aimed at the development, testing and application of validation procedures which are appropriate for more realistic, and thus more complex, models of social processes.

REFERENCES

Blalock, H.M. (1969). *Theory Construction: From Verbal to Mathematical Formulations.* Englewood Cliffs, NJ: Prentice-Hall.
Buckley, W. (1967). *Sociology and Modern Systems Theory.* Englewood Cliffs, NJ: Prentice-Hall.
Campbell, D.T. & Stanley, J.C. (1966). *Experimental and Quasi-experimental Designs for Research.* Chicago: Rand McNally.
Cavallo, R.E. (1979). *The Role of Systems Methodology in Social Science Research.* Boston: Martinus Nijhoff.
Comte, A. (1830/1842). *Cours de philosophie positive.* Paris: Bachelier.
Dent, J.B. & Blackie, M.J. (1979). *Systems Simulation in Agriculture.* London: Applied Science Publishers.
Deutsch, K.W. (1963). *The Nerves of Government: Models of Political Communication and Control.* New York: The Free Press of Glencoe.
Dijkum, C. van (1988). *Spelen met onderzoek* (Playing with research). Meppel, The Netherlands: Boom.
Dijkum, C. van (1997). From cybernetics to the science of complexity. *Kybernetes, 26,* 725-737.
Fisher, R.A. (1935). *The Design of Experiments.* London: Oliver & Boyd.
Forrester, J.W. (1968). *Principles of Systems.* Cambridge MA: Wright-Allen Press.
Geyer, F. & Zouwen, J. van der (1991). Cybernetics and social science: Theories and research in sociocybernetics. *Kybernetes, 20,* 81-92.
Geyer, F. & Zouwen, J. van der (1994). Norbert Wiener and the Social Sciences. *Kybernetes, 23,* 46-61.
Gödel, K. (1931). Über formal unentscheidbare Satzen der Principia Mathematica und verwandter Systeme. *Monatshefte für Mathematik und Physik, 38,* 173-198.
Hanneman, R.A. (1988). *Computer-assisted Theory Building: Modeling Dynamic Social Systems.* Newbury Park, CA: Sage.
Henshel, R.L. (1990). Credibility and confidence loops in social prediction. In F. Geyer & J. van der Zouwen (Eds.), *Self-referencing in Social Systems* (pp. 31-58). Salinas, CA: Intersystems Publications.
Henshel, R.L. (1997). Hypothesis Testing for Positive Feedback Models: Some Uses of Modified Poisson Distribution for Loops Involving the Self-fulfilling Prophecy. *Kybernetes 26,* 769-786.
Hilbert, D. & Bernays, P. (1934/1938). *Grundlagen der Mathematik I-II.* Berlin: Springer.
Kleijnen, J. (1999). Statistical Validation of Simulation, Including Case Studies. In C. van Dijkum, D. de Tombe & E. van Kuijk (Eds.), *Validation of Simulation Models* (pp. 112-127). Amsterdam: SISWO.
Klir, G.J. (1975). On the Representation of Activity Arrays. *International Journal of General Systems, 2,* 149-168.
Lakatos, I. (1970). Popper on Demarcation and Induction. In I. Worrall & G. Currie (Eds.), *The Methodology of Scientific Research* (pp. 139-168). Cambridge: Cambridge University Press.

Mankin, J.B., O'Neill, R.V., Shugart, H.H. & Rust, B.W. (1977). The Importance of Validation in Ecosystem Analysis. In G.S. Innis (Ed.), *New Directions in the Analysis of Ecological Systems*. Part 1. Simulation Councils Proceedings Series. Volume 5, Number 1, pp. 63-71.

Maruyama, M. (1963). The Second Cybernetics: Deviation-Amplifying Mutual Causal Processes. *American Scientist 51*, 164-179 & 250-256.

Meadows, D.L, Behrens III, W.W., Meadows, D.H., Naill, R.F., Randers, J. & Zahn, E.K.O. (1974). *Dynamics of Growth in a Finite World*. Cambridge, MA: MIT Press.

Parsons, T. (1952). *The Social System*. London: Tavistock.

Popper, K.R. (1934/1959). *The Logic of Scientific Discovery*. London: Hutchinson. (The original German version, Logik der Forschung, was published in Vienna in 1934.)

Popper, K.R. (1967). *The Open Society and Its Enemies*. London: Routledge and Kegan Paul.

Reichenbach, H. (1956). *The Direction of Time*, ed. M. Reichenbach. Berkeley, CA: University of California Press.

Richardson, G.P. & Pugh III, A.P. (Eds.) (1981) *Introduction to System Dynamics modeling*. Cambridge MA: MIT Press.

Spriet, J.A. & Steenkiste, G.C. van (1982). *Computer-aided Modelling and Simulation*. London: Academic Press.

Steinhorst, R.K. (1979). Parameter Identifiability, Validation and Sensitivity Analysis of Large System Models. In G.S. Innis & R.V. O'Neill (Eds.), *Systems Analysis of Ecosystems*. Fairland, MD: Inter-Cooperative Publishing House.

Takens, F. (1981). Detecting Strange Attractors in Turbulence. In D.A. Rand & L.S. Young (Eds.), *Dynamical Systems and Turbulence. Lecture Notes in Mathematics* (pp. 366-381). New York: Springer.

Tarski, A. (1936). Der Wahrheitsbegriff in den formalisierten Sprachen. *Studia Philosophica, 1*, 261-405.

Timm, N.H. (1975). *Multi-variate Analysis with Applications in Education and Psychology*. Monterey, CA: Brooks/Cole Publishing Company.

Vienna Circle (1929). *Wissenschaftliche Weltauffassung: Programmschrift des Wiener Kreises*. Vienna.

Wiener, N. (1948). *Cybernetics, or Control and Communication in the Animal and the Machine*. Cambridge, MA: MIT Press.

Wiener, N. (1950/1954) *The Human Use of Human Beings; Cybernetics and Society*. Boston: Houghton Mifflin.

Winer, B.J. (1971). *Statistical Principles in Experimental Design*. New York: McGraw-Hill.

Zouwen, J. van der (1997). The Validation of Sociocybernetic Models. *Kybernetes, 26*, 848-856.

INDEX

Action, 93; socially structured, 91
Activity, brain vs. mental, 44
Acton, John E.E.D., 26
Adaptive system, 193-94, 197, 199
Adilova, Fatima T., 181
Agriculture, self-organization of, 77-78
Ahl, V., 167-68
Ahlemeyer, Heinrich, 4, 60, 62, 70
Aitiai, 145-48
Alexander, J.C., 167
Allen, T.F.H., 167-68
Allopoiesis (or allopoietic system), 128, 144-45
Androgyny, 173, 174, 185, 186
Arieli, Amos, 49
Aristotle, 8, 142-45, 147-48, 150-53
Armstrong, Karen, 82
Arnopoulos, Paris, 3-4,
Arrow, Kenneth, 26
Artigiani, Robert, 5, 81, 83, 85
Ashby, W. Ross, 24, 59, 132, 135
Ashkenas, R., 132
Autocatalytic loop, 77
Autopoietic system, 111, 113, 118, 125, 127-29, 141, 160
Autopoiesis, 6, 8, 110-11, 118, 121, 125-27, 129, 134-36, 141-45, 147-150, 153-55, 159, 162, 182
Axelrod, Robert, 175, 202n6

Baecker, Dirk, 59, 61, 66
Bahr, D., 197
Bailey, Kenneth, 110
Baldacci, David, 22
Bales, Robert, 174
Balme, 148
Base rule, 194
Bateson, Gregory, 63, 135, 167
Behaviorism, 42
Benedict, Ruth, 177
Bernays, P., 228
Berry, J.W., 180
Bertalanffy, Ludwig von, 208
Betz, N.E., 174
Biggiero, Lucio, 8, 133-136
Blackie, M.J., 236
Blalock, Hubert M., 231
Boas, Franz, 177
Bogen, J., 151-52
Bohr, Niels, 22, 36
Boltzmann, Ludwig, 23
Bootstrap requirement, 146-48
Bossel, Hartmut, 175, 184
Bougon, M.G., 7.6
Boulding, Kenneth E., 111, 208
Boundary interchange, 100-101
Boundary of a system, 129, 131-32
Bourdieu, Pierre 142-43
Brans, M., 161, 164

Brecht, G., 112
Buckley, Walter, 4, 47, 54-55, 223
Buckner, C., 174

Calvin, William H., 52
Campbell, Donald T., 230
Carnap, Rudolf, 227
Carniero, B.L., 77
Carrithers, Michael, 83
Castells, Manuel, 96, 101
Causal recursion, 231-32
Causality, 228-30; forms of:
    determinism, 24; randomism, 24;
    voluntarism, 24
Cavallo, Roger E. 227
Cellular automaton (CA), 195-98
Central Intelligence Agency (CIA), 6
Chaos: theory, 23; edge of, 85
Choice submodel, 209, 211, 213-15
Chomsky, Noam, 200
Circular causality, 112
Clinton, President B., 99
Cognitive map, 185
Cognitive system, 175, 181-82
Collingwood, 149
Communication(s), 109-10, 116-17,
    119, 153-54, 162-63, 165
Communist Manifesto, 199, 202
Complexification, 2-3
Complexity, 59-61, 164-65, 167; as
    observer-bound, 61; and progress,
    86; simple, 61; societal, 3-4
Computer simulation, 10
Comte, Auguste, 227
Conceptual equivalence, 180, 181
Confucius, 84
Consciousness, 41-42, 83-85
Control, 19-22; primary, 19; secondary,
    19; social, 17, 31, 34-35; social vs.
    personal, 38; tertiary, 19
Cornell, D., 104
Correspondence (principle of), 228
Coupling (of [sub]systems), 225-26
Coutinho, A., 113
Cross-cultural research, 173, 183-86

Cultural relativism, 177-78, 180
Cybernetics, 1, 223; First-order, 1, 12;
    Second-order, 1, 12
Cyberoptimality, 38

Darwinism; simple, 28; social, 28
Dawkins, Richard, 194
Delays (in input-output
    transformation), 225
Democracy, 164
Democratic administration, 160-61,
    165
Democratic control, 160
Dent, J.B., 236
Deutsch, Karl W., 223
Differentiation, functional approach to,
    90; segmentationist theory of, 101;
    soci(et)al, 2-3; structural approach
    to, 90; (theories of) social, 89
Dijkum, Cor van, 11, 13, 208, 230, 232,
    238
Dilthey, Wilhelm, 81
Double contingency (of interaction),
    117, 118
Dougall, Colin, 8, 143, 150
Dretske, F. 109
Dunshire, A., 160
Durkheim, Emile, 2, 82, 96, 199
Dye, T.R., 162

Eder, K., 197
Educational expansion, 11, 205-208,
    219-20
Education submodel, 209-11
Eigen, Manfred, 198
Einstein, Albert, 21
Eliade, Mircea, 82
Embodied individual, 114, 115
Emic(s), 9, 178-80
Emotions, 55; in cognition and
    perception, 46
Empiricists, 44
Engels, Friedrich, 199
Enterprise model, 155-56
Entropy, 23; social, 33

Erikson, Erik H., 183
Escher, M.C., 112
Etic(s), 9, 178-81
Evaluation of models, 233-34
Expert systems, 91

Falsification (principle), 229, 233
Fararo, T.J., 195, 197-98, 200
Farmer, D.J., 194
Febbrajo, A., 125
Feedback loop, 225-27, 230
Feleppa, R., 179
Fernan, Barbara, 100
First-order cybernetics, 160, 223
Fischer, R., 83
Fisher, R.A., 231
Fitzgerald, H.E., 208
Fleischaker, Gail R., 129, 141
Flores, Fernando, 130, 144
Foerster, Heinz von, 1, 126, 135
Forrester, Jay W., 208, 231
Foucault, Michel, 104
Fox, C., 160
Frankfort, Henri, 81
Freeman, J., 133
Freeman, L.C., 191 202n6
Friedan, Betty, 173
Functional equivalence, 180, 181
Furth, M., 152-53

Galilei, Galileo, 73
Galtung, Johan, 97
Ganzeboom, Harry B.G., 11, 205, 219, 238
Geertz, Clifford, 82
Genetic algorithm (GA), 195-97
Geyer, Felix, 2, 141, 159, 223
Gibbs, Jack P., 20
Giddens, Anthony, 91, 120, 142-43
Giesen, B., 194
Gioia, D.A., 130
Glanz, J., 45
Glasersfeld, Ernst von, 135, 148
Globalization, 30
Goal adaptation, 226

Goal-seeking, 225
Gödel, Kurt, 24, 228
Gotthelf, A., 148
Governance, 159-61
Grene, M., 148

Habermas, Jürgen, 109, 192-93, 197-98, 200-201
Haefner, James W., 208
Hannan, M., 133
Hanneman, Robert A., 208, 231
Hanson, 230
Harris, Marvin, 178-80
Harrison, P.R., 162
Headland, T.N., 178, 179
Hegel, Friedrich, 54
Hegselman, Rainer, 197
Heidegger, Martin, 116, 144-45
Heintel, Peter, 67
Heisenberg, Werner, 22, 33
Hejl, Peter, 9, 159, 165-66, 168-69
Henshel, Richard L., 194
Hermeneutics, 176, 177
Hierarchy theory, 167
Hilbert, David, 228
Hildebrandt, H.J., 177
History, meaning of, 85
Hitzler, R., 176, 177
Holland, John H., 197
Homans, George C., 191
Homeostatic, 225
Honer, A., 176, 177
Hornung, Bernd, 9-10, 175-76, 181
Hornung, Charo, 9-10, 173
Hufford, Kevin D., 125, 141, 154-55
Hughes, P., 112
Hui, C.H., 180
Huizinga, Johan, 79
Hume, David, 37
Husserl, Edmund, 115-16
Huxley, Thomas Henry, 73
Hypothetico-deductive method, 230

Information, 50-51, 109, 110, 114-17; as relational, 55; vs. signal. 50

Interaction, 117
Interpenetration, 1, 182-83; of or among action and communication subsystems, 6, 89, 95-99; Interpenetration systems theory, 101-103; ubiquitousness of, 96

Jacob, François, 79
Jacobson, D., 96, 101
Janis, I.L., 130
Jarrillo, C.J., 132
Jaspers, Karl, 83
Jessop, B., 125

Kant, Immanuël, 149-50
Kenny, Vincent, 141
Kets de Vries, Manfred F.R., 131
Key, V.O., Jr., 162
Kickert, Walter J.M., 125, 135, 160
King, M., 148
Kleijnen, Jack P.C., 236
Klir, George J., 135, 208, 226
Klüver, Jürgen, 10, 193, 200-201
Knoke, David, 97-98, 100
Königswieser, Roswitha, 60
Korner, 149
Krainz, Ewald E, 67
Krogh, G. von, 125, 130, 136
Kuhn, Thomas S., 177

Lachs, John, 3
Lakatos, Imre, 229, 233
Lam, Niek, 11, 238
Langton, Christopher, 85
Language, 80-81
Laplace, Pierre, 23
Lash, Scott, 101
Laumann, Edward O., 97-98, 100
Lawson-Tancred, H., 149
Leibniz, Gottfried Wilhelm von, 148
Leinfellner, W., 198
Lennox, J.G., 148
Levine, R.L., 208
Lévi-Strauss, Claude, 175
Lewenstein, M., 197

Libertarianism vs. totalitarianism, 34
Lincoln, Abraham, 161, 168
Linear model, 214-15, 229
Little, John, 3, 8, 160
Löfgren, Lars, 61
Logistic (relation), 215-16
Loux, M., 149-50
Luhmann, Niklas, 2, 4, 6-8, 10, 60-62, 64-65, 89-93, 95-97, 101, 103-104, 109, 110, 116-20, 125, 129-30, 133, 135, 141-42, 153-54, 159, 161-66, 168-69, 176, 180, 182, 192-93, 200-201

Mach, Ernst, 44
Magnetic Resonance Imaging (MRI), 43
Magritte, René, 112
Mandelbrot, Benoit B., 29
Mankin, J.B., 234
Mann, L., 130
Mapping, 47
March, J.G., 130
Market, 65; global penetration of, 96
Maruyama, Magoroh, 229
Marx, Karl, 26, 54, 199-200
Maturana, Humberto, 6, 8, 109-12, 114, 118, 126-27, 129-30, 133, 135, 141-45, 147-50, 152-54, 156, 182
Maupertuis, Pierre Louis Moreau de, 22
Maxwell, James, 23
Mayntz, Renate, 193
McCullogh, W.S., 126
McMullin, B., 113
McSwite, O.C., 160
Mead, George Herbert, 47, 54
Meadows, Dennis L., 231
Meaning(s), 110, 114-16; conceptually structured, 91
Mediated society, 2
Merleau-Ponty, Maurice, 116
Merton, Robert K., 6
Metaphysics, 149-50
Meta rule, 194, 196, 200

Metric equivalence, 180, 181
Michalewicz, Z., 195
Michel, Robert, 26
Milgram, Stanly, 191
Miller, D., 131
Miller, H. 160
Mind-brain interaction, 41
Mingers, John, 7, 109-15, 117, 120, 141-44, 149-50, 154, 162-63
Model adequacy, 234
Model likelihood, 237
Model reliability, 234
Monod, Jacques, 75
Moravcsik, J., 145-47
Morgan, G., 125, 135
Morphogenesis, 226
Morris, Charles W., 109
Motowildo, S.J., 131
Multiple (or simultaneous) membership, 131, 133
Myth, 81

Nelson, R., 130
Nervous system, 113, 114
Networks, 67-68; network theory, 97
Neurath, Otto von, 227
Newton, Isaac, 25, 30, 73
Nonlinear model, 229
Norms and values, 5
Nowak, Andrezej, 197

Occam, William of, 37
Ojemann, George A., 52
Olsen, P., 130
Openness of a system, 224
Operational closure, 127-28, 134, 163, 169
Order out of chaos, 22
Organism-environment loop, 41-42, 53, 56; model, 46, 51
Organization(al) systems, 68; change and inovation in, 62; decisions in, 62, 64; function-oriented, 66; interlocking, 95

Organizational closure, 7, 110, 112, 114, 115, 117, 127, 182

Park, O.S., 131
Parsimony (of a model or theory), 227, 237
Parsons, Talcott, 6, 89-91, 93, 95, 97-99, 101, 103-105, 174, 223
Passerini, E., 197
Peat, D., 202n2
Perception, 48-49, 53, 55
Perturbation(s), 132-33
Peterson, S., 208
Pfeffer, J., 132
Phenomenalists, 44
Piaget, Jean, 167
Pike, Kenneth L., 178, 180
Pinker, S., 200
Planck, Max, 22
Plato, 148
Poincaré, Jules-Henri, 23, 29
Popper, Sir Karl R., 12, 194, 227-30, 233
Population submodel, 209-10
Postone, Moishe, 104
Powell, Walter W., 96, 101
Power, 22
Press, H., 239n1
Prigogine, Ilya, 74-75, 167
Probst, G.J.B., 125
Prophecy (self-denying or self-fulfilling), 226, 232
Public opinion, 162, 165
Pugh, A.P., III, 231, 233
Putnam, 149

Rand Corporation, 6
Rao, S. Chenchal, 49
Reality, levels of, 74
Redundancy, 60, 62
Reed, G.F., 52
Reflexivity, 226
Reichenbach, Hans, 229, 231
Reichertz, J., 176
Reiss, N., 181

Religion, 82-83; as autocatalytic information storage system, 82, as emergent information, 82
Rempel, Michael, 6, 92-93
Rescher, Nicholas, 149
Richardson, George P., 231, 233
Richmond, B., 208
Riesman, David, 3
Rituals, 80-81
Robb, Fenton F., 141
Rock, Irvin, 48, 49, 53
Roos, J., 130, 136
Rorty, Richard, 149-50
Ross, Edward A., 31
Rossbach, S., 161, 164
Rubino, Carl A., 83

Salancik, G.R., 132
Schacht, Richard, 5
Schlick, Morris, 227
Schmidt, Jörn, 10,
Schmookler, Andrew, 75
Schuster, Peter, 198
Schwartzman, H., 194
Second Law of Thermodynamics, 74
Second-order cybernetics, 126, 134-136
Self-cognizing system, 111, 113
Self-consciousness, 28-29; as emergent attribute, 83
Self-conscious system, 111
Self-influencing system, 111-12
Self-observation, 182
Self-organization, 74-75, 77, 86
Self-production, 142-43, 182
Self-recognizing system, 111, 113
Self-reference, 232
Self-referential system, 111-112, 163, 200
Self-regulating system, 111-12
Self-replicating system, 111, 113
Self-sustaining system. 111-12
Semantic network, 184-85
Semantic space, 184-85
Sense-making, 130

Sensory deprivation, 52
Shannon, Claude, 23, 50
Simon, Herbert A., 129-30, 167
Simplicity (of a theory or model), 196-97
Sims, H.P., Jr., 130-31
Simulation model, 206-208, 210-11, 220, 224
Six-point key (6PK), 154-56
Skvoretz, John, 195, 197
Smelser, Neil, 90, 98-99, 101
Snell, Bruno, 83
Social cybernetics, 223
Social development, 205
Social differentiation, 191-93, 198
Social distance, 191
Social evolution, 29, 194-95, 198, 200
Social network, 118, 119
Social roles, 79, 81
Social rules, 193-94
Social space (of interaction), 192-93
Social structure, 120
Social system(s), 119, 120; evolution of, 29; self-organization of, 79
Societal steering, 159
Society, 119
Sociocybernetics, 31, 36-37; 161, 167, 175, 180, 224, 235; limits of, 36
Sociodensity, 25
Sociomass, 25
Sociomotion, 25
Sociophysics, 18
Sociospace, 25
Socrates, 84
Spence, J.T., 174, 183
Spriet, J.A., 237
St. Augustine, 84
St. Mathew, 26
Stanley, Julian C., 230
State transition structure, 226
Steenkiste, G.C. van, 237
Steinhorst, R.K., 236
Stengers, Isabelle, 125-26
Stivers, C. 160
Stoica, C., 201

INDEX

Structural coupling, 182, 183
Structural invariance, 47
Studer, R., 182
Suber, P., 113
Subsystem, 120
Swenson, Rod, 141
Synreferentiality, 165-66
System dynamics model, 208, 232
Systemic Unification Model (SUM), 18

Takens, F., 237
Tarski, Alfred, 194, 228
Tennekes, Johannes, 177
Teubner, G., 125
Thelonius, 151-52, 156n2
Thompson, M., 180
Throughput, 212, 214, 216-18
Thurow, Lester, 206
Timm, N.H., 236
Toffoli, T., 197
Touraine, Alain, 142-43
Trajectory, 224
Treiman, D.J., 205, 219
Triandis, H.C., 180
TRISOC (3-dimensional society), 195-96, 202n5
Turing test, 238

Ulrich, H., 125
Understanding, 117, 163, 182, 183
Unfolding of dimensions, 199-200
Unity of science, 175-77
Uribe, Ricardo G., 109, 126
Urry, John, 101
Utterance, 117, 162

Validation (of a model), 224, 227, 230, 232-38

Varela, Francisco J., 6, 109-13, 125-29, 135, 141-43, 145, 148, 154, 156
Veld, Roel F. in 't, 159
Values, Ethics and Morals (VEMs), 76, 81-86
Vicari, S., 125, 136
Vienna Circle, 227-28
Vision, 48

Wallerstein, Immanuel, 96
Wamsley, G.L., 160
Watt, James, 44
Watzlawick, Paul, 62, 69
Weber, Max, 78, 96, 104
Weick, K.E., 130-31, 133
Whitaker, Randall, 166-67
Whitehead, Alfred North, 45, 80
Wiener, Norbert, 5, 44, 135, 208, 223
Williamson, O.E., 131
Wilson, Edward O., 75
Wimmer, R., 66, 68
Winer, B.J., 236
Winograd, Terry, 130, 144
Winter, S., 130
Wittgenstein, Ludwig, 133
Woodbridge, J., 145

Young, Arthur M., 20

Zahnley, T., 208
Zan, L., 133
Zeeuw, Gerard de, 141
Zeleny, Milan, 125-26, 129, 136, 141, 154-55
Zouwen, Johannes van der, 12, 13, 159, 223-24, 232, 236

ABOUT THE CONTRIBUTORS

HEINRICH W. AHLEMEYER is the Executive Director of *Sistema Consulting*, a firm specializing in organizational development and management consulting, based on sociocybernetic principles. He is a lecturer in organizational sociology at the University of Münster and Visiting Professor at the University of Vienna. sistema@t-online.de <http://www.sistema.de/>

PARIS ARNOPOULOS is professor in the Department of Political Science of Concordia University in Montreal, Canada. PARIS@vax2.concordia.ca

ROBERT ARTIGIANI is professor in the History Department in the US Naval Academy in Annapolis, Maryland. Artigian@NADN.NAVY.mil

LUCIO BIGGIERO is associate professor of organization in the Faculty of Economics of the LUISS University, Rome, Italy. lbiggier@luiss.it <http://www.luiss.it/facolta/economia/docenti/biggiero.htm>

WALTER BUCKLEY is emeritus professor of sociology at the University of New Hampshire in Durham, NH, where he now lives. walt.buckley@unh.edu

COR VAN DIJKUM is lecturer in the Department of Methodology and Statistics of the Faculty of Social Science of the University Utrecht, The Netherlands. c.vandijkum@fss.uu.nl <http://www.fsw.ruu.nl/ms/cvd/cvd.htm>

COLIN DOUGALL is lecturer in the School of Computing of Napier University, Edinburgh, United Kingdom. c.dougall@napier.ac.uk

About the Contributors

HARRY B. G. GANZEBOOM is professor of sociology at Utrecht University. The Netherlands. H.Ganzeboom@fss.uu.nl <http://www.fss.uu.nl/soc/hg/>

FELIX GEYER is a co-editor of this volume, and presently retired from SISWO, an interdisciplinary research institute of the Dutch universities. geyer@xs4all.nl <http://www.unizar.es/sociocybernetics/chen/felix.html>

BERND R. HORNUNG is senior researcher at the Institute of Medical Informatics of Marburg University, Germany. hornung@mailer.uni-marburg.de <http://www.euromise.cz/english/teachers/hornung.html>

CHARO HORNUNG is affiliated with the Faculty of Psychology of Marburg University, Germany. hornung@mailer.uni-marburg.de

JÜRGEN KLÜVER heads the Interdisciplinary Center for Research in Higher Education, HDZ-Computer project of the Universität Essen, Germany. juergen.kluever@uni-essen.de <http://www.uni-essen.de/hdz/compro/>

NIEK LAM works as a software developer at Royal & SunAlliance Levensverzekering, Capelle aan den IJssel, The Netherlands. nieklam@ision.nl

JOHN H. LITTLE is assistant professor of public administration for University College - Atlantic Region of Troy State University in Fort Meyer, Virginia, USA. jlittle@cox.rr.com <http://spectrum.troyst.edu/~little>

JOHN MINGERS heads the Operational Research and Systems Group of the Warwick Business School of the University of Warwick, Coventry, United Kingdom. orsjm@wbs.warwick.ac.uk <http://www.wbs.warwick.ac.uk/infosys/ors/jm.htm>

MICHAEL REMPEL is Deputy Research Director of the Center for Court Innovation in New York City. MREMPEL@courts.state.ny.us

JÖRN SCHMIDT leads the project "Computers in Higher Education" at the Interdisciplinary Center for Research in Higher Education, HDZ-Computer project of the Universität Essen, Germany. ydz020@sp2.power.uni-essen.de <http://www.uni-essen.de/hdz/computer_hochschule/start.htm>

JOHANNES VAN DER ZOUWEN is a co-editor of this volume and professor of social research methodology at the Vrije Universiteit, Amsterdam, The Netherlands. zouwen@scw.vu.nl

Lightning Source UK Ltd.
Milton Keynes UK
UKHW011830281219
356010UK00003B/119/P